Training International
Herausgegeben von Jochem Kießling-Sonntag

Susanne Watzke-Otte

Small Talk

deutsch – englisch

Der Herausgeber
Dr. Jochem Kießling-Sonntag (jks@trainsform.de) ist Managementtrainer, Organisationsentwickler und Gründer der Management-Beratung trainsform. Er begleitet Unternehmen bei Veränderungsprozessen, betreut umfassende Trainingsprojekte, leitet Führungs- und Teamtrainings und bildet Trainer aus.

The Editor
Dr. Jochem Kießling-Sonntag (jks@trainsform.de) is the founder of the management consultancy trainsform and also an experienced management trainer and organisation developer. He advises companies in change processes, is responsible for comprehensive training projects, conducts management and team trainings and also trains trainers.

Verlagsredaktion: Christine Schlagmann
Übersetzung: A&W Sprachendienst GmbH, Witten
Technische Umsetzung: Christian Jackmuth, Dormagen
Umschlaggestaltung: Gabriele Matzenauer, Berlin
Titelfoto: David De Lossy, getty images

Informationen über Cornelsen Fachbücher und Zusatzangebote:
www.cornelsen.de/berufskompetenz

1. Auflage

© 2007 Cornelsen Verlag Scriptor GmbH & Co. KG, Berlin

Das Werk und seine Teile sind urheberrechtlich geschützt.
Jede Nutzung in anderen als den gesetzlich zugelassenen Fällen bedarf der vorherigen schriftlichen Einwilligung des Verlages.
Hinweis zu § 52 a UrhG: Weder das Werk noch seine Teile dürfen ohne eine solche Einwilligung eingescannt und in ein Netzwerk eingestellt werden. Dies gilt auch für Intranets von Schulen und sonstigen Bildungseinrichtungen.

Druck: CS-Druck CornelsenStürtz, Berlin

ISBN 978-3-589-23934-4

Inhalt gedruckt auf säurefreiem Papier aus nachhaltiger Forstwirtschaft.

Inhaltsverzeichnis/Contents

Einführung: Warum Small Talk? 6

📖 Wie funktioniert Small Talk? – Die Regeln 12

Wie kommuniziere ich eigentlich? 16

1. Reflexion des persönlichen Kommunikationsverhaltens 16
2. Kommunikationsstile 20

Wie setze ich Gesprächstechniken richtig ein? ... 48

1. Aktives Zuhören 48
   📖 Voraussetzungen für aktives Zuhören 50
2. Fragetechnik 56
3. Positive Rhetorik 60

Was lasse ich besser? 62

1. Kommunikationssperren (nach Thomas Gordon) 64
2. Killerphrasen 74
3. Trigger (Reizformulierungen) 78

Wie kann ich über die Körpersprache einen guten Eindruck machen? ... 80

1. Körperhaltung 84
2. Distanzzonen 86
   📖 Distanzzonen 90
3. Gestik 92
4. Mimik 92
5. Stimme und Tonfall 96
6. Wie viel Körpersprache ist eigentlich gut? 100

1 Introduction: Why small talk? 7

📖 How does small talk work? – The Rules 13

2 How do I actually communicate? 17

2.1 Reflecting on Personal Communication Conduct ... 17
2.2 Communication Styles 21

3 How can I implement discussion techniques correctly? 49

3.1 Active Listening 49
   📖 Prerequisites for Active Listening 51
3.2 Questioning Technique 57
3.3 Positive Rhetoric 61

4 What shouldn't I do? 63

4.1 Communication Roadblocks (according to T. Gordon) 65
4.2 Killer Phrases 75
4.3 Triggers (Provocative Formulations) 79

5 How can I make a good impression with my body language? 81

5.1 Physical Posture 85
5.2 Distance Zones............. 87
   📖 Distance Zones 91
5.3 Gestures 93
5.4 Facial Expressions 93
5.5 Voice and Inflection 97
5.6 How much body language is actually good? 101

Inhaltsverzeichnis/Contents

6 Wie beginne ich den Small Talk? 102

7 Worüber spreche ich – und worüber besser nicht? ... 112

7.1 Small-Talk-Themen von A bis Z 114
7.2 Themenwechsel, bitte! 128
7.3 Tabu-Themen von A bis Z ... 132

8 Small Talk als Karrierefaktor 140

8.1 Small Talk mit Vorgesetzten 142
8.2 Small Talk mit Kolleginnen und Kollegen 144
8.3 Small Talk mit Kundinnen und Kunden 146
8.4 Small Talk bei Geschäftsessen 150
8.5 Small Talk bei Feiern und Events 150
8.6 Small Talk in Vorstellungsgesprächen 152

9 Small Talk im Ausland .. 154

9.1 Small Talk mit ausländischen Kunden 154
9.2 Landestypische Unterschiede 158
📝 Grundlegende Regeln für den Small Talk im Ausland .. 160

10 Wie kann ich Small Talk – höflich! – beenden? 186

Stichwortverzeichnis 194

6 How do I start small talk? 10

7 What do I talk about – and what do I avoid? 1

7.1 An Extensive List of Small Talk Topics 1
7.2 Can we change the subject, please! 12
7.3 The Entire Spectrum of Taboo Topics 1

8 Small Talk as a Career Factor 14

8.1 Small Talk with Superiors 14
8.2 Small Talk with Colleagues .. 14
8.3 Small Talk with Customers .. 14
8.4 Small Talk at Business Meals 1
8.5 Small Talk at Parties and Events 1
8.6 Small Talk in Job Interviews 15

9 Small Talk Abroad 15

9.1 Small Talk with Foreign Customers 15
9.2 Typical National Differences 15
📝 Fundamental Rules for Small Talk Abroad 16

10 How can I end small talk – politely?! 18

Index 19

Inhaltsverzeichnis/Contents

Wortschatz Deutsch-Englisch 196	**German-English Vocabulary** 196
Literaturverzeichnis 198	**Bibliography** 198
Die Autorin 199	**The Author** 199

1 Einführung: Warum Small Talk?
Vom Sinn und Nutzen des „kleinen Gesprächs"

Kaum ein Tag ist ohne Small Talk denkbar, im Privatleben genauso wenig wie im Berufsleben. Hier wie dort ist Small Talk gewissermaßen das Schmieröl im gesellschaftlichen Getriebe – er hält alles am Laufen, sowohl beim nachbarschaftlichen Gespräch über den Zaun als auch bei der kurzen Plauderei mit Arbeitskollegen in der Kantine.

Und das Schöne daran ist: Small Talk zu machen ist nicht schwer. Sie müssen keine Vorträge halten (was die meisten Menschen hassen), Sie brauchen keine druckreifen Sätze oder tiefschürfenden Weisheiten, noch nicht einmal besonders intelligente Formulierungen von sich zu geben.

Sie meinen, es gibt wichtigere Dinge, als mit dem Kollegen über das Wetter zu reden? – Natürlich haben Sie in gewisser Weise recht – Small Talk bleibt an der Oberfläche. Ein tiefsinniges, intellektuell herausforderndes Gespräch, das einen noch lange beschäftigt, sieht anders aus.

Aber auch Small Talk hat seine Funktion – er ist weit mehr als bloßer Zeitvertreib oder gar lästige Zeitverschwendung. Mit Small Talk können Sie nicht nur im privaten, sondern auch im beruflichen Bereich Kontakte knüpfen und intensivieren – und ohne diese Kontakte, ohne ein gewisses „Networking" ist beruflicher Erfolg auf Dauer kaum machbar.

Wer glaubt, ohne Small Talk auskommen zu können, verschenkt wichtige Chancen – auf interessante neue Bekanntschaften ebenso wie auf berufliches Weiterkommen.

Schwer zu glauben, Small Talk als Karrierefaktor? – Stimmt aber: Laut einer viel zitierten IBM-Studie aus den 1990er-Jahren, in der Abteilungsleiter und Personalreferenten befragt wurden, nach welchen Kriterien sie über eine Beförderung entscheiden, hängen Aufstiegschancen im beruflichen Umfeld vor allem von drei Faktoren ab:

- Erstens natürlich von der Leistung, die jemand am Arbeitsplatz zeigt – allerdings ist dies mit ca. 10 % der schwächste Faktor.
- Das Image, das jemand hat, der persönliche Stil, mit dem er auftritt, wiegt schon schwerer – dieser Faktor macht ca. 30 % aus.
- Und der wichtigste der drei Faktoren, die den beruflichen Aufstieg begünstigen, ist das Gesehen- und Wahrgenommenwerden – es macht ca. 60 % aus.

1 Introduction: Why small talk?

On the meaning and uses of "small talk"

A day without small talk is scarcely conceivable, both in one's private life and in the professional day-to-day. In both cases, small talk is sort of the lubricant in society's gearbox – it keeps things going, whether the scene is the neighbourly chat over the fence or a short break with co-workers in the cafeteria.

And the best thing is that small talk is not difficult. You don't need to hold a lecture (which most people hate anyway), you don't need any printable "soundbites" or deep gems of wisdom. You don't even need to relay particularly well-formed sentences.

You think there are more important things than chatting with colleagues about the weather? – Of course, you're right to a certain degree – small talk is basically superficial. A profound, intellectually challenging discussion that occupies one's thoughts for a while is a different animal.

But small talk also serves its function – it is far more than simply just "killing time" or even a burdensome waste of time. With small talk, contacts can be made and intensified, not just in one's private life, but more importantly, in one's professional life as well. And without these contacts, without a certain degree of "networking", professional success is virtually unimaginable.

Anyone who thinks they can get by without small talk is wasting important opportunities to make interesting new acquaintances and to further their career.

Hard to believe – small talk as a career factor? – But it's true: according to a frequently cited IBM study conducted in the 1990s, in which department managers and human resource managers were surveyed about what criteria they use to decide on promotions, opportunities for advancement in the professional environment depend on three primary factors:
- First of course is the job performance demonstrated at work – but with a significance of only around 10 %, this is actually the weakest factor.
- One's image, the personal style in someone's appearance carries more weight – this factor makes up some 30 %.
- And the most important of the three factors that positively affect job promotion opportunities is being seen and noticed – contributing approximately 60 %.

Einführung: Warum Small Talk?

Ernüchternd, aber wahr: Gut sein allein reicht nicht. Wie wir uns geben, wie wir auftreten und kommunizieren, ob und wie man uns wahrnimmt, ist also erheblich wichtiger, als es unsere fachlichen Leistungen sind. Daraus lässt sich zweierlei schlussfolgern:

- Es kommt zum einen darauf an, dass man Sie (und Ihre Leistungen!) überhaupt wahrnimmt. Dafür müssen Sie zur richtigen Zeit am richtigen Ort mit den richtigen Leuten Kontakt haben. Und das heißt eben nicht nur, eine tolle Präsentation zu halten oder in einer Besprechung durch intelligente Wortmeldungen zu punkten, sondern auch, in der Kantine beim Mittagessen mit Kolleginnen und Kollegen, auf einer Messe mit wichtigen Kunden oder auf einem Arbeitsessen mit dem Chef oder der Chefin zu plaudern.
- Zum anderen sollte bei all diesen Gelegenheiten der Eindruck, den Sie beim Small Talk hinterlassen, möglichst positiv sein – und das entscheidet sich oft buchstäblich in Sekundenschnelle: Experten haben herausgefunden, dass wir uns in nur dreißig Sekunden bis vier Minuten eine Meinung über unser Gegenüber bilden. Dies geschieht hauptsächlich aufgrund des Aussehens, der Stimme, der Körperhaltung, der Mimik und Gestik und (wenn auch zu einem deutlich kleineren Teil) aufgrund des Gesagten. Dieser erste Eindruck muss, wie wir sicher alle aus Erfahrung wissen, nicht immer den Tatsachen entsprechen, aber er bleibt trotzdem für lange Zeit (wenn nicht für immer!) entscheidend. Und natürlich bekommen wir für einen ersten Eindruck keine zweite Chance ... Nutzen Sie also schon die ersten Minuten eines Kontaktes, um einen positiven Eindruck zu hinterlassen. Wie das geht? Das erfahren Sie in den Kapiteln 2 bis 5.

Sie würden gern Small Talk machen, sind aber zu schüchtern und werden immer rot, wenn Sie etwas sagen? Und überhaupt: Ihnen fällt so schnell gar nichts ein? Und dann auch noch Small Talk mit Kunden, die man kaum kennt, oder mit dem Chef / der Chefin? – Stimmt, das macht die Sache nicht gerade einfacher. Aber zum Glück ist Small Talk ja ein Dialog! Soll heißen: Die Last der Konversation liegt nicht allein auf Ihren Schultern. Wenn Sie sich nicht als spritzige/-r Entertainer/-in im Small-Talk-Sektor profilieren können oder wollen, wie wäre es dann mit der Rolle des aufmerksamen, interessierten und einfühlsamen Zuhörers? Es gibt viele Menschen, die gern reden. Diejenigen, die konzentriert zuhören können und interessierte Fragen stellen, sind daher ausgesprochen beliebt (mehr dazu in Kapitel 3.1).

Introduction: Why small talk?

Sobering, but true: being good is not enough on its own. How we conduct ourselves, how we appear publicly and communicate, whether we are perceived and in what way, is significantly more important than our actual performance. This leads us to two conclusions:

- It depends on the one hand upon you (and your performance) being perceived, or noticed, at all! For this, you have to be in contact with the right people in the right place and at the right time. And this doesn't simply mean giving a great presentation or scoring points in a discussion with intelligent rhetoric. It also means chatting in the cafeteria at lunch with your co-workers, at a convention with important clients or at a business dinner with your boss.
- On the other hand, the impression you leave with your small talk at these types of occasions should be as positive as possible – and this is frequently decided quite literally in split seconds: experts have discovered that we form an opinion about the people we're talking to within a span of 30 seconds to four minutes. This happens mainly on the basis of appearance, voice, posture, facial expression and gesticulation, and (even if to a far lesser degree) on the basis of what we've said. As we all know from experience, this first impression doesn't necessarily always correspond with the facts, but it does remain decisive for a long time (if not forever!). And naturally, there's no second chance to make a first impression ... So, use the first few minutes of a contact to leave a positive impression. How does one do that? You'll learn that in Chapters 2 to 5.

You'd love to be able to make small talk, but you're shy and you always blush when you have to say something? And you can't think of anything that quickly anyway? And then having to make small talk with clients you hardly know, or with the boss? – You're right that this doesn't make things any easier. Fortunately, however, small talk is actually a dialogue! This means that the burden of bearing up the conversation doesn't rest solely on your shoulders. If you can't or don't want to present yourself as the lively entertainer in the small talk sector, then how about taking on the role of the attentive, interested and empathetic listener? There are lots of people who like to talk. And that's why people who can listen in a focused manner and ask interesting questions are extremely popular (more on this in Chapter 3.1).

Einführung: Warum Small Talk?

Wenn Sie selbst gern mehr erzählen möchten:

> *Die Fähigkeit zur flüssigen Plauderei ist zum Glück erlernbar. Es gibt eine Reihe von Tricks und Regeln, die Sie sich aneignen und trainieren können.*

Falls Sie also (wenn auch vielleicht nur zähneknirschend) die Wichtigkeit des Small Talks im Berufsleben akzeptieren, wenn Sie an Ihren Small-Talk-Fähigkeiten arbeiten oder sie vielleicht nur noch perfektionieren wollen: Herzlich willkommen!

Schauen wir uns zunächst an, welche Regeln beim Small Talk zu beachten sind.

Kann ich mich auf Small Talk vorbereiten? – Ja! Natürlich können Sie sich nicht auf jede Small-Talk-Situation vorbereiten, aber es gibt durchaus einiges, das planbar ist. Gehen Sie dabei wie folgt vor:

- Fragen Sie sich, bei welchen Gelegenheiten Sie im Beruf Small Talk machen könnten. Denken Sie dabei sowohl an alltägliche Situationen (in der Kantine, am Kopierer etc.) als auch an seltenere, aber wichtige Gelegenheiten (z.B. Messen, Kongresse, Betriebsfeiern), und tragen Sie zehn solcher Gelegenheiten in die folgende Tabelle ein.

- Anschließend notieren Sie die Small-Talk-Partner, die Sie bei den entsprechenden Gelegenheiten treffen könnten – entweder konkret mit Namen oder mit ihrer Funktion (Kunde, Kollege etc.).

Small-Talk-Gelegenheit	Small-Talk-Partner

Introduction: Why small talk?

If you would like to be able to speak more easily, then ...

> ... the good news is that the art of chatting fluently is learnable. There is a series of tricks and rules that you can adopt and train.

So, in the event that you accept the importance of small talk in professional life (even begrudgingly), if you want to improve your small talk skills, or if you're already a talented small talker who perhaps just wants to perfect the skills you already have, then: welcome aboard!

Let's look first at the rules that need to be observed in small talk.

Can I prepare for small talk? – Yes! Of course, you can't prepare specifically for every small talk situation, but there are certainly aspects that can be planned. Proceed like this:

- Ask yourself which situations in your job you can use small talk in. Consider daily situations (in the cafeteria, at the copier, etc.) and other, less frequent but no less important occasions (for example, conventions, conferences, company parties), and enter ten of these types of situations into the following chart.

- In conclusion, note the small talk partners that you might meet in the corresponding situations – either specifically by name or by their function (client, colleague, etc.).

Small Talk Situations	Small Talk Partners

Wie funktioniert Small Talk? – Die Regeln

Small Talk ist eine von vielen Gesprächsarten und unterliegt wie alle anderen auch bestimmten Regeln und Gesetzmäßigkeiten.

> Als Small Talk bezeichnet man ein „kleines" Gespräch, d.h., anders als etwa bei Sach-, Informations-, Problemlösungs- oder Konfliktgesprächen bleibt die Konversation an der Oberfläche, die ausgewählten bzw. geeigneten Themen sind wenig kontrovers und werden nicht vertieft.

> Die Sachebene des Gespräches ist nachrangig; wichtig ist die Beziehungsebene: Es geht nicht um den Austausch wichtiger Informationen, um ein Gesprächsergebnis oder eine Konfliktlösung. Entscheidend ist, dass Sie auf Ihr Gegenüber sympathisch wirken und dass sich Ihr Gesprächspartner gut unterhalten fühlt: Die angenehme und entspannte Gesprächsatmosphäre, der Aufbau und die Pflege von Beziehungen zählen.

> Um sich zu unterhalten, braucht man beim Small Talk keine Vertrauensbasis – im Gegenteil, Small Talk muss auch und gerade bei wildfremden Menschen funktionieren, denn: Das Ziel beim Small Talk heißt: Kontakte knüpfen und Beziehungen pflegen. Small Talk ist dann erfolgreich, wenn Sie einen guten Eindruck hinterlassen und positiv im Gedächtnis bleiben.

> Umgekehrt hilft Small Talk natürlich auch Ihnen, sich ein Urteil über Ihre/-n Gesprächspartner/-in zu bilden: Wirkt er/sie sympathisch, gibt es gemeinsame Interessen? Würden Sie den Kontakt gern vertiefen?

> Small Talk ist nicht nur ein kleines, sondern auch ein kurzes Gespräch – er dauert nur wenige Minuten. Daher ist das „Timing" besonders wichtig: Es kommt darauf an, zum richtigen Zeitpunkt das passende Thema zu wählen und zum richtigen Zeitpunkt das Gespräch wieder abzuschließen.

> Das Timing ist vor allem dann wichtig, wenn Small Talk das „eigentliche" Gespräch nur einleiten bzw. abschließen soll. Nahezu jedes Gespräch beginnt und endet nämlich mit Small Talk: Das Vorstellungsgespräch ebenso wie Beratungs- und Verkaufsgespräche mit Kunden oder Besprechungen im Kollegenkreis. Small Talk in der richtigen Dosierung trägt also zur Entspannung und Lockerung der Gesprächsatmosphäre, zur Öffnung Ihres Gegenübers bei. Er baut Distanz ab und fördert Vertrauen.

How does small talk work? – The Rules

Small talk is a form of discussion, and as with all others, it is subject to certain rules and standards.

Small talk is characterized as a "brief" talk, i.e., in contrast to technical, informational, problem-solving or conflict discussions, with small talk, the conversation remains superficial; the selected or appropriate topics are less controversial and are not discussed in depth.

The factual level of the talk is not of primary importance; what's important is the relationship level. The focus is not on the exchange of important information, on a discussion result or the resolution of a problem. Instead, the point is to make a congenial impression on the other party and to give them the feeling of being pleasantly entertained: the things that count are an enjoyable, relaxed discussion atmosphere and the build-up and maintenance of relationships.

You don't need a basis of trust to converse in small talk – on the contrary, small talk has to work as well and in particular with complete strangers, because: The aim of small talk is making contacts and maintaining relationships. Small talk is successful when you make a good impression and are remembered positively in the mind of the other party.

Conversely, small talk also helps you to form an opinion of the person you're talking to: does he/she seem friendly, do we have common interests? Would you like to intensify the contact?

Small talk is not only a "small talk"; it's also a brief talk – it only lasts a few minutes. That's why "timing" is particularly important: the point is to pick the right topic at the right time, and then to end the conversation at the right time.

The timing is especially important when small talk is an introduction or conclusion to the "actual" discussion. Almost every conversation begins and ends with small talk, be it a job interview, an advisory or sales discussion with a client or a discussion with co-workers. In the right dosage, small talk contributes to a relaxation and loosening up of the conversational atmosphere, and to your discussion partner opening up. It reduces distance and promotes trust.

- Analysieren Sie nun **Ihr (mutmaßliches) Small-Talk-Gegenüber:**
  - Mit wem haben Sie es zu tun?
  - Wissen Sie schon etwas über ihn/sie oder können Sie etwas in Erfahrung bringen, beispielsweise über den beruflichen Hintergrund, über Einstellungen, Interessen, Vorurteile, Hobbys oder Vorlieben?
  - Mit welchen Themen könnten Sie Ihr Gegenüber erreichen, überzeugen, locken?

- Spielen Sie nun den **Gesprächsablauf** einer solchen Small-Talk-Situation übungshalber gedanklich durch:
  - Wie eröffnen Sie den Small Talk?
  - Was sind für diesen Gesprächskontakt geeignete Themen?
  - Auf was wollen Sie bezüglich Ihres Kommunikationsverhaltens achten (den anderen anschauen, laut genug sprechen usw.)?

- Denken Sie auch daran, **welchen Eindruck Sie hinterlassen wollen:**
  - Möchten Sie intelligent, kompetent, gebildet, freundlich, nett, hilfsbereit wirken?
  - Wie können Sie diesen Eindruck erreichen?
  - Welche Themen eignen sich dafür, welche Gesprächstechniken helfen Ihnen dabei, wie können Sie den Eindruck durch Ihre Körpersprache unterstützen?

Natürlich sollten Sie in der realen Situation nicht auf Biegen und Brechen ein vorher geplantes „Programm" ablaufen lassen; vieles entwickelt sich aus der Situation heraus. Aber: Sie können Strategien entwickeln. Und vielleicht tauchen dabei auch noch einige Fragen auf, beispielsweise:

- Was zeichnet erfolgreiche Small Talker/-innen aus?
- Wie kommuniziere ich überhaupt mit anderen Menschen?
- Auf was sollte ich dabei achten – verbal und nonverbal?
- Wie knüpfe ich Kontakte und wie eröffne ich Gespräche, ohne aufdringlich zu wirken?
- Welche Themen sind für Small Talk geeignet und welche nicht?
- Wie funktioniert Small Talk mit Vorgesetzten, Kollegen oder Kunden?
- Erfordern besondere berufliche Situationen wie Tagungen, Messen, Betriebsfeiern etc. besondere Maßnahmen, was den Small Talk angeht?

Introduction: Why small talk?

Now analyse your (probable) small talk partner:
- Who are you dealing with?
- Do you already know something about him/her, or can you find out something, for example, about their professional background, attitudes, interests, prejudices, hobbies or preferences?
- What topics could you address to reach, persuade or entice your small talk partner?

- Now, mentally go through the course of a conversation in this type of small talk situation:
    - How do you open up the small talk?
    - What are appropriate topics for this contact?
    - What do you want to pay attention to in relation to your communication conduct (look at the other person, speak loudly enough, etc.)?

- Also think about what impression you want to leave:
    - Do you want to appear intelligent, competent, well-educated, friendly, nice or helpful?
    - How can you make this impression?
    - What topics are in line with this, what conversational techniques can help you with this, how can you reinforce this impression with your body language?

Of course, in the real situation you shouldn't force yourself to stay within the confines of a previously planned "programme"; lots of things develop simply from the situation itself. But you can develop strategies. And it's possible that some additional questions will arise in the process, for example:
- What distinguishes the successful small talker?
- How do I communicate with other people in the first place?
- What should I pay attention to in the process – verbal and non-verbal?
- How can I make contact and how can I open a conversation without seeming pushy?
- Which topics are appropriate for small talk, and which ones aren't?
- How does small talk function with bosses, co-workers or clients?
- Do special job-related situations like conferences, conventions, company parties, etc. require special measures in regard to small talk?

- Welche Regeln gibt es für Small Talk mit Kunden und Geschäftspartnern im Ausland?
- Wie beende ich Gespräche höflich?

Fragen über Fragen ... Die Antworten finden Sie in diesem Buch.

Erfolgreiche Small Talker/-innen ...

- reflektieren ihr persönliches Kommunikationsverhalten,
- kennen Gesprächstechniken – und wenden sie auch an,
- sind an anderen Menschen interessiert und gehen auf sie zu,
- wissen, worüber man beim Small Talk spricht – und worüber nicht,
- formulieren positiv und wirken dadurch positiv,
- stellen Fragen, ohne indiskret oder penetrant zu sein,
- kennen die Don'ts der Kommunikation und arbeiten daran, sie zu vermeiden,
- zeigen Interesse, Aufgeschlossenheit und positive Emotionalität – auch in ihrer Körpersprache.

2 Wie kommuniziere ich eigentlich?
Individuelle Kommunikationsweisen

„Die Art, sich zu geben und die zwischenmenschlichen Kontakte und Beziehungen zu gestalten, bestimmt das private Glück und das berufliche Fortkommen in hohem Maße mit."

Friedemann Schulz von Thun (in: *Miteinander reden. Stile, Werte und Persönlichkeitsentwicklung.* Reinbek 1989, S. 11.)

2.1 Reflexion des persönlichen Kommunikationsverhaltens

Wo immer und wann immer wir verbal oder nonverbal mit Menschen kommunizieren, machen wir uns aufgrund verschiedenster Signale ein Bild vom anderen – und der/die andere macht sich ein Bild von uns. Das passiert in der Regel spontan und unbewusst: Wir nehmen z.B. körpersprachliche Signale oder Äußerlichkeiten wahr und schließen daraus auf die Persönlichkeit unseres Gegenübers, schreiben ihm oder ihr bestimmte Eigenschaften, Absichten und Befindlichkeiten zu – mal mehr, mal weniger zutreffend.

Diese „Schnellschussurteile" haben meistens durchaus ihren Sinn: So können wir uns ohne langes Nachdenken aufgrund unserer gespeicherten Erfahrungen und unseres Wissens schnell auf eine Situation und das Gegenüber einstellen und – im Idealfall – ein

- What rules apply for small talk with clients and business partners abroad?
- How can I end conversations politely?

One question after the other ... You'll find the answers in this book.

> **Successful small talkers ...**
> - think about their personal communication conduct,
> - know conversational techniques – and use them,
> - are interested in other people and approach them,
> - know what to talk about – and what not to – in small talk,
> - formulate what they say in a positive manner, and so make a positive impression,
> - pose questions without being indiscreet or pushy,
> - know the communication "don'ts", and work to avoid them,
> - show interest, openness and positive emotionality – also in their body language.

2 How do I actually communicate?

Individual Means of Communication

"The way in which one presents oneself and arranges interpersonal contacts and relationships determines to a large degree one's private happiness and professional progress."

Friedemann Schulz von Thun (in: *Miteinander reden. Stile, Werte und Persönlichkeitsentwicklung. [Speaking To Each Other: Styles, Values and Personality Development]* Reinbek 1989, p. 11.)

2.1 Reflecting on Personal Communication Conduct

Wherever and whenever we communicate with people, either verbally or non-verbally, we form an image of the other person(s) on the basis of a large variety of signals – and the other person or people do the same with us. This generally happens spontaneously and unconsciously: for example, we perceive body language signals or outward appearances and subsequently make judgments about the personality of our discussion partner, attributing certain characteristics, intentions and attitudes to him or her – sometimes more, and sometimes less accurately.

These "snapshot appraisals" are usually perfectly useful: they allow us, without a longer period of contemplation and based on the experiences and knowledge we've gathered up to that point, to

situationsadäquates Verhalten zeigen. Pech nur, wenn unsere Wahrnehmung (oder die Interpretation unserer Wahrnehmung) uns auf den Holzweg führt.

> *„Da habe ich doch gedacht, das ist eine ganz Nette und Kompetente, so wie die auf mich gewirkt hat. Und als ich dann ihre Ansichten zum Thema Mitarbeiterführung gehört habe – da bin ich fast umgefallen!"*

Genauso kann es natürlich umgekehrt passieren, dass sich jemand ein Bild von Ihnen macht, das Ihrem Selbstbild überhaupt nicht entspricht ...

Das wirft spannende Fragen auf:
- Wie werde ich eigentlich von anderen gesehen?
- Welchen Eindruck bekommt man von mir, wie wirke ich auf andere?
- Wie kann ich mich, meine Persönlichkeit, meinen Kommunikationsstil gezielt reflektieren und hinterfragen?

Beim Small Talk wird die Persönlichkeit des Gesprächspartners, sein Auftreten, sein Kommunikationsstil deutlicher wahrgenommen als in anderen Gesprächsformen, in denen man sich stärker auf die Sache konzentriert und beispielsweise ein Problem lösen, über etwas informieren, etwas erklären oder einen Konflikt bewältigen muss.

Im Small Talk hingegen ist die Sachebene eher unwichtig; hier ist die Beziehungsebene die Hauptsache.

Kennen Sie das Johari-Fenster? Dieses Modell wurde von den amerikanischen Sozialpsychologen Joseph (Jo) Luft und Harry (hari) Ingham entwickelt und zeigt die unterschiedlichen Aspekte der Selbst- und Fremdwahrnehmung.

Nutzen Sie dieses Modell zur Selbstreflexion:
- Wie sieht Ihr Verhalten im Bereich der „öffentlichen Person" aus? Wie verhalten Sie sich in Gesprächen – sprachlich und körpersprachlich?
- Haben Sie Angewohnheiten, die Ihnen nicht bewusst sind – und vielleicht in der Kommunikation stören? Bitten Sie andere Menschen um Feedback, damit Sie Ihren „blinden Fleck" verkleinern können.
- Was gehört zu Ihrer „Privatperson", was möchten Sie schützen und – zumindest im Small Talk – nicht zum Thema machen?

quickly adjust to a particular situation, and – ideally – to demonstrate conduct appropriate for the situation. It's just bad luck if our perception (or the interpretation of our perception) leads us down the garden path.

> *"The impression she made on me led me to believe she was genuinely nice and really competent. But when I heard her views on employee management, I almost fell out of my chair!"*

And of course, precisely the same thing can happen the other way around, with someone forming an image of you that has nothing to do with your own perception of yourself ...

That raises some interesting questions:
- How am I actually viewed by others?
- What impression do others get from me, how do I seem to others?
- How can I specifically reflect upon and scrutinise myself, my personality and my communication style?

In small talk, the personality of the discussion partner, their appearance and their communication style are more clearly perceived than in other forms of discussion in which one is more focused on a particular subject in order to, for instance, solve a problem, provide information, explain something or settle a conflict.

> *By contrast, in small talk, the factual level is of rather less importance; the relationship level is the main thing here.*

Are you familiar with the Johari Window? This model was developed by the American social psychologists Joseph (Jo) Luft and Harry (hari) Ingham, and it depicts the various aspects of self-perception and the perception of others.

Use this model for self-reflection:
- How does your conduct appear in the "Public Person" section? How do you behave in discussions – verbally and in relation to body language?
- Do you have habits you're not conscious of – and that might disrupt communication? Ask others for feedback so that you can reduce your "blind spot".
- What is a part of your "Private Person", what would you like to protect, and – at least in small talk – avoid as a topic?

	Mir bekannt	Mir unbekannt
Anderen bekannt	**Öffentliche Person** Dieser Anteil unseres Verhaltens ist uns selbst und anderen bekannt. Wir agieren i.d.R. authentisch, weil unbeeinträchtigt von Ängsten und Vorbehalten. Da das Verhalten bewusst ist, kann es auch willentlich verändert und an Situationen oder Personen angepasst werden.	**Blinder Fleck** Dies ist der Anteil unseres Verhaltens, der uns selbst nicht bewusst ist, von anderen jedoch meist deutlich wahrgenommen wird (unbedachte Gewohnheiten, Verhaltensmuster, Vorurteile, Zu- und Abneigungen). Er wird meist auf der nonverbalen Ebene, etwa durch Gesten und Tonfall, kommuniziert und kann durch Feedback bewusst gemacht werden.
Anderen unbekannt	**Privatperson** Dies ist der Bereich unseres Denkens und Handelns, den wir als Intim- und Privatsphäre bewusst vor anderen verbergen: Werte, politische Gesinnung, religiöse Überzeugungen, heimliche Wünsche, empfindliche Stellen und tiefe Ängste.	**Unbekanntes** In diesem Bereich ist unbewusstes Wissen verborgen, das weder uns noch anderen unmittelbar zugänglich ist. Es kann durch tiefenpsychologische Methoden (zumindest teilweise) bewusst gemacht werden.

Das Johari-Fenster

2.2 Kommunikationsstile

„Wie sprechen Menschen mit Menschen? Aneinander vorbei."
  Kurt Tucholsky (1890–1935), dt. Schriftsteller

Aufbauend auf Ihren Ergebnissen der Selbstreflexion können Sie nun mehr über Ihren Kommunikationsstil herausfinden.

Der Kommunikationspsychologe Friedemann Schulz von Thun hat acht deutlich voneinander unterscheidbare Kommunikationsstile definiert (ausführlich in: *Miteinander reden. Stile, Werte und Persönlichkeitsentwicklung*. Reinbek 1989):

- den bedürftig-abhängigen Stil,
- den helfenden Stil,
- den selbstlosen Stil,
- den aggressiv-entwertenden Stil,
- den sich beweisenden Stil,

How do I actually communicate?

	Known to me	Unknown to me
Known to others	**Public Person** This part of our behaviour is known to us and others. We generally react authentically because we're not burdened by fears and reservations. Since this behaviour is conscious, we can also change it at will and adapt it to situations or persons.	**Blind Spot** This is the part of our behaviour that we are not conscious of, but which is in large part clearly perceived by others (unconscious habits, behavioural patterns, prejudices, inclinations and aversions). It is primarily communicated at the non-verbal level, perhaps through gestures and inflection, and we can become conscious of it through feedback.
Unknown to others	**Private Person** This is the area of our thinking and actions that we consciously conceal from others as our private sphere: values, political opinions, religious convictions, secret desires, sensitive points, and deep fears.	**Unknown** This area conceals subconscious knowledge that is not directly accessible for us or others. It can be made conscious through deep-reaching psychological methods (at least to some extent).

The Johari Window

2.2 Communication Styles

"How do people speak with people? At cross purposes."
Kurt Tucholsky (1890–1935), German author

Expanding on the results of your self-reflection, you can now find out more about your communication style.

Communications psychologist Friedemann Schulz von Thun has defined eight clearly distinguishable communication styles (comprehensively covered in: *Miteinander reden. Stile, Werte und Persönlichkeitsentwicklung*. Reinbek 1989):

- the Needy-Dependent Style,
- the Helpful Style,
- the Selfless Style,
- the Aggressive-Demeaning Style,
- the Self-Praising Style,

- den bestimmend-kontrollierenden Stil,
- den sich distanzierenden Stil,
- den mitteilungsfreudig-dramatisierenden Stil.

Lesen Sie die Erläuterungen dazu auf den folgenden Seiten, die zur Veranschaulichung manchmal bewusst etwas überspitzt formuliert sind. Dabei wird auch deutlich, dass alles zwei Seiten hat: Keiner der Kommunikationsstile ist nur „gut" oder „schlecht", schon gar nicht gibt es den „besten" oder „idealen" Kommunikationsstil – jeder hat seine Stärken und Schwächen. Schließlich gibt es auch kein immer gleiches ideales Kommunikationsverhalten:

> *Das ideale Kommunikationsverhalten ist situationsabhängig.*

Deshalb gelten für ein gelungenes Small-Talk-Gespräch andere Regeln als etwa für ein gelungenes Konfliktgespräch.

Die wenigsten Menschen lassen sich eindeutig einem einzigen Stil zuordnen, weshalb es durchaus sein kann, dass Sie sich in verschiedenen Stilen wiedererkennen. Überlegen Sie also, was für Sie charakteristisch ist.

Natürlich ist es sinnvoll, eine gewisse **kommunikative Grundkompetenz** zu haben oder zu erwerben. Dazu gehören z.B. Gesprächstechniken wie das aktive Zuhören (vgl. Kapitel 3.1). Darüber hinaus aber sollte man – je nach Art des individuellen Kommunikationsverhaltens – unterschiedliche Strategien für den Kontakt zu und die Gespräche mit anderen Menschen beherrschen. Und die kann jede/-r von uns umso leichter entwickeln, je besser er/sie seine bevorzugten Kommunikationsstile kennt und versteht. Behalten Sie deshalb folgende Fragen im Hinterkopf, wenn Sie die Charakterisierungen der verschiedenen Kommunikationsstile auf den folgenden Seiten lesen:

- Was ermöglicht oder erleichtert Ihnen Ihr Kommunikationsstil?
- Was ersparen Sie sich möglicherweise durch Ihren Kommunikationsstil?
- Was verbaut Ihnen der Stil auf der anderen Seite, woran hindert er Sie?
- Was würde passieren, wenn Sie bewusst, auf der Basis Ihrer neuen Erkenntnisse, anders reagieren?
- Was bedeutet das für Ihr (zukünftiges) Kommunikationsverhalten – auch beim Small Talk?

> How do I actually communicate?

- the Determining-Controlling Style,
- the Self-Distancing Style,
- the "News Scoop"-Dramatising Style.

Read the explanations of these styles on the following pages. For demonstration purposes, they may sometimes seem a little exaggerated in their formulation. They also make it clear that everything has two sides: none of the communication styles is only "good" or "bad", and there's absolutely no "best" or "ideal" style of communication – everyone has their strengths and weaknesses. After all, there's also no type of communication conduct that's always ideal:

> *The ideal communication conduct depends on the situation.*

That's why a successful small talk discussion has different rules than a successful conflict discussion, for instance.

Very few people can be clearly classified within one single style, which is why it's entirely possible that you can recognise yourself in different styles. So think about what's characteristic of you.

Naturally, it makes sense to have or acquire a certain basic **communicative competence**. This includes conversational techniques such as active listening, for instance (see Chapter 3.1). Beyond this, one should, depending on the type of individual communication behaviour, be proficient in strategies for contact and discussions with other people. And each one of us can develop these skills even easier the better we know and understand our preferred communication styles. So for this reason, keep the following questions in the back of your mind while you're reading about the characterisations of the various communication styles in the following pages:

- What makes your own communication style possible or easier?
- What are you possibly sparing yourself from through your communication style?
- How does the style of your discussion partner block you; what does it hinder you from?
- What would happen if you, on the basis of the new knowledge you've acquired, were to react differently?
- What does this mean for your (future) communication conduct – also in small talk?

1. Der bedürftig-abhängige Stil

Wer in diesem Stil kommuniziert, gibt sich hilflos, überfordert, überlastet und fordert vom Gegenüber Unterstützung – meist nonverbal. Typisch für diesen Stil sind der herzerweichende, hilfesuchende Blick, die Körperhaltung, die deutlich macht, welche Last auf den Schultern ruht, und ein entkräfteter bis flehender Tonfall. Reicht das als Appell nicht aus, wird man deutlicher: Von Bitten bis zu drängenden und dringlichen Forderungen reicht die Bandbreite dieses oft manipulativen Kommunikationsstils, der häufig zum Erfolg führt …

Small Talk unter Arbeitskollegen in der Kantine

- *„Hallo Michael – na, wie sieht's aus?"*
- *„Ach, Klaus – hallo!" (tiefes Seufzen)*
- *„Klingt ja nicht gut – schlecht drauf?"*
- *„Na ja, wir haben doch in der letzten Woche dieses neue EDV-Programm in unserer Abteilung eingeführt – totaler Stress, sage ich dir."*
- *„Ja, stimmt, habe ich gehört."*
- *„Du kennst dich doch so gut mit solchen Sachen aus – hast du vielleicht nach der Pause mal ganz kurz Zeit, mir was zu erklären?"*
- *„Äh, ich muss eigentlich …"*
- *„Mensch, das wär echt hilfreich, ich komm sonst wirklich nicht weiter – und ich muss morgen was beim Chef abgeben, dafür brauche ich das Programm." (flehender Blick und Tonfall)*
- *„Also, das passt mir jetzt wirklich nicht so gut, ich muss heute Nachmittag nämlich selbst noch eine Terminsache fertig machen."*
- *„Ach so." (tonlose, ersterbende Stimme, enttäuschter Blick)*
- *„Aber, ich meine – vielleicht schaffe ich es ja, morgen früh mal kurz vorbeikommen. Dann gucken wir uns die Sache mal an."*
- *„Mmmh." (hängende Schultern, gesenkter Blick)*
- *„Ach, was soll's – wenn ich aufgegessen habe, komme ich mit rüber."*
- *„Echt? Super! Vielen Dank!" (dankbarer Blick, freudiger Tonfall)*

Haben Sie sich in diesem Stil erkannt? Dann beachten Sie folgende Tipps:

- Sind Sie wirklich so passiv und hilfsbedürftig? Versuchen Sie, sich selbst anders wahrzunehmen und sich auch in Ihren Formulierungen anders darzustellen: *„Ich will das einfach nicht"* ist etwas anderes als das hilflose *„Ich kann das einfach nicht"*, und *„Ich werde"* ist eine deutlich aktivere und selbstbestimmtere Formulierung als *„Ich muss"*.

1. The Needy-Dependent Style

People communicating in this style present themselves as helpless, out of their depth, overloaded and in need of support, mostly non-verbal, from their discussion partner. Typical of this style are the heartrending, helpless looks, a posture that signifies just how great the load is on the person's shoulders and an inflection that is either disempowered or simply pleading. If that's not sufficient as a "call for help", then they get more specific: the range of this frequently manipulative communication style stretches from requests to pushy, pressing demands, and it's often successful ...

Small talk among co-workers in the cafeteria

- "Hello Michael – how's it going?"
- "Oh, Dave – hello!" (Deep sigh)
- "That doesn't sound good – in a bad mood?"
- "Ah, y'know, we introduced this new DP program in our department last week – nothing but stress, I'm telling you."
- "Yeah, I heard something about that."
- "You know all about stuff like that – have you maybe got a minute after the break to explain something to me?"
- "Umm, actually I've got to ..."
- "Oh man, it would be a big help. I don't know where to start otherwise – and I've got to turn something in to the boss tomorrow morning. I need the program for that." (Pleading look and inflection)
- "Y'know, today's really bad timing for me. I've got a deadline myself this afternoon for something."
- "Oh, I see." (Monotonous, fading voice, dejected look)
- "But, well – maybe I can pop by early in the morning for a minute. Then we could have a look at it."
- "Mmmh." (Hanging shoulders, eyes lowered)
- "Ah, what the hell – when I'm finished eating, I'll come with you."
- "Really? Great! Thanks a lot!" (Thankful look, happy inflection)

Did you recognise yourself in this style? Then pay attention to the following tips:
- Are you really so passive and in need of help? Try to perceive yourself differently and also to present yourself differently in how you formulate your speech: *"I just don't want to"* is a little different from the helpless *"I just can't"*, and *"I will"* is a far more active and self-determined formulation than *"I have to"*.

Die Art der Formulierungen beeinflusst nicht nur, was andere von uns halten, sondern lässt auf Dauer auch bei uns selbst ein anderes Selbstbewusstsein entstehen.

- Wenn Sie Hilfe benötigen, bitten Sie offen statt manipulativ (z.B. über hilfesuchende, flehende Körpersprache) darum. Akzeptieren Sie ein Nein und versuchen Sie nicht, es doch noch zu einem *„Na gut, meinetwegen"* zu ändern.
- Geben Sie die Verantwortung nicht komplett an andere ab – meist ist Ihnen schon mit einer partiellen Unterstützung geholfen.
- Lassen Sie sich nicht von anderen (die vielleicht einen helfenden Kommunikationsstil haben, s.u.) in die abhängige Rolle des Hilfesuchenden drängen.

2. Der helfende Stil

Dieser Kommunikationsstil ist gewissermaßen das Gegenstück zum bedürftig-abhängigen Stil – und dessen „Wunschpartner". Wer im helfenden Stil kommuniziert, braucht scheinbar selbst weder Hilfe noch Unterstützung. Er hat alles im Griff, ist jederzeit stark, kompetent und souverän – und ohne langes Bitten für alle anderen da: als geduldiger Zuhörer, allzeit bereiter Ratgeber und Helfer in allen Lebenslagen. Auf Dauer kann das natürlich nicht gut gehen: Wer permanent für andere da ist, ist irgendwann auch mal überfordert und gereizt – und fällt dann aus der Rolle. Und das ist dann für die anderen nicht nachvollziehbar.

Der Helfer wartet nicht unbedingt, bis jemand um Hilfe bittet – er hilft auch ungefragt. Ungerecht, wie das Leben nun mal ist, wird das dann oft als Besserwisserei geschmäht ...

Small Talk am Fotokopierer

- „Hallo Gabi!"
- „Monika, hallo! Wie geht's dir? Dein neuer Chef soll ja ganz schön fordernd sein – jede Menge Überstunden, hört man."
- „Mir geht's prima, danke. Und mit dem neuen Chef komme ich sehr gut klar."
- „Und – macht ihr wirklich so viel Überstunden?"
- „Du, die paar Überstunden sind überhaupt kein Problem für mich, das klappt alles wunderbar. Sag mal, brauchst du noch länger?"
- „Ein bisschen dauert es noch – das sind alles Unterlagen für die Besprechung von meinem Chef morgen. Ist ihm eben erst eingefallen – mal wieder typisch!"

The manner of our verbalisation influences not only what others think about us, but in the long term, it even allows a different self-consciousness to emerge within ourselves.

- When you need help, ask for it openly instead of manipulatively (i.e., helpless, pleading body language). Accept "No", and don't try to change it into a *"Yeah, OK. If you say so"*.
- Don't give up the responsibility entirely to others – you're usually helped as much as you need with a little bit of support.
- Don't let others (who may have a "helpful" communication style – see below) force you into the role of the help-seeker.

2. The Helpful Style

To a certain degree, this communication style is the exact opposite of the needy-dependent style – and it's also its "preferred partner". People who communicate in the helpful style apparently need neither help nor support for themselves. They've got everything under control, they're always strong and independent – and they don't need much persuasion to help anyone else as a patient listener, ever-ready advisor and helper for any situation that life throws at you. Of course, this can't always work in the long run: anyone who's permanently there for others is bound at some point to be overwhelmed and irritable – and subsequently unable then to fulfil their "helpful" role. And when that happens, the others can't understand it.

Helpers don't necessarily wait to be asked for help – they also help without being asked. And unfair as life so often is, this is frequently misinterpreted as being a "know-all" ...

Small talk at the copier

- *"Hello Gabi!"*
- *"Monika, hello! How are you? Your new boss sounds pretty demanding – rumour has it that you're all having to put in lots of overtime."*
- *"I'm doing fine, thanks. And I'm getting along great with the new boss."*
- *"And are you really getting stuck with so much overtime?"*
- *"Ah, a couple of hours of overtime are no problem for me, everything's going fine. Say, are you going to stay long?"*
- *"I've still got a little bit to do – all this is documentation for my boss's meeting tomorrow. He's just remembered it now – that's so typical!"*

- *„Weißt du, Gabi, du könntest das etwas beschleunigen, indem du beidseitig kopierst und gleichzeitig schon lochen und heften lässt."*
- *„Ach – das geht?"*
- *„Ja, pass auf: Ich gebe hier die gewünschten Funktionen ein – und schon läuft es."*
- *„Toll."*
- *„Ja, so sparst du zwei weitere Arbeitsgänge – das solltest du grundsätzlich so machen, ist einfach viel effektiver."*
- *„Hm, danke."*
- *„Dieser Kopierer hat doch eine Menge Funktionen mehr als der alte – wenn du mal Zeit hast, erkläre ich sie dir gern."*
- *„Mmmhm."*

Haben Sie sich in diesem Stil erkannt? Dann beachten Sie folgende Tipps:

- Hilfsbereit zu sein und andere zu unterstützen, ist natürlich grundsätzlich etwas Gutes, das Sie beibehalten sollten. Sie sollten allerdings auf ein ausgeglichenes Verhältnis zwischen Geben und Nehmen achten. Wenn Sie schon oft das Gefühl hatten, dass Ihre eigenen Bedürfnisse zu kurz kommen, sollten Sie anfangen, etwas daran zu ändern.
- Lernen Sie also, sich stärker abzugrenzen und gelegentlich ohne schlechtes Gewissen Nein zu sagen. Deswegen sind Sie noch lange nicht egoistisch.
- Immer alles im Griff zu haben, immer perfekt zu sein – das schafft kein Mensch. Werden Sie sensibel für Ihre eigenen Bedürfnisse, gestehen Sie sich diese Bedürfnisse zu und bitten Sie auch mal selbst um Hilfe.

3. Der selbstlose Stil

Ähnlich wie Menschen, die im helfenden Stil kommunizieren, wollen auch Selbstlose vor allem für andere da sein. Wo der eine jedoch hilft und damit seine souveräne, kompetente, sogar überlegene Haltung betonen will, dient der Selbstlose eher: Gefühle von Schwäche, sogar Bedeutungs- oder Wertlosigkeit spiegeln sich bei ihm in einer gewissen Unterwürfigkeit und Opferbereitschaft wider. Das Gegenüber wird aufgewertet, Schwächen und Fehler heruntergespielt oder komplett übersehen.

Die eigene Person wird hingegen permanent abgewertet – und zwar nicht mit dem Hintergedanken, „fishing for compliments" zu betreiben. Im Gegenteil: Bekommt der Selbstlose Anerkennung und Komplimente, nimmt er nichts davon an, weil er glaubt: *„Die wollten doch nur nett sein."*

> How do I actually communicate?

- "You know, Gabi, you could speed that up by copying on both sides and having the holes punched and the sheets compiled at the same time."
- "Oh – can you really do that?"
- "Yeah, just watch: I just enter the desired function here – and off it goes."
- "Great."
- "Yeah, this saves you having to do two other work processes – you should do it like that all the time. It's just more efficient."
- "Hm, thanks."
- "This copier has lots more functions than the old one – when you've got time, I'll be glad to explain it to you."
- "Mmmhm."

Did you recognise yourself in this style? Then pay attention to the following tips:

- Being ready to help and support others is of course fundamentally a good thing that you should continue. Nevertheless, you should make sure that there's a balanced relationship between giving and taking. If you've often had the feeling that your own needs are getting the short stick, then you should start to change some things.
- Learn to set firmer limits for yourself and to say "No" once in a while without a guilty conscience. Doing so doesn't make you egotistical at all.
- Always being in control, always being perfect – nobody's up to that. Learn to be sensitive to your own needs, admit to yourself that you have these needs and don't be afraid to ask for help yourself occasionally.

3. The Selfless Style

In a manner similar to people who communicate in the helpful style, selfless folks also want first and foremost to be there for others. But while the one helps in a spirit of emphasising their confident, competent and even superior posture, the selfless person is more of a servant-type: feelings of weakness, even insignificance or worthlessness are reflected in such people in the form of a certain servility and willingness to sacrifice. The discussion partner is over-appreciated, and their weaknesses and mistakes are played down or completely overseen, while the selfless person permanently devalues their own worth – and without a thought of "fishing for compliments". On the contrary: if the selfless person receives recognition and compliments, these are dismissed in the belief that, *"They were just being nice"*.

Während der Selbstlose jederzeit ein offenes Ohr für die Sorgen und Nöte anderer hat und geradezu glücklich ist, sich irgendwie nützlich machen zu können, spricht er eigene Probleme nicht an: Er möchte schließlich nicht lästig sein – und im Grunde sind seine Sorgen – so meint er – ja auch völlig unwichtig verglichen mit den Schwierigkeiten anderer.

Small Talk zwischen Kollegen, Frühstückspause

- *„Das ist ja ein Superwetter heute! Viel zu schade zum Arbeiten – gut, dass heute Freitag ist!"*
- *„Ja, da haben Sie wirklich recht."*
- *„Was haben Sie denn Schönes vor am Wochenende? Ich habe gehört, Sie sind umgezogen – da ist sicher noch viel zu tun?"*
- *„Ach, das geht schon. Was haben Sie denn vor?"*
- *„Ich werde zum Golfen gehen – und zwar an beiden Tagen."*
- *„Oh ja, das ist sicher sehr schön."*
- *„Haben Sie schon mal gespielt?"*
- *„Nein, ich bin leider total unsportlich und habe gar kein Ballgefühl."*
- *„Das kann man lernen, dafür gibt es schließlich Kurse."*
- *„Ach nein, ich war schon in der Schule furchtbar ungeschickt. Aber Sie spielen sicher sehr gut."*
- *„Geht so, ich habe Handicap 14."*
- *„Das ist doch toll!"*
- *„Na ja, ich arbeite daran, wird schon werden."* (lacht)
- *„Ja, bestimmt."* (lacht auch)
- *„Hauptsache, das Wetter hält sich – bloß kein Regen!"*
- *„Stimmt, das wäre gar nicht schön."* (schaut besorgt)

Haben Sie sich in diesem Stil erkannt? Dann beachten Sie folgende Tipps:

- Selbstbewusstsein statt Selbstlosigkeit: Lernen Sie, an sich zu denken, „Ich" zu sagen und eventuelle Konflikte auszuhalten.
- Auf das Lernen des Ich-Sagens folgt das Lernen des Nein-Sagens – gern auch in Kombination: *„Nein, das möchte ich nicht.", „Nein, das finde ich falsch."*
- Reflektieren Sie Ihre Sprache: Benutzen Sie oft Formulierungen, die Sie selbst herabsetzen? *„Ich bin ja leider nur …", „Wahrscheinlich liege ich da völlig falsch."* Verzichten Sie in Zukunft darauf.
- Nehmen Sie Anerkennung an und werten Sie sie nicht ab. *„Danke!"* statt: *„Ach, das war doch nichts …"*
- Äußern Sie Ihre Meinung, ohne sie abzuschwächen: *„Das gefällt mir nicht"* statt: *„Also, ich kann mich ja irren, aber irgendwie ist das doch ein bisschen eigenartig, oder nicht? Aber vielleicht macht man das jetzt ja auch so, ich habe ja da wenig Ahnung."*

How do I actually communicate?

While Mr or Ms Selfless always has an ear for the worries and problems of others and is virtually overjoyed at the prospect of possibly being useful in some way, they don't talk about their own problems. They just don't want to be a burden, and basically – in their own minds – their own worries are completely unimportant compared to the difficulties others are having anyway.

Small talk between co-workers, morning coffee break

- "Great weather today! Much too good to waste working – good thing it's Friday!"
- "Yes, you're absolutely right."
- "So what kind of plans have you got for the weekend? I heard that you moved – you must have a lot to do?"
- "Oh, it's OK. What are you up to?"
- "I'm playing golf – on both days!"
- "Oh yeah, I'm sure that'll be fun."
- "Have you ever played?"
- "Nah, unfortunately, I'm not much of an athlete and I don't really have any feeling for the ball."
- "You can learn that. They've got instructors, y'know?"
- "Ah, no. I have always been awfully clumsy, even back in school. But I'm sure you play really well."
- "It's OK. I've got a handicap of 14."
- "But that's great!"
- "Well, I'm working on it. I'll get it right one day." (Laughs)
- "Yeah. For sure." (Also laughs)
- "The main thing is that the weather holds up – no rain, please!"
- "Right, that wouldn't be good at all." (Looks worried)

Did you recognise yourself in this style? Then pay attention to the following tips:

- Self-assurance instead of selflessness: learn to think of yourself, to say "I" and to endure possible conflicts.
- And once you've learnt to say "I", then learn to say "No" – you can even combine the two: *"No, I don't want that.", "No, I think that's wrong."*
- Think about your speech: do you often find yourself formulating phrases that put yourself down? *"Unfortunately I'm only ...", "I'm probably completely wrong on that"*. Avoid these in the future.
- Accept recognition and don't devalue it. *"Thanks!"* instead of, *"Ah, that was nothing, really."*
- Express your opinion without diluting it: *"I don't like that"* instead of: *"Well, I might be wrong, but somehow that's a little strange, isn't it? But maybe that's how this is done these days. I don't really know much about it."*

4. Der aggressiv-entwertende Stil

„Ach, das ist doch Unsinn!", „Was erzählen Sie da für einen Quatsch – das ist doch wohl nicht Ihr Ernst?!"

Wie schaffe ich es, mein Gegenüber offen oder versteckt (z.B. durch ironische, als Witz getarnte Bemerkungen) abzuwerten, ihn/sie schuldig erscheinen zu lassen?

Das scheint zunächst mal das Ziel zu sein, wenn jemand in diesem Stil kommuniziert. Klingt nicht gut? Und doch steckt in den meisten von uns auch etwas von diesem Kommunikationsverhalten.

Warum kommuniziert jemand so? Sie kennen den Spruch „Harte Schale, weicher Kern": Bevor man selbst verletzt wird, holt man lieber zum Präventivschlag aus. Das schützt den eigenen weichen Kern. Dass dies die Kommunikation nicht fördert, ist klar: Abwertende Äußerungen, Ironie, Spott, Schuldzuweisungen, Unterbrechungen, Körpersprache, die Langeweile signalisiert – all das ist typisch für den aggressiv-entwertenden Stil und schlecht für das Miteinander.

Aber dieser Stil hat auch positive Aspekte: Jemand, der so kommuniziert, hat es gelernt, sich zu behaupten (wenn auch mit eher unschönen Methoden). Außerdem ist er in der Lage, Kritik offen zu äußern (jedoch leider meist unfair).

Small Talk bei der Messe, die Prokuristin Frau Kruse begrüßt einen wichtigen Kunden

– *„Herr Schulte, ich grüße Sie! Wie finden Sie unseren Stand?"*
– *„Sieht gut aus – da weiß ich doch gleich, wo mein Geld bleibt, ha ha! Habe ich alles mitbezahlt, was!"*
– *„Es sieht gut aus, nicht wahr? Sie wissen doch, wie wichtig Marketing ist – Ihr Unternehmen ist ja sehr erfolgreich."*
– *„In der Tat – liegt wahrscheinlich daran, dass wir keine horrenden Summen für irgendeinen Schickimicki ausgeben."*
– *„Darf ich Ihnen einen Kaffee anbieten, Herr Schulte?"*
– *„Nee, hatte ich schon bei Ihrer Konkurrenz. Hat allerdings nach nix geschmeckt – vielleicht stecken die ihr ganzes Geld in die Produkte, ha ha."*
– *„Haben Sie sich schon unsere Neuentwicklungen im Bereich des Brandschutzes angesehen? Da hat sich einiges getan, wir haben schon viele positive Rückmeldungen bekommen."*
– *„Wurde auch höchste Zeit, meine Liebe, die Konkurrenz schläft schließlich nicht."*

Haben Sie sich in diesem Stil erkannt? Dann beachten Sie folgende Tipps:

4. The Aggressive-Demeaning Style

"Ah, that's nonsense!", "What kind of horsefeathers are you telling there – you can't be serious?!"

How can I devalue my discussion partner, openly or covertly (for example, with ironic comments disguised as jokes), or make them appear guilty?

This would initially seem to be the aim when someone communicates in this style. Sounds bad? But still, there seems to be at least a grain of this type of communication conduct in most of us.

Why does someone communicate like that? Do you know the saying, "His bark is worse than his bite"? It's a bit like striking a preventative blow to keep from getting hurt first. This protects one's own soft core. It's no mystery that this doesn't promote communication. Demeaning statements, irony, ridicule, apportioning blame, interruptions, body language that signalises boredom – this is all typical of the aggressive-demeaning style, and bad for co-operation.

But, believe it or not, this style also has its positive aspects: someone who communicates in this way has learned to assert themselves (even if the methods aren't exactly appealing). Additionally, they're also capable of levelling criticism (but usually unfairly).

Small talk at a trade fair; Company Officer Ms Kruse greets an important client

- *"Mr Schulte, hello! How do you like our stand?"*
- *"Looks nice – now I know where my money's going, ha ha! I helped pay for this, didn't I!"*
- *"It does look good, doesn't it? You know well enough how important marketing is – your company certainly is very successful."*
- *"That's a fact – that's probably because we don't spend horrendous amounts of money on overpriced junk."*
- *"Can I get you a cup of coffee, Mr Schulte?"*
- *"Nah, your competition beat you to it. Tasted like mud, though – maybe they put all their money into their products, ha ha."*
- *"Have you already seen our latest development in the fire protection sector? A lot has happened there, and we've already had lots of positive reactions."*
- *"About time, too, my dear. The competition's not taking a nap, you know."*

Did you recognise yourself in this style? Then pay attention to the following tips:

- Versuchen Sie, sich nicht nur auf die negativen Seiten anderer zu fokussieren. Hat Ihr Gegenüber nicht auch eine Menge Positives zu bieten? Möglicherweise stecken sogar in dem, was Sie als Schwäche ansehen, gewisse Stärken: Da ist ein ruhiger, schüchterner Mensch – negativ gesehen muss man ihm jedes Wort einzeln aus der Nase ziehen. Positiv gesehen ist er ein guter Zuhörer und angenehm zurückhaltend.
- Verzichten Sie grundsätzlich auf abwertende Formulierungen, auf Ironie und Sarkasmus – auch wenn das alles als Witz getarnt daherkommt.
- Arbeiten Sie an Ihrem Taktgefühl: Wie kann man Dinge formulieren, ohne dass sie verletzend klingen? Besonders wichtig ist das, wenn Sie Kritik üben:

> *Bemühen Sie sich, den Sachverhalt ohne plumpe Schuldzuweisungen (denn die lösen das Problem ja nicht) konstruktiv zu formulieren.*

Statt *„Sind Sie eigentlich zu blöd, den richtigen Knopf zu drücken?"* z.B.: *„Beim nächsten Mal drücken Sie bitte auf diesen Knopf hier, das ist der richtige."*
- Denken Sie auch mal daran, wie Sie sich fühlen würden, wenn jemand so mit Ihnen umginge …

5. Der sich selbst beweisende Stil

Beim aggressiv-entwertenden Stil setzt man andere herab, um sich überlegen zu fühlen und vor Verletzungen zu schützen. Wer den sich selbst beweisenden Stil einsetzt, gewinnt seinen Selbstwert hingegen nicht dadurch, dass er andere herabsetzt, sondern indem er sich selbst als besonders kompetent und intelligent darstellt. Das kostet viel Kraft: Bloß nicht versagen, sich keine Blöße geben! Es reicht nicht, einfach nur richtig gut zu sein. Nein, alle anderen müssen es merken. Je stärker die Selbstzweifel an uns nagen, umso wichtiger ist die nach außen getragene Botschaft: „Schaut her: Ich habe alles im Griff, ich bin perfekt! Meine Karriere, mein Haus, mein Auto, mein Boot! Ich habe die besten Beziehungen, ich bin da, wo die Musik spielt!"

Dieses „Selbstmarketing" kann sehr laut und plump, aber auch durchaus dezent und geradezu beiläufig daherkommen. Die Reaktionen der Umwelt können von der gewünschten Anerkennung über ein entnervtes *„Schon klar – keiner ist so toll wie du!"* bis hin zur Ablehnung (*„Was bildet die sich eigentlich ein!"*, *„Angeber!"*) reichen.

> *How do I actually communicate?*

- Try to avoid focusing solely on other people's negative sides. Doesn't the person you're talking to also have a lot of positive aspects? It's even possible that certain strengths are contained in what you see as weakness: there's a quiet, shy person – from a negative viewpoint, you practically need pliers to get a word out of him. Viewed positively, he's a good listener who is pleasantly reserved.
- Fundamentally avoid demeaning formulations, irony and sarcasm – even if it's all disguised as a joke.
- Work on your sense of tact: how can one phrase things in a way that doesn't sound hurtful? This is particularly important when you are criticising someone:

   Try to formulate the facts as you see them constructively and without heavy-handed "finger-pointing" (because that won't actually solve the problem).

   Instead of *"Are you just too stupid to push the right button?"*, try for example: *"Next time, please push this button here. That's the right one."*
- And think about how you would feel if someone treated you the same way …

5. The Self-Praising Style

In the aggressive-demeaning style, one puts others down as a defence mechanism and to feel superior. In contrast, those using the self-praising style massage their own sense of value not by demeaning others, but rather by depicting themselves as particularly competent and intelligent. That takes a lot of energy: don't fail, for heaven's sake, don't expose your own weaknesses! Simply being really good just isn't enough. No, everyone else has to notice it, too. The more self-doubt gnaws at us, the more important it is to project the message, "Hey, look at me! I've got everything under control, I'm perfect! My career, my house, my car, my boat! I've got the best connections, I'm where it's all happening!"

This "self-marketing" can come in a way that's very loud and pompous, but also subtly and almost casually. Reactions to it can stretch from the desired recognition to an irritated *"Of course – nobody's as good as you!"*, and up to rejection (*"Who does she think she is?!"*, *"Show-off!"*).

Wie kommuniziere ich eigentlich?

Small Talk bei einer Fachtagung über Qualitätsmanagement in der Kaffeepause

- „War ja wirklich ganz interessant, der Vortrag eben. Wir müssten bei uns im Unternehmen wohl noch einiges ändern, wenn wir wirklich zertifiziert werden wollen."
- „Ja? In meiner Abteilung – ich bin Abteilungsleiter – habe ich bereits alles dafür vorbereiten lassen, wenn auch, das muss ich zugeben, andere bei uns noch ziemlich hinterherhinken."
- „Wo arbeiten Sie denn?"
- „Bei der Winter AG – wie gesagt, als Abteilungsleiter. Kennen Sie sicher, wir sind im Bereich Sicherheitstechnik tätig. Ich bin von Haus aus Diplom-Ingenieur und Betriebswirt und habe öfter im Ausland zu tun, hauptsächlich in den USA und in Japan. Da ist man im QM ja schon viel weiter, da habe ich viel mitgenommen."
- „Klingt interessant. Ich arbeite bei Zettlach & Söhne, kennen Sie die? Ich werde jetzt ab nächsten Monat das gesamte QM für unseren Betrieb übernehmen."
- „Ach ja, Zettlach & Söhne – ich kenne Ihren Chef ganz gut, netter Kerl, wir waren schon mal zusammen golfen."
- „Mmmh. Tja, mal sehen, was der nächste Vortrag bringt, den hält ein Professor, hoffentlich wird es nicht zu theoretisch."
- „Glaube ich nicht, ich kenne den Prof aus anderen Veranstaltungen, sehr sympathischer Mann – wir haben uns öfter unterhalten. Erinnert mich an einen Professor, bei dem ich studiert habe – Professor Bethmann, ist Ihnen sicher ein Begriff?"
- „Nein, kenne ich nicht."
- „Hat einen enormen Ruf in seinem Fach, fordert einen im Studium aber ordentlich – da kommen nur die Besten durch!"
- „Aha. Na, dann gehe ich mal wieder in den Saal. Bis dann."

Haben Sie sich in diesem Stil erkannt? Dann beachten Sie folgende Tipps:
- Wer viel macht, macht auch Fehler:

    Gestehen Sie sich und anderen solche Fehler ein – das wirkt menschlich.

- Trauen Sie sich, unperfekt zu sein: Niemand muss und kann immer der/die Schnellste, Beste, Erste sein, niemand muss alles wissen und können. Geben Sie auch mal zu, etwas nicht zu können oder zu wissen. Nicht perfekt sein zu müssen, nimmt eine Menge Druck von Ihnen und bringt Entspannung – Ihnen und Ihren Kollegen, Bekannten, Familienmitgliedern.
- Leistung ist nicht alles im Leben. Da war doch noch etwas ...

How do I actually communicate?

> **Small talk during a coffee break at a symposium on quality management**
>
> - *"That lecture was really interesting. We're going to have to make some changes in our company if we really want to get certification."*
> - *"Really? In my department – I'm the Department Manager – I've already got everything prepared for that, even though, I have to say, others in the company are still lagging behind."*
> - *"Where is it you work?"*
> - *"At Winter Ltd – like I said, Department Manager. You must know us. We're in the safety technology sector. I'm an engineering and business administration graduate, and I travel abroad a lot, mainly to the USA and Japan. They're a lot further along in QM, and I've picked up a lot from them."*
> - *"Sounds interesting. I work for Zettlach & Sons. Do you know the company? Starting next month, I'm taking over QM for the whole company."*
> - *"Oh, yeah, Zettlach & Sons – I know your Director pretty well. Nice guy, we've played golf together."*
> - *"Hmm. Well, let's see what the next lecture has in store for us. It's from a professor. Hope it won't be too theoretical."*
> - *"I don't think so. I know the professor from other seminars. Very nice guy – we've talked several times. He reminds me of a professor of mine from college – Professor Bethmann, you must've heard of him."*
> - *"No, I don't know him."*
> - *"He's got a great reputation in his field. He really pushes you as a student – only the best make it through!"*
> - *"Uh-huh. Yeah, well, guess I'll go on back inside. See you later."*

Did you recognise yourself in this style? Then pay attention to the following tips:

- Those who do a lot, make a lot of mistakes:

    Admit mistakes like that to yourself and others – it humanises you.

- Allow yourself to be imperfect: nobody has to be or always can be the fastest, best, first; nobody has to know and be able to do everything. Admit sometimes to not knowing or being able to do something. Not having to be perfect takes a lot of pressure off you and facilitates a more relaxed atmosphere for you and your co-workers, friends and family members.
- Achievement is not everything in life. Wasn't there something else?

6. Der bestimmend-kontrollierende Stil

Wenn wir im bestimmend-kontrollierenden Stil kommunizieren, versuchen wir nach Kräften, alles – Dinge ebenso wie Menschen – so zu ordnen und zu steuern, dass es unseren Vorstellungen entspricht. Warum? Weil wir unter allen Umständen die Kontrolle behalten wollen, weil wir (negative) Überraschungen fürchten und vermeiden möchten – es könnte ja ein nicht mehr zu steuerndes Chaos entstehen ...

Der Mensch, der im bestimmend-kontrollierenden Stil agiert, weiß, was richtig ist – er hat klare Regeln und Strukturen und festgelegte Rituale. Dementsprechend geht er mit anderen um: Er lenkt und dirigiert (schließlich kennt er ja die richtige Richtung), er erwartet, dass sich die anderen an diesen Vorgaben orientieren. Andere Verhaltensweisen, Einwände oder gar Widerspruch – das bringt den Bestimmend-Kontrollierenden schier zum Verzweifeln: *„Dass die Leute aber auch immer so eigensinnig sein müssen! Es könnte doch allen besser gehen, wenn sie nur auf mich hören würden!"*

Dabei sind wir, wenn wir in diesem Stil kommunizieren, zwar oft durchaus tüchtig und zuverlässig – aber eben leider auch unflexibel bis stur, fantasielos und wenig kreativ.

Small Talk bei einem Empfang

- *„Hm, dieses Nachtischbuffet sieht absolut verlockend aus – eigentlich bin ich zwar auf Diät, aber das ist ja die reine Versuchung!"*
- *„Ich nehme grundsätzlich nur Obstsalat – das ist kalorienarm, gesund und trotzdem sehr lecker."*
- *„Bewundernswert, diese Disziplin. Aber haben Sie die Mousse au Chocolat gesehen? Und die Crème Brulée, die Eistörtchen, die Vanillecreme? Also, ich werde da schwach."*
- *„So geht es natürlich nicht. Sie sollten unbedingt versuchen, konsequent zu bleiben! Ansonsten bereuen Sie es nachher."*
- *„Ja, spätestens morgen früh auf der Waage! Ach, was soll's – man lebt nur einmal!"*
- *„Meistens sind doch die Augen größer als der Magen. Probieren Sie doch nur kleine Häppchen von allem und dann haben Sie bestimmt keine Lust auf mehr."*
- *„Im Gegenteil – wenn ich erst mal anfange, dann gibt es kein Halten mehr!" (lacht)*
- *„Na ja, Sie müssen ja wissen, was Sie tun." (guckt missbilligend)*

Haben Sie sich in diesem Stil erkannt? Dann beachten Sie folgende Tipps:

6. The Determining-Controlling Style

When we communicate in the determining-controlling style, we try our best to arrange and direct everything around us – things as well as people – to fit in with our ideas. Why? Because we want to retain control at all costs, because we're afraid of (negative) surprises and we try to avoid them – otherwise, uncontrollable chaos could arise …

Someone acting in the determining-controlling style knows what's right – they have clear rules, structures and established rituals. And that's how they treat others: they steer and direct (after all, they're sure about the right direction), and they expect others to orientate themselves according to these requirements. Other modes of behaviour, objections or, heaven forbid, disagreements drive the determining-controlling person to despair: *"Why do they always have to be so obstinate?! Things would be better for everybody if they'd just listen to me!"*

While we're often capable and reliable when we communicate in this style, we're unfortunately just as often also inflexible or even stubborn, unimaginative and uncreative.

Small talk at a reception

- *"Hm, this dessert buffet looks absolutely stunning – actually I'm on a diet, but this is such a temptation!"*
- *"I only ever take fruit salad – that's low in calories, healthy and still delicious."*
- *"Your discipline's really admirable. But did you see the chocolate mousse? And the crème brulée, the baked alaska or the vanilla cream? That's just hard to resist."*
- *"You can't do things that way. You really have to try to be consistent! You'll regret it later otherwise."*
- *"Yep, probably tomorrow morning when I weigh myself! Ah, what the hell – you only live once!"*
- *"The eyes are usually bigger than the stomach, y'know. Just try a little bit of everything and then you won't be hungry for it anymore."*
- *"Are you kidding? Once I get started, there's no stopping me!"* (Laughs)
- *"Well, it's up to you, I guess."* (Looks disapprovingly)

Did you recognise yourself in this style? Then pay attention to the following tips:

- Versuchen Sie, nicht immer alles zu kontrollieren. Lassen Sie andere Menschen die Dinge ruhig mal so erledigen, wie diese es für richtig halten.
- Verzichten Sie auf Rat-„Schläge".
- Lenken Sie Gespräche nicht zu stark in die von Ihnen gewünschte Richtung – überlassen Sie sich mal dem Gesprächsverlauf, ohne direktiv einzugreifen. Gehen Sie auf das Gesagte Ihres Gegenübers ein, hören Sie aktiv zu. Bewerten Sie nicht (vor allem nicht negativ!) und verzichten Sie auf moralisierende und kontrollierende Bemerkungen („*Man muss natürlich immer...*", „*Sie dürfen jetzt vor allem nicht ...*").

7. Der sich distanzierende Stil

Wenn wir in diesem Stil kommunizieren, brauchen wir vor allem eins: Abstand, sowohl physisch als auch psychisch. Dadurch, dass man sich unpersönlich, korrekt und sachlich gibt, entsteht diese Distanz fast automatisch. Andere Menschen nehmen den sich Distanzierenden als abweisend, vielleicht sogar arrogant wahr, als jemanden, mit dem man einfach nicht warm wird.

Der/die sich Distanzierende ist im Gespräch sehr sachlich, stellt Fragen, drückt sich überlegt und präzise aus – Fakten, nicht Emotionen zählen. Das heißt aber nicht, dass er keine Emotionen hat: Er kann sie nur nicht ausdrücken. Distanz statt Nähe – das schafft für diesen Kommunikationstyp Sicherheit, denn aus der Distanz wird man nicht so schnell verletzt und macht sich nicht abhängig.

Die eher steife und verschlossene Grundhaltung dieses Stils drückt sich auch in der Körpersprache aus: Man hält Abstand zu anderen und erwartet dies auch von seinem Gegenüber; körperliche Berührungen sind tabu.

Alle Gespräche, bei denen die Beziehungsebene wichtiger als die Sachebene ist, fallen uns, wenn wir in diesem Stil kommunizieren, sehr schwer. Und Small Talk – das geht irgendwie gar nicht: Keine Fakten, nur lockere Plauderei – wie furchtbar!

> **Small Talk im Flugzeug** – die Kollegen Frau Kohler und Herr Clemens fliegen nach einem beruflichen Auslandsaufenthalt wieder nach Haus, Frau Kohler beginnt das Gespräch
>
> - *„So, jetzt noch zwei Stunden und dann sind wir endlich wieder zu Hause, herrlich, nicht wahr?"*
> - *„Ja, das ist wirklich angenehm."*

- Try to avoid controlling everything all the time. Let other people take care of things the way they see fit.
- Avoid using advice like a blunt instrument!
- Don't steer conversations too heavily in the direction you want – let others take the conversational lead sometimes without intervening directly. Talk about what your discussion partner has brought up, and listen actively. Don't analyse (above all, not negatively!), and avoid preachy, controlling remarks (*"You always have to ...", "First and foremost, you just can't ..."*).

7. The Self-Distancing Style

When we communicate in this style, we need one thing above all: distance, both physical and mental. By behaving in a manner that's impersonal, proper and businesslike, this distance comes almost automatically. Others perceive the self-distancing person as aloof, maybe even arrogant and someone you just can't warm to.

The distancing person is very businesslike in conversation, posing questions and choosing their words very precisely – facts are what count, not emotions. This doesn't mean that they don't have any emotions, however: they just can't express them. Distance instead of closeness – for this type of communicator, distance provides security, because one is not as vulnerable or dependent at a distance.

This sort of stiff, unapproachable attitude is also reflected in the body language: one maintains a distance to others and expects the same from the discussion partner. Body contact is taboo.

When we communicate in this style, every conversation in which the relationship level is more important than the factual level is very difficult for us. And small talk – well,forget it: no facts, just casual chat – how awful!

Small talk on an aeroplane — work colleagues Ms Cole and Mr Clemens are flying back home from a business trip abroad. Ms Cole starts the conversation

- *"So, just two more hours to go and then we're finally back home. Great, isn't it?"*
- *"Yes, that'll be good."*

- „Wir waren ja ganz schön lange hier. Ich merke immer, dass es für meine Familie nicht so leicht ist, wenn ich weg bin. Ganz abgesehen davon, was im Büro alles liegen bleibt."
- „Es wird zweifellos einiges aufzuarbeiten sein."
- „Ich bin zugegebenermaßen etwas enttäuscht, dass wir den letzten Auftrag nicht auch noch bekommen haben."
- „Das ist tatsächlich bedauerlich."
- „Andererseits: Alles in allem haben wir doch gut abgeschnitten, sogar noch besser als geplant, nicht wahr?"
- „Durchaus, das Auftragsvolumen liegt 18% über dem Plan."
- „Haben wir gut gemacht, was?"
- „Insgesamt fällt das Resümee der Reise sicher positiv aus."

Haben Sie sich in diesem Stil erkannt? Dann beachten Sie folgende Tipps:

- Versuchen Sie, etwas von sich zu erzählen, etwas preiszugeben – am Anfang z.B. einfach, was Sie mögen und was Sie nicht mögen. Im nächsten Schritt sprechen Sie auch mal über das, was in Ihnen vorgeht: dass Sie z.B. nervös, ratlos, begeistert sind. So werden Sie für andere Menschen nachvollziehbarer – und meist auch sympathischer und nahbarer.
- Statt nur sachorientierte Fragen zu stellen, üben Sie die Technik des aktiven Zuhörens, die in Kapitel 3.1 beschrieben wird. Gerade beziehungsorientierte Gespräche verlaufen spürbar angenehmer, wenn man auf die Emotionen des Gegenübers eingeht, statt sie zu ignorieren.
- Small Talk zu halten ist eine gute Übung: Verlassen Sie die distanzierte, rein sachliche Ebene des Gespräches, und lernen Sie zu plaudern.

8. Der mitteilungsfreudig-dramatisierende Stil

Jemand, der in diesem Stil kommuniziert, redet gern und unaufhörlich und ist kaum zu stoppen. Er liebt es, im Mittelpunkt zu stehen und viel Publikum zu haben. Wo er ist, ist immer etwas los. Typisch für diesen Stil ist eine starke Emotionalität, die sich durch mitreißende Rhetorik ebenso wie durch eine lebhafte Körpersprache zeigen kann.

Der ideale Small-Talk-Typ? Nicht ganz: Auch hier lauern Tücken. Zwar hat der Mitteilungsfreudige keine Scheu vor fremden Menschen, tut sich leicht damit, Kontakte zu knüpfen, und kann fesselnd erzählen. Er gerät jedoch oft in Gefahr zu vergessen, dass Small Talk ein Dialog sein soll.

How do I actually communicate?

- "We were here for a pretty long time. I always notice that it's not so easy for my family when I'm gone. Not to mention all the work that stacks up in the office."
- "There'll certainly be some catching up to do."
- "I have to admit I'm a little disappointed that we didn't get that last order, too."
- "Yes, regrettable."
- "On the other hand, I think we did pretty well all in all, even better than originally planned, didn't we?"
- "Certainly. Our order volume is 18 % higher than the forecast."
- "So we did good, huh?"
- "I'm sure the overall appraisal of the trip will be positive."

Did you recognise yourself in this style? Then pay attention to the following tips:

- Try to tell a little about yourself, to reveal something – start for example simply with your likes and dislikes. As the next step, talk a little about what you're thinking: for instance, that you're nervous perplexed, enthusiastic. This makes you more comprehensible for others – and usually also more sympathetic and approachable.
- Instead of asking only factually-oriented questions, try the technique of active listening described later in Chapter 3.1. Relationship-oriented conversations run noticeably smoother when one acknowledges the emotions of the discussion partner instead of ignoring them.
- Making small talk is good practice: get away from a distanced, purely factual level of conversation and learn to shoot the breeze!

8. The "News Flash"-Dramatising Style

People who communicate in this style like to talk unceasingly and preferably without taking a breath! They love to be in the spotlight at the centre of a large audience. Wherever they are, that's where things are happening. One of this style's typical features is great emotionality that demonstrates itself both in gripping rhetoric and in lively body language.

The ideal person for small talk? Not exactly: perils are hiding here, too. While these gregarious types have no fear of people they don't know, no problem making contacts and a real talent for storytelling, they nevertheless sometimes forget that small talk is supposed to be a dialogue.

Wie kommuniziere ich eigentlich?

Er neigt zu Monologen – und zwar meist über sein Lieblingsthema, nämlich über sich selbst. Und so erfahren Gesprächspartner sehr viel und oft sehr viel mehr, als sie wissen wollten ...

Small Talk beim Geschäftsessen

— *"Waren Sie dieses Jahr schon im Urlaub?"*
— *"Oh ja! Ich bin mit meiner Familie zum Tauchen an die Algarve geflogen – fantastisch, kann ich Ihnen sagen, einfach unglaublich! Ich tauche jetzt seit zwölf Jahren, und ich muss sagen, ich kann mir kaum etwas Schöneres vorstellen. Diese Unterwasserwelten, die Farben – so etwas kann man kaum mit Worten beschreiben! Ich bin mittlerweile schon fast süchtig danach!"*
— *"Klingt wirklich interessant. Wir haben dieses Jahr allerdings mal was ganz anderes gemacht – eine Städtereise nach San Francisco."*
— *"Da war ich auch schon mal, eine unglaubliche Stadt! Diese verrückten Hügel und Straßen, die Cable Cars – ich glaube, ich bin damals Stunden damit gefahren, das war wirklich cool. Und das Fisherman's Wharf – ein absolut tolles Viertel. Da sind wir Stunden rumgelaufen, und ich weiß noch, einmal, da hatte ich plötzlich ..."*
— *"Ja, da waren wir auch, hat uns gut gefallen. Wir sind auch ein bisschen in die umliegende Gegend gefahren, unter anderem ins Napa Valley ..."*
— *"Da war ich auch! Ist es dort nicht fantastisch? Die Weine! Ich glaube, ich habe sie alle probiert – drei Tage im Alkoholnebel, ha ha! Zinfandel und Chardonnay sind seit damals meine absoluten Lieblingsweine, superlecker – stehen die hier eigentlich nicht auch auf der Karte? Ober – kommen Sie bitte mal zu uns!"*

Haben Sie sich in diesem Stil erkannt? Dann beachten Sie folgende Tipps:
- Small Talk ist (wie die meisten Gespräche) als Dialog gedacht. Achten Sie daher bewusst auf Ihren Redeanteil und verringern Sie ihn gegebenenfalls.
- Lassen Sie Ihren Gesprächspartner auch mal zu Wort kommen und lassen Sie ihn dann auch ausreden.
- Vermeiden Sie es, zu oft und zu lange über sich selbst zu sprechen. Das funktioniert am leichtesten, wenn Sie Fragen stellen.
- Hören Sie stattdessen aktiv zu – nutzen Sie vor allem die Technik des aufnehmenden Zuhörens. Wie das geht? Dazu mehr in Kapitel 3.1.
- Achten Sie auf die Distanzzonen Ihres Gesprächspartners, lassen Sie ihm auch körperlich Raum, sich auszudrücken (vgl. Kap. 5.2).

How do I actually communicate?

They lean towards the monologue – usually about their favourite subject, namely themselves. This means that their discussion partners find out a lot, and often a lot more than they really wanted to know ...

Small talk at a business dinner

- *"Have you already been on holiday this year?"*
- *"Oh yes! I flew with my family to the Algarve – fantastic, I'm telling you, simply unbelievable! I've been diving for twelve years, and I have to say that I can hardly imagine anything more beautiful. These underwater worlds, the colours – it's hard to put it into words! I'm afraid I'm pretty much hooked on it now!"*
- *"Sounds really interesting. This year we did something completely different and did a 'city' holiday to San Francisco."*
- *"Oh, I've been there before, too. What an incredible city! Those insane hills and streets, the cable cars – I must've spent hours just riding around back then. It was great! And Fisherman's Wharf – what a great area. We walked around there for hours, and now I remember one time when I suddenly..."*
- *"Yeah, we went there, too. We also liked it. We also drove around the surrounding areas outside the city. One of the places we went to was Napa Valley ..."*
- *"Hey, I've been there, too! Isn't it just fantastic? The wine! I think I tried them all – a real three-day drunk, ha ha! Zinfandel and Chardonnay have been my absolute favourites ever since – say, don't they have them on the wine list here, too? Waiter – could you please come here!"*

Did you recognise yourself in this style? Then pay attention to the following tips:
- Small talk is (as with most discussions) intended as a dialogue. So keep an eye on whether you're dominating the conversation and tone it down if need be.
- Allow your discussion partner to speak, too, and let them speak until they're finished.
- Avoid speaking about yourself too often and for too long. This is easiest when you ask questions.
- Instead of hogging the discussion, listen actively – use the technique of absorbent listening first and foremost. How does that work? Find out more in Chapter 3.1.
- Pay attention to your discussion partner's distance zone. Leave them some physical space and allow them to express themselves (see Chapter 5.2).

> *Wie kommuniziere ich eigentlich?*

Um erfolgreich(er) zu kommunizieren, kann die Kenntnis des eigenen Kommunikationsverhaltens hilfreich sein – vorausgesetzt, wir nutzen dieses Wissen, um unser Verhalten situationsgerecht und gezielt zu steuern: Die ideale Kommunikation ist wie gesagt die situationsgerechte.

> *Lernen Sie also, Ihre verschiedenen Kommunikationsstile entsprechend der jeweiligen Gesprächssituation erfolgreich einzusetzen.*

Das Wissen über Kommunikationsverhalten fördert aber auch das Verständnis für unser Gegenüber – es versetzt uns in die Lage, Gesprächspartner und -situationen besser einzuschätzen und dementsprechend souveräner zu reagieren.

Ihnen ist sicher aufgefallen, das sich manche Kommunikationsstile auf den ersten Blick perfekt zu ergänzen scheinen: Der Hilfsbedürftige und der Helfende, der sich selbst beweisende und der selbstlose Stil – Gespräche mit diesen Paarungen werden weitgehend problemlos verlaufen. Andere Paare werden sich hingegen in Gesprächen weit weniger wohl fühlen: Stellen Sie sich ein Gespräch zwischen dem Mitteilungsfreudigen und dem sich Distanzierenden vor – oder zwischen dem bestimmend Kontrollierenden und dem aggressiv Entwertenden ...

Unsere Gesprächspartner/-innen sind nun mal nicht immer so, wie wir es am liebsten hätten. Daran lässt sich nichts ändern. Was wir aber ändern können, sind unsere Reaktionen und unser Verhalten im Gespräch. Und über unser Verhalten können wir wiederum das Verhalten unserer Gesprächspartner beeinflussen.

Sie kennen das: Unterhalten Sie sich z.B. mit einem schüchternen Menschen und ermutigen Sie ihn, aus sich herauszugehen, bestätigen Sie ihn durch Worte und nonverbale Signale der Ermunterung (Lächeln, Kopfnicken etc.), wird Ihr Gegenüber wahrscheinlich an Sicherheit gewinnen, sein Verhalten also verändern.

Gesprächstechniken wie etwa das aktive Zuhören oder die Fragetechnik helfen Ihnen dabei.

Sie fragen sich, wie Sie diese Gesprächstechniken der Situation entsprechend einsetzen? Dazu erfahren Sie mehr im folgenden Kapitel.

> *How do I actually communicate?*

Knowledge of one's own communication conduct can be helpful in learning to communicate more successfully – that is, if we use this knowledge to control our behaviour specifically according to the situation: as said before, the ideal communication is appropriate for the situation.

> *So learn to implement your different communication styles according to the discussion situation at hand.*

Knowledge about communication conduct also promotes our understanding of our discussion partner – it puts us in a position to better assess our discussion partners and situations, allowing us to react more confidently.

You've surely noticed that some communication styles appear to perfectly complement others, at least at first glance: the helpless discussion partner and the helper, the self-praising and the selfless style – discussions between partners paired up in this way should go smoothly for the most part. Other pairs, on the other hand, will feel significantly less comfortable with each other. Imagine a discussion between someone in the "News Flash" style and a self-distancing person – or between a determining-controlling person and an aggressive-demeaning partner ...

Our discussion partners are simply not always how we would like them to be. And we can't change that. What we can change, however, are our reactions and our behaviour in a discussion. And with our own behaviour, we can also influence the conduct of our discussion partner.

Familiar situation: have a chat with a shy person, for instance, and encourage them to open up a little. Reinforce the person with your own words and non-verbal signals (laughter, nodding your head, etc). The person will most likely become more confident and alter their behaviour.

Conversational techniques such as active listening or questioning techniques can help you with this.

You're probably asking yourself how to apply these conversational techniques in accordance with the situation. You'll learn more about that in the next chapter.

3 Wie setze ich Gesprächstechniken richtig ein?

Die Grundkompetenzen der Kommunikation

„Niemand würde viel in Gesellschaften sprechen, wenn er sich bewusst wäre, wie oft er die anderen missversteht."
Johann Wolfgang von Goethe (1749–1832)

Gelungene Kommunikation ist kein Zufall. Aber obwohl wir den ganzen Tag mit anderen Menschen kommunizieren, wissen wir oft zu wenig über die Gesetzmäßigkeiten der Kommunikation.

Was man tun kann, um Kommunikation positiv zu beeinflussen und Gespräche erfolgreich zu gestalten? Nun, Gesprächstechniken wie die folgenden sind das Werkzeug für gelungene Kommunikation – nicht nur beim Small Talk.

3.1 Aktives Zuhören

„Was ich sage, will gesagt, was ich dir sage – gehört werden."
Elazar Benyoetz (*1937), isr. Aphoristiker

Was wünschen Sie sich von Ihren Gesprächspartnern? Wahrscheinlich unter anderem, dass sie Interesse zeigen an dem, was Sie erzählen, dass sie aufmerksam zuhören und sich bemühen zu verstehen, was Sie sagen wollen. Und so geht es den meisten Menschen: Hören Sie deshalb auch selbst zu. Und zwar richtig – es genügt natürlich nicht, so zu tun, als ob!

Richtig zuzuhören heißt, dem Gegenüber das Gefühl zu geben, dass er/sie in diesem Moment für Sie der interessanteste Mensch weit und breit ist. Damit das gelingt, müssen einige Voraussetzungen erfüllt sein, die Sie der folgenden Übersicht entnehmen können.

Sind Sie ein neugieriger, einfühlsamer, offener und toleranter Mensch? Dann haben Sie es in Gesprächen leicht gerade was das Zuhören angeht – Sie machen oft intuitiv alles richtig. Aber Zuhören kann man auch lernen.

Drei Stufen des Zuhörens lassen sich unterscheiden: das aufnehmende Zuhören, das Paraphrasieren und das Verbalisieren.

1. Aufnehmendes Zuhören

Dies ist die einfachste Form des Zuhörens: Sie sagen selbst nichts oder wenig und konzentrieren sich auf das, was Ihr Gegenüber sagt. Durch Blickkontakt, Aufmerksamkeitslaute und das Spiegeln der

3 How can I implement discussion techniques correctly?

The Basic Skills of Communication

"No one would speak much in company if they were aware of just how often they misunderstand the other persons."
  Johann Wolfgang von Goethe (1749–1832)

Successful communication is no accident. But although we communicate with other people all day long, we often know too little about the rules of communication.

What can one do to positively influence communication and arrange discussions successfully? Discussion techniques like the ones listed below are the tools of successful communication – and not just in small talk.

3.1 Active Listening

"What I say wants to be said. What I say to you wants to be heard."
  Elazar Benyoetz (*1937), Israeli aphorist

What do you want from your discussion partners? This would probably include the partner showing interest in what you're saying, listening attentively and trying to understand what you want to say.

And that's how most people feel: so listen yourself. And do it right – pretending to listen is just not enough!

Listening correctly means giving the discussion partner the feeling that they are the most interesting person within reach at the moment. For this to work, there are some prerequisites to fulfil that you can learn from the following overview.

Are you a curious, empathetic, open and tolerant person? Then conversation is easy for you, especially in relation to listening – often, you intuitively do everything right. But listening can also be learnt.

There are three distinguishable levels of listening: absorbent listening, paraphrasing and verbalising.

1. Absorbent Listening

This is the simplest form of listening: you yourself say little or nothing, concentrating instead on what your discussion partner is saying. Through eye contact, attentive comments and reflecting the

Voraussetzungen für aktives Zuhören

Konzentration

Konzentrieren Sie sich voll und ganz auf den Gesprächspartner. Ob Sie konzentriert sind, merkt man u.a. am Blickkontakt, der signalisiert: Mich interessiert, was Sie sagen, ich höre zu. Blickkontakt heißt natürlich nicht, dass Sie dem anderen permanent in die Pupillen starren – ein lockerer Blickkontakt zum Gesichtsfeld des anderen reicht aus. Keinen Blickkontakt zu halten, weckt hingegen beim anderen negative Gefühle: Entweder denkt er, er sei uninteressant und langweilig – oder er hält sein Gegenüber für arrogant und überheblich ... Halten Sie sich in Gesprächen an eine einfache Regel: Derjenige, der zuhört, hält den Blickkontakt, derjenige, der erzählt, darf den Blick auch mal schweifen lassen. Auch kleine Aufmerksamkeitslaute (*„Aha!", „Mhmm"*) zeigen, dass Sie zuhören.

Anteilnahme

Anteilnehmen an dem, was der andere sagt, bedeutet, sich in ihn hineinzuversetzen und nachzufühlen, was er erzählt. Ob Sie das tun, kann man an Ihrem Gesicht ablesen: Wenn Sie Anteil nehmen, „spiegeln" Sie nämlich die Emotionen Ihres Gesprächspartners. Verweigert ein Gesprächspartner hingegen diese Anteilnahme, zeigt die Mimik auch das.

Einfühlungsvermögen

Nicht nur hören, was der andere sagt, sondern auch, wie er es sagt – das macht richtiges Zuhören aus. Trainieren Sie dafür Ihre Wahrnehmung der Körpersprache Ihres Gegenübers. So können Sie manches Fettnäpfchen vermeiden oder zumindest schnellstmöglich wieder verlassen.

Unvoreingenommenheit

Haben Sie sich, schon bevor Sie die ersten Worte mit jemandem gewechselt haben, ein Bild von ihm gemacht? Sind Sie überzeugt davon, dass der erste Eindruck selten täuscht? Glauben Sie von sich, ein guter Menschenkenner zu sein? Wenn Sie diese Fragen für sich mit Ja beantwortet haben, ist es schon vorbei mit der Unvoreingenommenheit ... Alles, was Ihr Gesprächspartner nun sagen oder tun wird, läuft durch Ihren persönlichen Filter – und das heißt, Sie hören das, was Sie heraushören möchten. Richtiges Zuhören bedeutet, sich von diesen (Vor-)Urteilen zu befreien und zu hören, was tatsächlich gesagt wird, eventuell auch mal nachzufragen, wie etwas gemeint ist.

Prerequisites for Active Listening

Concentration

Concentrate completely on your discussion partner. Whether you're concentrating can be noticed from your eye contact, which signalises, "I'm interested in what you have to say, and I'm listening". Naturally, eye contact doesn't mean permanently staring at the other person's pupils – loose eye contact with the other person's field of vision is enough. In contrast, maintaining no eye contact awakens negative feelings in the other person, who will either feel that they are uninteresting and boring, or that you are arrogant and condescending ... Observe one simple rule in discussions: The listener maintains eye contact; the talker can occasionally avert their gaze. And little attentive comments (*"Aha!"*, *"Um-hmm"*) show that you're listening.

Interest

Showing interest in what the other person says means putting yourself in their place and appreciating what they are saying. And your face shows whether you're doing this: If you are sympathising, you "reflect" the emotions of your discussion partner. If, however, one isn't interested, then this is also demonstrated in their facial expression.

Empathy

Not just hearing what the other person says, but also how they say it – that's what distinguishes proper listening. Train your perception of the other person's body language for this. This can occasionally help you to avoid putting your foot in your mouth, or at least help you to quickly pull it back out again!

Impartiality

Have you already formed an opinion about someone, even before you've spoken to them at all? Are you convinced that first impressions are seldom wrong? Do you think you're a good judge of character? If you've answered these questions with "Yes", then impartiality is already out the window ... Everything that your discussion partner now says or does will be put through your personal filter – and that means you're only hearing what you want to hear. Listening properly means liberating yourself from these prejudices and listening to what's actually being said, and if need be, asking what the other person means with something you haven't entirely understood.

Wie setze ich Gesprächstechniken richtig ein?

Emotionen Ihres Gesprächspartners zeigen Sie, dass Sie am Gespräch teilnehmen – auch wenn Sie nur wenig sagen. Diese Form des Zuhörens sollten Sie natürlich nicht ausschließlich praktizieren, schließlich wollen und sollen Sie ja ab und zu auch mal etwas sagen ... Besonders bewährt hat sich das aufnehmende Zuhören immer dann, **wenn Ihr Gesprächspartner sehr emotional ist,** beispielsweise, weil er sich gerade furchtbar aufgeregt hat (*"Also, Sie glauben ja nicht, was der Meyer aus der Buchhaltung gerade zu mir gesagt hat ..."*) oder weil er etwas extrem Interessantes erlebt hat (*"Mahlzeit! Also, ich war ja gerade beim Chef, um mit ihm die Quartalszahlen durchzugehen, als plötzlich ..."*).

In solchen Situationen hören Sie am besten aufnehmend zu – und zwar so lange, bis der andere alles losgeworden ist.

2. Paraphrasieren

Auf der nächsten Stufe des aktiven Zuhörens „paraphrasieren" Sie: **Sie wiederholen mit eigenen Worten Informationen oder Argumente des Gesprächspartners** – und zwar am besten in Frageform formuliert, um ggf. eine Korrektur zu ermöglichen: *„Sie meinen also, ...", „Habe ich Sie richtig verstanden, dass ..."*

Beim Paraphrasieren reicht es tatsächlich aus, nur das Gehörte kurz zurückzuspiegeln – bitte keine negativen oder ironischen Bemerkungen (*„Habe ich Sie richtig verstanden, dass ...? Aber das ist doch sicher nicht Ihr Ernst?"*), keine Ergänzungen oder oberlehrerhaften Verbesserungen: *„Sie fanden also den Vortrag nicht so interessant? Sie sollten aber natürlich bedenken, dass ..."*

Paraphrasieren hilft zum einen, **Missverständnisse auszuschließen** und die Sichtweise des Gesprächspartners zu verstehen, zum anderen **gewinnen Sie mit dieser Technik Zeit,** um gut zu überlegen, was Sie antworten wollen. Und für den Fall, dass Ihnen jemand beim Small Talk ganz haarsträubende Dinge erzählt, schaffen Sie es durch Paraphrasieren besser, Ihre Emotionen zu kontrollieren: *„Sie finden also, dass berufstätige Mütter ihre Kinder vernachlässigen?", „Wenn ich Sie richtig verstehe, sind Sie ein Befürworter der Prügelstrafe an Schulen?"*

Falls Sie es in solchen Fällen auch noch schaffen, Ihre Körpersprache zu kontrollieren, also etwa das Entgleisen der Mimik oder das Entsetzen in der Stimme zu verhindern: Respekt!

3. Verbalisieren

Auf dieser dritten Stufe des aktiven Zuhörens sprechen Sie nicht mehr nur die Sachinhalte des Gesprächs an, sondern **Sie gehen auf die emotionalen, manchmal versteckten Botschaften ein.** Sie geben

emotions of your discussion partner, you show that you are participating in the conversation – even if you're actually saying very little. Of course, no one should use this form of listening exclusively; after all, you want to say something once in a while, too. Absorbent listening is most appropriate when your discussion partner is very emotional, for example, because they're upset about something (*"You won't believe what that guy in Accounting just said to me ..."*), or because they have experienced something of great interest (*"Hi! I've just been in the boss's office to go through the quarterly figures, when suddenly ..."*).

In situations like these, you're best off listening absorbingly for as long as it takes the other person to say everything they want to say.

2. Paraphrasing

At the next level of active listening, you "paraphrase": you repeat your discussion partner's information or arguments in your own words – and you do so ideally phrased in question form in order to enable a correction if needed: *"So you think ...",* *"Did I understand correctly that ..."*

In paraphrasing, it's actually enough to briefly reflect what you've heard, without any negative or ironic comments (*"Did I understand you right that ...? But you can't seriously mean that?"*), no supplements or patronising corrections: *"So, you didn't think the lecture was very interesting? But you should remember that ..."*

Paraphrasing is a technique that, on the one hand, helps to eliminate misunderstandings and to get a better grip on the viewpoint of the discussion partner, while also giving you sufficient time to consider how you want to respond on the other hand. And in the event that someone tells you something during small talk that's genuinely outrageous, paraphrasing will help you control your emotions more effectively: *"So you think that working mothers are neglecting their children?",* *"If I understand you right, you're in favour of corporal punishment in schools?"*

And all respect to you if you manage to control your body language in such instances by maintaining a calm facial expression or keeping an even inflection!

3. Verbalising

At this third level of active listening, you don't just address the factual content of the discussion any more. Instead, you respond to the more emotional, sometimes hidden messages. You use your own

Wie setze ich Gesprächstechniken richtig ein?

mit eigenen Worten die vermutlichen Stimmungen und Emotionen des Gesprächspartners wieder – vorausgesetzt, die Gesprächsatmosphäre gestattet dies. Schärfen Sie dafür Ihre Wahrnehmung für Zwischentöne: Nicht nur, was gesagt wird, sondern vor allem, wie es gesagt wird, ist interessant.

Um beim Verbalisieren deutlich zu machen, dass es sich um Ihre Wahrnehmung handelt und Sie bereit sind, Korrekturen und Widerspruch zu akzeptieren, formulieren Sie moderat: *„Ich habe den Eindruck, dass …", „Es kommt mir so vor, als ob …"*

Achten Sie immer darauf, dass gute Kommunikation umkehrbar sein muss: Darf Ihr Gegenüber das Gleiche auch zu Ihnen sagen, ohne dass Sie irritiert oder gar gekränkt wären?

Wie aktiv hören Sie zu? Testen Sie sich mit folgender Übung:

Welche Antwort ist Ihrer Meinung nach die beste, wenn Sie aktiv zuhören möchten?

1. *„Die Umgestaltung des Foyers finde ich absolut misslungen, der Innenarchitekt sollte den Beruf wechseln!"*
   a) *„Das finde ich auch!"*
   b) *„Sie finden, man hätte es anders machen sollen?"*
   c) *„Wieso? Die Wandgestaltung zum Beispiel finde ich gelungen, das sieht sehr elegant aus."*

2. *„Dass unser Projekt so gut gelaufen ist, hatte viel mit der Atmosphäre im Team zu tun."*
   a) *„Sie sind alle gut miteinander klargekommen?"*
   b) *„Ja, das spielt natürlich eine große Rolle!"*
   c) *„Ich denke, auch die strategische Planung und das Controlling sind immer ganz wichtig."*

3. *„In der Firma, in der ich vorher war, haben wir vieles ganz anders gemacht – na ja, man muss sich halt umstellen."*
   a) *„Gefällt es Ihnen hier denn nicht?"*
   b) *„In Ihrem vorherigen Job sind Sie anders vorgegangen?"*
   c) *„Sie haben recht, man muss einfach flexibel sein heutzutage."*

4. *„Also, mein Sohn, der hat ja jetzt Abitur gemacht, Spitzennoten, sage ich Ihnen, Spitzennoten! Der kann sich jetzt aussuchen, was er studieren will, dem stehen alle Karrierewege offen!"*
   a) *„Dann hoffen wir mal, dass weiter alles gut läuft – man liest ja so viel von arbeitslosen jungen Akademikern."*
   b) *„Das ist ja schön."*
   c) *„Da sind Sie bestimmt sehr stolz auf ihn."*

words to express the probable moods and emotions of the discussion partner – on the condition that the discussion atmosphere allows for it. So for this, sharpen up your perception of what's "between the lines": not only what's been said, but above all, how it's said is interesting here.

In order to clarify in verbalising that your perception is at issue and that you are prepared to accept corrections and contradiction, formulate your responses moderately: *"I have the impression that ...", "It seems to me like ..."*

Always remember that good communication has to be reciprocal: can your conversation partner say the same thing to you without your becoming irritated or even upset?

How actively do you listen? Test yourself with the following exercise:

> **Which one of the following answers is the best one if you want to listen actively?**
>
> 1. *"The way the foyer has been renovated is just awful. The interior decorator should change professions!"*
>   a) *"I think so, too!"*
>   b) *"You think it should've been done differently?"*
>   c) *"Why? I think he did a great job on the wall design, for instance. It looks very elegant."*
>
> 2. *"The atmosphere in the team was a big contributing factor to our project going so well."*
>   a) *"So you all got along well with each other?"*
>   b) *"Yes, of course that played a big role!"*
>   c) *"I think that strategic planning and controlling are also always really important."*
>
> 3. *"At the company where I used to work, we did lots of things very differently – oh well, you just have to adjust."*
>   a) *"Don't you like it here, then?"*
>   b) *"Things worked differently in your old job?"*
>   c) *"You're right. These days, you just have to be flexible."*
>
> 4. *"Hey, my son just finished school with top grades, I'm telling you, top grades! He can take his pick of colleges now; he can have any career he wants!"*
>   a) *"Then let's hope the good luck streak continues – you read so much these days about out-of-work young graduates."*
>   b) *"That's nice."*
>   c) *"You must be very proud of him."*

Wie setze ich Gesprächstechniken richtig ein?

5. „Früher war hier doch alles anders. Immer weniger Leuten, immer mehr Arbeit, und die Kunden werden ja auch immer schwieriger. Da kann eine Betriebsfeier wie heute auch nichts mehr bringen."
   a) „Kopf hoch – so schlimm ist es ja auch nicht!"
   b) „Klingt so, als wären Sie ziemlich frustriert."
   c) „Sie haben ja so recht – und ich glaube, es wird noch schlimmer."

6. „Das ist doch mal wieder typisch – wir in unserer Abteilung erfahren immer alles als Letzte!"
   a) „Sie fühlen sich nicht genügend einbezogen?"
   b) „Ach, regen Sie sich doch nicht so auf – meinen Sie denn, uns erzählt jemand was?"
   c) „So ist das eben hier in der Firma – und seit wir den neuen Geschäftsführer haben, ist alles noch schlimmer als früher."

7. „Und Sie glauben wirklich, dass Small Talk im Beruf wichtig ist?"
   a) „Absolut – je eher Sie das einsehen, umso besser für Sie und Ihre Karriere!"
   b) „Es gibt in der Tat viele Untersuchungen, die dies belegen."
   c) „Sie sind da noch skeptisch?"

Auflösung: 1b, 2a, 3b, 4c, 5b, 6a, 7c

3.2 Fragetechnik

„Fragensteller sind Weichensteller."
  Hans Leopold Davi (*1928), schweizer. Schriftsteller

Sie sind interessiert an Ihrem Gegenüber? Sie wollen etwas genauer wissen? Sie möchten ein Gespräch eröffnen, aber nicht gleich zu Beginn so viel erzählen? Sie würden gern andere in das Gespräch einbeziehen? Dann stellen Sie Fragen! Fragetechniken zu beherrschen, heißt zu wissen, welche Frageform man wie einsetzt. Folgende Frageformen gibt es:

Offene Fragen

Sie heißen so, weil sie ein Gespräch (er)öffnen. Offene Fragen sind W-Fragen, beginnen also mit Fragewörtern wie *warum, wie, womit, wann, wodurch*:

> „Wie war Ihre Anreise?"
> „Welchen Eindruck hatten Sie denn von dem Vortrag?"

Zu indiskret dürfen diese Fragen allerdings nicht sein – es gibt Dinge, die möchten wir eher verschlossen halten: *„Wie alt sind Sie eigentlich?", „Warum heiraten Sie eigentlich nicht?"*

Implement discussion techniques correctly

5. *"It was all different here before. Now there are fewer people, there's more work and the customers are getting more and more difficult. Not even a company party like we're having today can change that."*
   a) *"Chin up – it's not all that bad!"*
   b) *"Sounds like you're pretty frustrated."*
   c) *"You're right – and I think it's going to get even worse."*

6. *"That's so typical – in our department, we're always the last to know!"*
   a) *"Not feeling included enough?"*
   b) *"Ah, calm down – you think they tell us anything?"*
   c) *"That's just how it is at this company – and since the new Director's been here, it's worse than ever."*

7. *"And you really think that small talk is important to one's career?"*
   a) *"Absolutely – the sooner you realise that, the better for you and your career!"*
   b) *"There are actually lots of studies that prove it."*
   c) *"Are you still sceptical about that?"*

Answers: 1b, 2a, 3b, 4c, 5b, 6a, 7c

3.2 Questioning Technique

"Questioners are signalmen."
   Hans Leopold Davi (*1928), Swiss author

You're interested in your discussion partner? You want more precise information about something? You want to open a conversation, but don't want to do the lion's share of talking at the beginning? You'd like to include others in the conversation? Then ask questions! Being in command of questioning techniques means knowing which form of question to use and how to use it. The following **question forms** exist:

Open Questions

They're called "open" because they open a conversation. Open questions begin with interrogatives such as *why, which, how* and *when*:

> *"How was your trip?"*
> *"What was your impression of the lecture?"*

These questions must not be too indiscreet, however – there are some things we'd rather keep to ourselves: *"How old are you, actually?"*, *"Why aren't you getting married after all?"*

Geschlossene Fragen

Diese Fragen erfordern als Antwort nur ein Ja oder Nein und lassen ein Gespräch sehr viel schwerer als bei offenen Fragen aufkommen.

> *„Haben Sie gut hergefunden?" – „Ja, danke."*
> *„Gefiel Ihnen der Vortrag?" – „Ja."*

Aber auch diese Frageform hat ihren Platz: Immer da, wo Sie das Gespräch „schließen" wollen, passen geschlossene Fragen.

Manipulative oder suggestive Fragen

Diese Frageform sollten Sie grundsätzlich vermeiden – nicht nur beim Small Talk.

> *„Sie als Fachmann fanden den Vortrag doch bestimmt sehr langweilig?"*
> *„Gefiel Ihnen dieser merkwürdige Vortrag etwa?"*

Sie hinterlässt einen unangenehmen Nachgeschmack bei demjenigen, der so bedrängt wurde.

Alternativ-Fragen

Alternativ-Fragen können ebenfalls manipulativ wirken – nämlich dann, wenn einem nur zwei Alternativen angeboten werden, man aber weiß, dass es noch eine Menge mehr gibt:

> *„Möchten Sie Kaffee oder Tee?" – „Am liebsten hätte ich ein Wasser."*

Rhetorische Fragen

Das sind keine echten Fragen. Sie bedürfen also keiner Antwort:

> *„Ist das nicht ein herrliches Wetter heute?"*

Und deshalb sollten Sie sie im Small Talk vermeiden – denn der soll ja ein Dialog sein ...

Frageketten

Diese Variante schließlich ist absolut tabu. Hier werden mehrere Fragen direkt hintereinandergehängt:

Closed Questions
These kinds of questions require only a "yes" or "no" as an answer, making it much more difficult to start a conversation than with open questions.

> *"Did you find your way here easily enough?"* — *"Yes, thanks."*
> *"Did you enjoy the lecture?"* — *"Yes."*

But this form of question also has its place: closed questions are appropriate at the point where you want to "close" the discussion.

Manipulative or Suggestive Questions
You should fundamentally avoid this form of question – and not just in small talk.

> *"As an expert, you must've been bored to tears with that lecture?"*
> *"You didn't actually like that ridiculous lecture, did you?"*

They leave a bitter aftertaste with the person subjected to them.

Alternative Questions
Alternative questions can equally have a manipulative effect in the event that one is only offered two alternatives, when it's nevertheless clear that there are more:

> *"Would you like coffee or tea?"* — *"Actually I would prefer water."*

Rhetorical Questions
These are not genuine questions, and as such, they don't require an answer:

> *"Great weather today, huh?"*

And that's why you should avoid them in small talk, since it's supposed to be a dialogue …

Question Chains
In conclusion, this variation is an absolute taboo! This is when numerous questions follow one another consecutively:

> *Wie setze ich Gesprächstechniken richtig ein?*

> *„Wo kommen Sie eigentlich her? Und was machen Sie denn so beruflich? Sind Sie verheiratet? Und haben Sie Kinder?"*

So schön es ist, dass da jemand derart interessiert ist – es erinnert doch fatal an eine Verhörsituation. Und wissen Sie bei der vierten Frage noch, wie die erste lautete?

3.3 Positive Rhetorik

Wo immer es geht – und auch ehrlich klingt! –, äußern Sie etwas Positives. Mit Kritik, Besserwisserei und Ironie dagegen hält man sich besser zurück – vor allem natürlich, was die Anwesenden, speziell Gastgeber oder Veranstalter, betrifft. Die meisten von uns finden ein Gespräch mit Menschen, die eine positive Einstellung haben, deutlich angenehmer als eines mit jemandem, dem man es nie recht machen kann.

Wenn Sie bei Ihrem Gesprächspartner also positive Gefühle wecken möchten, gelingt Ihnen das, indem Sie aktiv zuhören, interessierte und höfliche Fragen stellen – und positiv formulieren. Und das bedeutet:

> *Positive Dinge sollten auch wirklich uneingeschränkt positiv dargestellt werden.*

Sie meinen, das ist doch klar? – Dann achten Sie mal darauf, wie viele Menschen etwas *„gar nicht mal schlecht"* statt *„gut"* finden.

Fortgeschrittene Rhetoriker schaffen es sogar, negative Formulierungen in positive umzuwandeln. Versuchen Sie es selbst:

> **Ersetzen Sie die negativen Formulierungen aus den Beispielsätzen durch positive, ohne die Sachaussage zu verändern.**

Negative Formulierung	Positive Formulierung
1. *„Das ist ein großes Problem."*	
2. *„Diese Veranstaltung ist ja leider völlig überfüllt."*	
3. *„Das ist nervenaufreibend!"*	
4. *„Sie haben einen Einwand?"*	

Implement discussion techniques correctly

> "Where are you actually from? And what's your profession? Are you married? And do you have children?"

As nice as it can be that someone is so interested, it still smacks of an interrogation! And after the fourth question, can you still remember what the first one was?

3.3 Positive Rhetoric

Wherever you can, and as long as it still sounds genuine, express yourself positively. In contrast, be reserved with criticism, "knowing-it-all" and irony – above all of course in regard to present company, especially hosts or event organisers. Most of us find a conversation with persons who have a positive attitude far more pleasant than one with someone who just can't be satisfied.

So if you want to awaken positive feelings in your discussion partner, you'll be able to do so by listening actively, asking interesting and polite questions and formulating your words positively.

> *And this means that positive things should genuinely be depicted positively, without reservation.*

You're thinking that this goes without saying? – Then pay attention to how many people describe something as *"not so bad"* instead of *"good"*.

Advanced rhetoricians even manage to transform negative formulations into positive ones. Try it yourself:

> Substitute the negative formulations in the following sample sentences with positive ones, without changing the basic statement.

Negative Formulation	Positive Formulation
1. *"That's a big problem."*	
2. *"Unfortunately, this event is completely overcrowded."*	
3. *"That's nerve-racking!"*	
4. *"You have an objection?"*	

Wie setze ich Gesprächstechniken richtig ein?

5. „Das ist doch unnormal!"

6. „Keine schlechte Idee."

7. „Was für eine Affenhitze!"

Auflösung:
1. „Das ist eine echte Herausforderung."
2. „Diese Veranstaltung ist wirklich ausgesprochen gut besucht."
3. „Ziemlich spannend!"
4. „Sie haben eine Frage?"
5. „Das ist ja außergewöhnlich!"
6. „Eine gute Idee!"
7. „Das ist ja ein tropisches Klima!"

Sie mögen einwenden, dass das doch alles nur oberflächlich und reine Verpackung ist. Und natürlich haben Sie recht! Aber genau diese Verpackung kann bewirken, dass der gleiche Inhalt besser aufgenommen wird:

Mal angenommen, Sie haben Geburtstag und bekommen Geschenke. Eines davon ist lieblos in die leicht angeschmuddelte Tüte eines Lebensmitteldiscounters gesteckt und mit Paketband verklebt. Die anderen Geschenke sind sorgfältig in schönes Papier verpackt, mit edlen Bändern und Schleifen verschnürt und dekoriert.

Ist er wirklich egal, der äußere Schein? Zählt tatsächlich nur der Inhalt?

4 Was lasse ich besser?

Die Don'ts der Kommunikation

Es gibt Dinge, die tut man besser nicht. In der Kommunikation zählen dazu vor allem die so genannten Kommunikationssperren, Killerphrasen und Trigger. Sie haben eines gemeinsam: Gespräche verändern sich durch sie zum Negativen, können sogar vorzeitig abgebrochen werden, Gesprächspartner sind verärgert oder verletzt. Trotzdem benutzen wir sie:
- manchmal aus Unkenntnis,
- manchmal aus Bequemlichkeit – man kann doch nicht jedes Wort auf die Goldwaage legen …,
- manchmal aus mangelnder Sensibilität – worüber der sich schon wieder aufregt …

Implement discussion techniques correctly

5. "That's completely abnormal!"

6. "Not a bad idea."

7. "The heat is awful!"

Answers:
1. *That's a real challenge.*
2. *This event is exceptionally well attended.*
3. *Pretty exciting!*
4. *You have a question?*
5. *That's really unusual!*
6. *Good idea!*
7. *That's a tropical climate here!*

You want to argue that this is all purely superficial and just different "packaging". And of course, you're right! But it's precisely this packaging that can make the same content more acceptable:

Let's assume it's your birthday and you receive presents. One of them is contained in a wrinkly bag from a discount supermarket chain and closed up with packaging tape. The others are carefully packed in appealing wrapping paper, decorated with ribbons and bows.

Is outward appearance really unimportant? Is the content really all that counts?

4 What shouldn't I do?

The "Don'ts" of Communication

There are things one is just better off not doing. In communication, these include first and foremost the so-called **communication roadblocks, killer phrases and triggers**. They all have one thing in common: their appearance turns discussions into negatives. They can even cause a discussion to be broken off and discussion partners to be irritated or offended. But we still use them,

- sometimes due to a simple lack of knowledge,
- sometimes out of convenience – you can't weigh up every word …,
- and sometimes because of a lack of sensitivity – what's he so upset about again?

Schauen Sie sich die folgenden Don'ts der Kommunikation an und überlegen Sie, wann und wie oft Sie sie selbst schon benutzt haben. Schaffen Sie es, den Gebrauch von Kommunikationssperren, Killerphrasen und Triggern sukzessive zu verringern? Ihre Gesprächspartner werden Ihnen dankbar sein!

4.1 Kommunikationssperren (nach Thomas Gordon)

Was halten Sie von folgendem Small-Talk-Dialog?

Die Situation
Ein Fortbildungskongress zum Thema „Neue Wege der Kundenbindung", 11.00 Uhr, Pause nach dem ersten Referat an der Kaffeebar. Einer der Teilnehmer, Reinhard Schniedermeyer, entdeckt eine Kollegin, Sabine Schröder, die im gleichen Unternehmen wie er arbeitet, allerdings in einer Filiale in einer anderen Stadt. Die beiden kennen sich bereits aus anderen Weiterbildungsveranstaltungen. Herr Schniedermeyer eröffnet den Small Talk:

— „Hallo, Frau Schröder! Hatten Sie eine gute Anreise? Oder war Stau? Sie sind ja sicher mit dem Auto hier, oder sind Sie ausnahmsweise mal mit der Bahn gefahren?"
— „Guten Morgen, Herr Schniedermeyer, schön, Sie zu sehen! Ja, ich bin mit dem Auto hier und ja, ich habe auf der A 45 im Stau gestanden – ziemlich lange sogar, es hat fast eine Stunde lang gedauert. Zum Glück bin ich aber noch pünktlich hier angekommen."
— „Ach, eine Stunde Stau, das ist doch überhaupt nicht viel, da können Sie sich nicht beklagen. Wissen Sie, was mir letzten Monat passiert ist? Als ich geschäftlich nach München musste, da habe ich sage und schreibe vier Staus gehabt und mehr als drei Stunden nur gestanden! Das war wirklich heftig, sage ich Ihnen!"
— „Ja, das klingt wirklich unangenehm, da waren Sie ja sehr lange unterwegs. Wie fanden Sie denn das Einstiegsreferat eben?"
— „Na ja, war ja nichts wirklich Neues. Und der Referent, der schien mir doch alles andere als sicher zu sein. Wahrscheinlich macht er das zum ersten Mal und ist nervös, das sehe ich ja an seiner Körpersprache. Ich habe gesehen, wie er mit den Unterlagen hantiert hat – total hibbelig."
— „Fanden Sie? Mir haben vor allem seine Beispiele gut gefallen, die waren doch sehr praxisnah, so richtig aus dem Leben gegriffen. Da habe ich oft unsere Kundengespräche wiedererkannt."
— „Manchmal schon, das stimmt. Aber rhetorisch ist der Gute eben nicht gerade beschlagen, na ja, das freie Reden ist nicht jedermanns Sache."
— „Das Referat nach der Pause klingt auch interessant, die Rednerin kennen wir ja aus einer anderen Fortbildung, das war letzten

> *What shouldn't I do?*

Have a look at the following "Don'ts" of communication and think about when and how often you've used them yourself. Can you manage to successively reduce your own use of communication roadblocks, killer phrases and triggers? Your discussion partners will thank you for it!

4.1 Communication Roadblocks (according to Thomas Gordon)

What do you think of the following small talk dialogue?

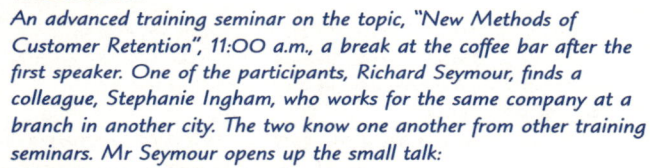

> **The situation**
> *An advanced training seminar on the topic, "New Methods of Customer Retention", 11:00 a.m., a break at the coffee bar after the first speaker. One of the participants, Richard Seymour, finds a colleague, Stephanie Ingham, who works for the same company at a branch in another city. The two know one another from other training seminars. Mr Seymour opens up the small talk:*
>
> – *"Hello, Stephanie! Did you have a good drive, or did you get caught in traffic? You came by car, didn't you, or did you break the bank and come by train this time?"*
> – *"Good morning, Richard. Nice to see you! Yes, I drove and I got stuck in traffic on the motorway — pretty long this time, too. It took almost an hour to loosen up, but luckily I still managed to get here on time."*
> – *"Ah, an hour in traffic? That's nothing! You can't complain about that. You know what happened to me? I had a business trip last month where I swear I got caught in four different traffic jams. I spent over three hours just sitting there! That was really awful, I'm telling you!"*
> – *"Yeah, that really sounds bad. That's a long time to be stuck. So, what did you think about the first speaker just now?"*
> – *"Well, it wasn't really anything new. And the speaker himself didn't seem all that confident. It's probably his first time and he was nervous. I could see that in his body language. I could see how he was fiddling with his papers — really flustered."*
> – *"Did you think so? I really liked his examples. They were very practical, straight out of real life. I was often reminded of our own client discussions."*
> – *"Yeah, here and there. But he's not great with rhetoric. I guess public speaking just isn't for everyone."*
> – *"The lecture after the break also sounds interesting. We've already heard her speak once in another seminar last autumn. Remember? She uses humour a lot and she's also good at getting complicated things across simply."*
> – *"I didn't think so."*

Was lasse ich besser?

> *Herbst in Hamburg. Erinnern Sie sich? Sie hat viel Humor und schafft es, auch komplizierte Dinge locker rüberzubringen."*
> – *"Fand ich gar nicht."*
> – *"Bleiben Sie denn beide Tage hier, Herr Schniedermeyer? Es fällt einem ja oft schwer, sich so lange frei zu machen im Betrieb."*
> – *"Damit habe ich keine Probleme: Delegation, liebe Kollegin, das ist das Zauberwort! Sie müssen einfach die richtigen Prioritäten setzen und auch mal entsprechend delegieren, dann können Sie sich auch für solche wichtigen Weiterbildungen freimachen. Generell hängt doch alles am persönlichen Zeitmanagement. Ich sage immer: Gute Planung ist die halbe Arbeit!"*
> – *"Das ist sicher richtig."*
> – *"Sie müssen unbedingt das Buch ‚Zeit nutzen, statt sie zu verschwenden' lesen! Das ist von diesem berühmten Wissenschaftler, Professor Börger. Wissen Sie was: Ich schicke es Ihnen nächste Woche mal zu, dann gucken Sie sich das mal genau an."*
> – *"Das ist nett, danke."*
> – *"Das wird Ihnen gefallen, dieses Buch. Sie sind doch eine clevere Person, Sie haben sogar studiert, oder? Eine richtige Karrierefrau, ha ha! Wenn Sie da kein gutes Zeitmanagement haben, droht Ihnen irgendwann der Burn-out! Und dann werden Sie bereuen, dass Sie nicht eher was verändert haben!"*
> – *"Ach, ich sehe da vorn gerade eine Bekannte, die muss ich unbedingt begrüßen. Wir sehen uns ja sicher später noch, Herr Schniedermeyer – tschüss!"*

Wenn Ihnen Frau Schröder im Verlauf des Gespräches zunehmend leidtat und Ihnen Herr Schniedermeyer immer unsympathischer wurde, liegt das daran, dass seine Gesprächsbeiträge allesamt aus Kommunikationssperren bestanden.

Können Sie diese identifizieren und beschreiben, was genau er da tut? Versuchen Sie es mal:

> *"Hallo, Frau Schröder! Hatten Sie eine gute Anreise? Oder war Stau? Sie sind ja sicher mit dem Auto hier, oder sind Sie ausnahmsweise mal mit der Bahn gefahren?"*

Fragen zu stellen ist prima und absolut erwünscht. Das zeigt Ihrem Gesprächspartner, dass Sie interessiert sind. Eine ganz andere Sache sind Frageketten, bei denen der Gefragte gar nicht weiß, worauf er zuerst antworten soll. Auch bohrende oder indiskrete Fragen sind unerwünscht – und die Kommunikationssperre, die Herr Schniedermeyer hier benutzt, lautet dementsprechend: Ausfragen, verhören – statt fragen.

> *What shouldn't I do?*

- "Are you staying both days, Richard? Sometimes it's really hard to leave the office for so long."
- "I've got no problem with that! Delegation, my dear, that's the magic word! You just have to set your priorities right and delegate accordingly, and then you can take time too for these kinds of important advanced training sessions. Generally speaking, it's all about personal time management. I always say, 'Good planning is half the job done'!"
- "I guess that's right."
- "You've just got to read the book, 'Using Time Instead Of Wasting It'! It's by that famous scientist, Professor Burger. You know what? I'll send it to you next week. Then read it yourself."
- "That's nice, thanks."
- "You'll like this book. You're a clever person. You even went to college, didn't you? A real career woman, ha ha! If you don't manage your time right, then at some point you'll face a burn-out, and you'll regret not having changed things earlier!"
- "Oh, I see someone I know over there. I've got to go say hello. Probably see you later, Richard – bye!"

If you found yourself feeling increasingly sorry for Ms Ingham during the course of the conversation, while Mr Seymour appeared ever more unpleasant, this is because all of his contributions to the discussion consisted of communication roadblocks.

Can you identify these and describe exactly what he's doing there? Try it one time:

> "Hello, Stephanie! Did you have a good drive, or did you get caught in traffic? You came by car, didn't you, or did you break the bank and come by train this time?"

It's OK and even absolutely desirable to ask questions. That shows your discussion partner that you're interested. Question chains, however, are something completely different, in which the person being questioned has no idea what they should answer first. Probing or indiscreet questions are not desired – and the communication roadblock that Mr Seymour uses here reads: quizzing, interrogating – instead of asking.

> *„Ach, eine Stunde Stau, das ist doch überhaupt nicht viel, da können Sie sich nicht beklagen."*

Eine beliebte Kommunikationssperre: das Herunterspielen und Verharmlosen von etwas, das man Ihnen erzählt, das Beschwichtigen des Gesprächspartners: *„Ach, so schlimm ist das doch gar nicht ...", „Morgen sieht das schon ganz anders aus!"*

Ist doch nett gemeint? – Vielleicht. Meist sieht es aber eher nach Interesselosigkeit (*„Und was geht mich das an?"*) oder sogar nach Unverständnis (*„Über welche Kleinigkeiten regt der sich eigentlich auf?"*) aus. In jedem Fall fühlt sich der Gesprächspartner mit seinem Problem nicht ernst genommen – und das fördert den Gesprächsverlauf nicht.

> *„Wissen Sie, was mir letzten Monat passiert ist? Als ich geschäftlich nach München musste, da habe ich sage und schreibe vier Staus gehabt und mehr als drei Stunden nur gestanden! Das war wirklich heftig, sage ich Ihnen!"*

Sie haben es erkannt? Da redet jemand lieber von sich, holt – vielleicht um abzulenken oder auszuweichen, etwa weil ihm das Thema unangenehm ist – den Ball in seine Spielhälfte: *„Das kenne ich! Bei mir war es damals ja so, dass ..."* Und aus (leidvoller) Erfahrung wissen wir: Da bleibt der Ball dann häufig auch, mit dem Dialog war es das erst einmal. Small Talk sollte aber möglichst ausgeglichene Redeanteile aller Gesprächspartner haben.

Also: Eigene Ansichten oder Erfahrungen beizutragen, ist völlig okay, dauernd und in langen Monologen von sich zu reden hingegen nicht. In Kombination mit der vorhergehenden Kommunikationssperre von Herrn Schniedermeyer, nämlich dem Herunterspielen der Erfahrungen des Gegenübers, wirkt es umso unangenehmer, dass er nur von sich redet.

> *„Na ja, war ja nichts wirklich Neues. Und der Referent – der schien mir doch auch alles andere als sicher zu sein. Wahrscheinlich macht er das zum ersten Mal und ist nervös, das sehe ich ja an seiner Körpersprache. Ich habe gesehen, wie er mit den Unterlagen hantiert hat – total hibbelig."*

Eine ausgesprochen verbreitete Kommunikationssperre ist es, dem Gesprächspartner eine Diagnose seines Verhaltens zu stellen: Wir

> *What shouldn't I do?*

> *"Ah, an hour in traffic? That's nothing! You can't complain about that."*

One popular communication roadblock: downplaying and trivialising something that someone tells you, or placating the discussion partners: *"Ah, that's not so bad ...", "By tomorrow you'll have forgotten about it!"*

It's meant well? – Maybe. But usually it just seems like a lack of interest (*"And what does that have to do with me?"*), or even a lack of understanding (*"Some people get upset about nothing."*). In any case, the discussion partner is left feeling that their problem isn't being taken seriously – and that doesn't advance the course of the conversation.

> *"You know what happened to me? I had a business trip last month where I swear I got caught in four different traffic jams. I spent over three hours just sitting there! That was really awful, I'm telling you!"*

Did you recognise it? Here's someone who prefers to talk about themselves. Perhaps it's to divert attention or avoid a subject that's somehow unpleasant for them, but what they're doing is moving the ball into their own court: *"I know how that is! For me back then it was like ..."* And from (bitter) experience, we know that that's where the ball is likely to stay, and that was that for the dialogue this time. But small talk should be equally divided as much as possible among all of the discussion partners.

So, it's OK to contribute one's own views or experiences, but it's a no-no to continuously, repeatedly talk about oneself in long monologues. In combination with Mr Seymour's previous communication roadblock, namely downplaying the experiences of the other person, it's even more unpleasant that he only talks about himself.

> *"Well, it wasn't really anything new. And the speaker himself didn't seem all that confident. It's probably his first time and he was nervous. I could see that in his body language. I could see how he was fiddling with his papers — really flustered."*

A particularly widespread communication roadblock is to diagnose the conduct of the discussion partner: we not only believe we know

glauben nicht nur zu wissen, warum sich jemand auf die beobachtete Weise verhält, wir melden es ihm oder ihr auch zurück. Widerspruch ist sinnlos: *„Ich kenne dich doch!"*

Dass das den anderen nervt, ist klar. Jemand, der glaubt, uns und unser Verhalten beurteilen zu können, wirkt überheblich und fördert den gleichberechtigten Dialog nicht. Also: Geben Sie Interpretationen und Diagnosen im Gespräch am besten nur auf Nachfrage ab.

Was hat Herr Schniedermeyer uns noch zu bieten? Die nächste Kommunikationssperre erkennen Sie bestimmt sofort:

> *„Aber rhetorisch ist der Gute eben nicht gerade beschlagen, na ja, das freie Reden ist nicht jedermanns Sache."*

Jawohl, er kritisiert – und das eben nicht konstruktiv: Er spottet, er ist ironisch. Auch wenn man generell beim Small Talk vorsichtig mit Kritik sein sollte: Konstruktive Verbesserungsvorschläge sind in Maßen okay; spöttische, herabsetzende Bemerkungen hingegen sind tabu – ebenso wie Ironie.

Auf den diplomatischen Versuch seiner Kollegin, dem Gespräch eine etwas positivere Richtung zu geben, reagiert Herr Schniedermeyer mit einer weiteren Kommunikationssperre:

> *„Das Referat nach der Pause klingt auch interessant, die Rednerin kennen wir ja aus einer anderen Fortbildung, das war letzten Herbst in Hamburg. Erinnern Sie sich? Sie hat viel Humor und schafft es, auch komplizierte Dinge locker rüberzubringen."*
> *„Fand ich gar nicht."*

Auch diese Kommunikationssperre ist weit verbreitet: Wir stellen – oft ungeprüfte und nicht durch Argumente belegte – Gegenbehauptungen auf: *„Stimmt doch gar nicht!"*

Wenn Sie widersprechen möchten, sollten Sie Ihre Gegenbehauptung stets argumentativ belegen. Beim Small Talk können und sollten Sie aber durchaus auch gewagte Behauptungen mal einfach stehen lassen, statt in eine Diskussion einzusteigen: *„Das ist eine interessante Sichtweise."* Oder, wenn Ihnen nichts anderes dazu einfällt: *„Aha."*

Es gibt noch mehr Kommunikationssperren – und Herr Schniedermeyer kennt sie alle:

What shouldn't I do?

why someone behaves in the way we've observed, we also go on to report it back to them. Protest is useless: *"I know you!"*

It's no mystery that this gets on the other person's nerves. Someone who believes they're capable of judging our behaviour comes across as condescending and doesn't promote an equitable dialogue. So as a rule, only express interpretations and diagnoses in a conversation when asked.

What else does Mr Seymour have in store for us? You're sure to recognise the next communication roadblock right away:

> *"But he's not great with rhetoric. I guess public speaking just isn't for everyone."*

Of course, he criticises – and he doesn't do it constructively. Instead, he's scoffing, he's ironic. Even though one should generally be careful with criticism in small talk, constructive suggestions for improvement are OK in small doses; but derisive, disparaging comments are out of bounds – just like irony.

In response to the diplomatic attempt by his colleague to turn the conversation in a somewhat more positive direction, Mr Seymour reacts with yet another communication roadblock:

> *"The lecture after the break also sounds interesting. We've already heard her speak once in another seminar last autumn. Remember? She uses humour a lot and she's also good at getting complicated things across simply."*
> *"I didn't think so."*

This communication roadblock is also very widespread. We contradict, often with no verifiable basis or argument: *"That's not true!"*

If you want to contradict something, then you should always substantiate your argument. In small talk, however, you should by all means simply let claims, even bold assertions, stand as they are instead of getting involved in a discussion about them: *"That's an interesting viewpoint."* Or, if you just can't think of anything else: *"Aha."*

There are even more communication roadblocks – and Mr Seymour knows them all:

> 👁 *„Delegation, liebe Kollegin, das ist das Zauberwort! Sie müssen einfach die richtigen Prioritäten setzen und auch mal entsprechend delegieren, dann können Sie sich auch für solche wichtigen Weiterbildungen freimachen."*

Ein echter Besserwisser, nicht wahr? Herr Schniedermeyer tut hier etwas, das viele Menschen auf die Palme treibt: Er liefert Lösungen. Klingt zunächst doch gut, sogar hilfreich? Im Prinzip schon, nur: Er liefert die Lösung erstens ungefragt und zweitens für ein Problem, das er der Kollegin unterstellt, das sie aber möglicherweise gar nicht hat.

Wenn wir jemanden um eine Lösung bitten, freuen wir uns meist über einen Ratschlag. Etwas völlig anderes sind ungebetene Ratschläge. Daher gilt: Ganz gleich, wie gut wir uns mit einem Thema auskennen – auf Nachfragen geben wir gern Empfehlungen, unerbeten niemals. Denn wer will schon beim Small Talk als Besserwisser – wie Herr Schniedermeyer – dastehen?

Und der arbeitet weiter eifrig daran, sich unbeliebt zu machen:

> 👁 *„Generell hängt doch alles am persönlichen Zeitmanagement, ich sage immer: Gute Planung ist die halbe Arbeit!"*

Schwer, etwas darauf zu erwidern – im Grunde hat er ja recht. Und trotzdem reizt der Satz irgendwie ...

Lebensweisheiten zum Besten geben, kommt in der Tat bei den meisten Gesprächspartnern nicht gut an. Sie kennen solche Sprüche, haben sich vielleicht sogar schon dabei ertappt, dass Sie sie selbst anbringen: *„Wer A sagt, muss auch B sagen!" „Es geht im Leben eben nicht immer alles nach Wunsch!"* Ein echter Dialog kann so kaum aufkommen. Lassen Sie's besser sein – befreien Sie Ihre Kommunikation von derartigen moralisierenden Sinnsprüchen und weitgehend inhaltsfreien Lebensweisheiten.

Was hat Her Schniedermeyer noch im Köcher?

> 👁 *„Sie müssen unbedingt das Buch ‚Zeit nutzen, statt sie zu verschwenden' lesen! Das ist von diesem berühmten Wissenschaftler, dem Professor Börger. Wissen Sie was: Ich schicke es Ihnen nächste Woche mal zu, dann gucken Sie sich das mal genau an."*

Auffordern, anordnen, befehlen – eine weitere Kommunikationssperre. Auch hier gilt: In einer entsprechenden Situation jemanden aufzufordern, etwas zu tun, ist in Ordnung. Im Small Talk mit einer Kollegin im Befehlston zu kommunizieren, ist es nicht.

> *What shouldn't I do?*

> "Delegation, my dear, that's the magic word! You just have to set your priorities right and delegate accordingly, and then you can take time too for these kinds of important advanced training sessions."

A real know-all, isn't he? Mr Seymour does something here that drives many people nuts: he's offering solutions. Sounds good at first, even helpful, doesn't it? Essentially, yes. However, first of all, he's offering the solution without being asked, and second, it's for a problem he's implying his colleague has, and that might not be the case at all.

When we ask someone for a solution, we're usually happy to get a piece of advice. Unrequested advice is a completely different story. So the rule is no matter how well we know our way around a particular topic – when asked, we're happy to make recommendations; if not asked, then never. After all, who wants to be remembered from a small talk discussion as a know-it-all like Mr Seymour?

And off he goes again in his quest to be unpopular:

> "Generally speaking, it's all about personal time management. I always say, 'Good planning is half the job done'!"

Hard to retort – because fundamentally, he's right. But still, that statement is irritating somehow...

In fact, treating people to "nuggets of wisdom" is usually not well received by most discussion partners. You know the kind of sayings, and may even have caught yourself using them: *"Don't start something you're not prepared to finish!", "Life's not a bowl of cherries!"* But a genuine dialogue can hardly emerge in this way. Resist the temptation – liberate your communication from those types of moralising aphorisms and generally meaningless, allegedly "wise" sayings.

What's Mr Seymour still got up his sleeve?

> "You've just got to read the book, 'Using Time Instead Of Wasting It'! It's by that famous scientist, Professor Burger. You know what? I'll send it to you next week. Then read it yourself."

Demanding, ordering, commanding – just one more communication roadblock. Here again, it's OK to demand something of someone in the appropriate situation. But it's not OK in small talk to communicate with a colleague in a commanding tone.

> *Was lasse ich besser?*

> *"Das wird Ihnen gefallen, dieses Buch. Sie sind doch eine clevere Person, Sie haben sogar studiert, oder? Eine richtige Karrierefrau, ha ha!"*

Herr Schniedermeyer lobt. Aber Loben ist doch gut? Ja, stimmt. Allerdings darf das Lob niemals gönnerhaft klingen, dann verfehlt es seine Wirkung komplett: *"Das machen Sie doch schon sehr schön."*, *"Hätte ich Ihnen ja gar nicht zugetraut, dass Sie das schaffen."* Auch allzu durchschaubare Schmeicheleien machen keinen guten Eindruck. Ehrliche Anerkennung dagegen, die darf es jederzeit und zwar reichlich geben – aber die sieht eben anders aus als in diesem Beispiel.

> *"Wenn Sie da kein gutes Zeitmanagement haben, droht Ihnen irgendwann der Burn-out! Und dann werden Sie bereuen, dass Sie nicht eher was verändert haben!"*

Die nächste Kommunikationssperre: Herr Schniedermeyer mahnt und warnt. Das zeigt deutlich, wie hier jemand unter Druck gesetzt werden soll. Die (angeblich unausweichlichen!) Konsequenzen werden drastisch benannt – das ist eine häufig angewandte **Manipulationsstrategie**: Kann man jemanden nicht von der gewünschten Verhaltensänderung überzeugen, dann versucht man, ihm ein schlechtes Gewissen zu machen, etwa so: *"Bitte, wenn du das nicht willst. Dir sollten aber die Konsequenzen klar sein …"*, *"Sie müssen ja wissen, was Sie da tun."*

Es gibt Dinge, die unterlässt man im Gespräch besser – jedenfalls dann, wenn man ein konstruktives und angenehmes Gesprächsklima anstrebt.

Reflektieren Sie Ihre Kommunikationsgewohnheiten. Ist Ihnen erst einmal bewusst, was Sie tun, können Sie es auch verändern.

Vorausgesetzt natürlich, Sie wollen es. Aber wer will schon ein Herr Schniedermeyer sein …

4.2 Killerphrasen

Jeder kennt sie, diese Phrasen, die das Gespräch regelrecht abwürgen:
- *"Das kann ich mir nicht vorstellen."*
- *"Das bringt doch sowieso nichts."*
- *"Das hat noch nie funktioniert."*
- Und die absolute Lieblingsphrase im Job: *"Das haben wir aber noch nie so gemacht!"*

> *"You'll like this book. You're a clever person. You even went to college, didn't you? A real career woman, ha ha!"*

Mr Seymour is paying a compliment. And complimenting is good, right? Yes, of course. But praise should never sound patronising, because this undermines its effect completely: *"You're doing fine on that after all.", "I would never have thought you'd get it done."* And flattery that's all too obvious also doesn't make a genuinely good impression. In contrast, honest praise is permitted anytime and in generous helpings – but such praise sounds different than what we see in this example.

> *"If you don't manage your time right, then at some point you'll face a burn-out, and you'll regret not having changed things earlier!"*

The next communication roadblock: Mr. Seymour admonishes and warns. This clearly shows how someone is supposed to be pressured. The (allegedly inevitable!) consequences are drastically specified. This is a frequently used manipulation strategy. Failing to persuade someone else to change their conduct in the desired manner, the protagonist then tries to make them feel guilty, for example: *"OK, if you don't want to. But you should be aware of the consequences ...", "You're old enough to know better."*

There are things that should be avoided in a conversation – in any case, if you're trying to achieve a constructive, pleasant discussion climate.

Think about your communication habits. Are you aware of what you're doing? Can you also change it?

And of course, that's on the condition that you want to change it. But hey, who wants to be a Mr Seymour anyway ...

4.2 Killer Phrases

Everybody knows them; the phrases that genuinely strangle a conversation:
- *"I can't imagine that."*
- *"That won't do any good anyway."*
- *"That's never worked before."*
- and the all-time, absolute favourite job phrase: *"But we've never done it like that before!"*

> Was lasse ich besser?

Killerphrasen sind weit verbreitet; sie werden beispielsweise gern zur Abwehr eingesetzt: Wenn wir uns auf das Gesagte einließen, hätte das ja Konsequenzen, wir müssten etwas tun, das uns nicht so angenehm erscheint ...

👁 Zwei Kolleginnen unterhalten sich in der Mittagspause

- *„Du hast doch auch immer so schreckliche Rückenschmerzen – ich habe da jetzt etwas entdeckt, das mir hilft: Ich gehe zweimal die Woche zum Pilates, das ist so eine Art Gymnastik, die die Muskeln stärkt. Und seit Kurzem sind meine Rückenschmerzen wie weggeblasen!"*
- *„Kann ich mir gar nicht vorstellen."*
- *„Doch, wirklich! Es ist zwar ganz schön anstrengend, ich hatte die ersten Wochen furchtbaren Muskelkater, aber jetzt geht es mir super – komm doch mal mit."*
- *„Bei mir funktioniert das sowieso nicht."*

Das Prinzip ist klar, nicht? Wer also im Gespräch nicht stur, uneinsichtig und träge wirken möchte, sollte seine Blockadehaltung aufgeben und sich den Gebrauch von Killerphrasen abgewöhnen.

Und was macht man, wenn der Gesprächspartner beim Small Talk ein sturer Killerphrasenbenutzer ist? – Wenn Sie das Gespräch nicht ohne weiteres beenden können, weil Sie z.B. beim Geschäftsessen neben dem Chef oder einem wichtigen Kunden sitzen, können Sie entweder das Thema wechseln oder mittels Fragetechnik versuchen, die Blockadehaltung aufzuweichen.

Nehmen wir an, Sie erzählen Ihrem Gesprächspartner, dass Sie dabei sind, ein Haus zu bauen. Sie haben die Planung gemeinsam mit einem Architekten erstellt und wollen jetzt – aufgrund Ihrer Erfahrungen als Projektmanager – den ganzen Ablauf selbst managen und steuern. Ihr Gesprächspartner: *„Das klappt sowieso nicht, das werden Sie schon sehen. Hat bei uns auch nicht funktioniert."*

Wenn Sie jetzt dranbleiben wollen, können Sie es mit zwei unterschiedlichen Frageformen probieren:

- **Die analysierende, forschende W-Frage:** *„Wie sind Sie denn bei Ihrem Hausbau vorgegangen?"*
  Jetzt wird Ihr Gesprächspartner Ihnen zwar vermutlich alles aufzählen, was nicht geklappt hat – aber immerhin sind Sie weiter im Gespräch. Und vielleicht kriegen Sie sogar ein paar nützliche Hinweise, worauf Sie beim Hausbau wirklich achten sollten.

What shouldn't I do?

Killer phrases are widespread; for example, they're used often as defence mechanisms: if we were to accept what's been said, then that would have consequences, and we'd have to do something that doesn't seem very pleasant …

Two co-workers are talking in the lunch break

- *"You've always got such terrible back pain, too. I've found something now that helps me: I go to Pilates twice a week. It's a kind of gymnastic exercise that strengthens the muscles. And lately it's like my back pain has vanished!"*
- *"I can't imagine that."*
- *"No, really! OK, it's pretty exhausting, and for the first few weeks my muscles were awfully sore. But now I feel great – come with me sometime."*
- *"It won't work for me anyway."*

The principle is clear, isn't it? So if you don't want to appear stubborn, contrary and lethargic in conversation, then relinquish your blockade posture and get out of the habit of using killer phrases.

And what can you do if your small talk discussion partner is a dyed-in-the-wool killer phrase user? – If you can't just end the conversation as such, for example, because you're at a business dinner and you're sitting next to the boss or an important client, then you can either change the subject or use questioning techniques to soften up the blockade posture.

Let's assume you're telling your discussion partner about how you're in the process of building a house. You've finished the planning with the architect and now – thanks to your experience as a project manager – you want to manage and control the entire course of construction. Your discussion partner: *"That won't work anyway. You'll see. It didn't work for us, either."*

If you now want to continue, then you can try with two different question forms:

- The analysing, inquisitive open question: *"How did you go about it with your house?"*
  Now your discussion partner will probably go on to tell you about everything that didn't work out – but you're still talking with one another. And maybe you'll even get some valuable tips about what you really need to pay attention to in building your house.

- Sie können die W-Frage auch konstruktiv stellen bzw. nach der analysierenden eine konstruktive Frage formulieren: *„Was würden Sie aufgrund Ihrer Erfahrung denn heute anders machen?"* Und jetzt kann Ihr Gesprächspartner nicht mehr einfach nur negativ sein – jetzt muss er konstruktiv werden.

4.3 Trigger (Reizformulierungen)

Genauso, wie es positive Formulierungen mit entsprechender Wirkung gibt, gibt es auch Wörter und Floskeln, die eine spürbar negative Wirkung auf uns haben. Dass solche Reizwörter oder -formulierungen im Small Talk nichts zu suchen haben, leuchtet ein. Lassen Sie folgende Sätze auf sich wirken:

> *„Aber Sie müssen doch zugeben ..."*
> *„Das müssen Sie doch einsehen!"*
> *„Sie müssen schon entschuldigen, aber ..."*

Das Wort „müssen" löst in der Regel eine Gegenreaktion aus: Muss ich wirklich? ... und schon bin ich auf Widerstand gepolt.

Ähnlich sieht es aus, wenn uns jemand erzählt, dass wir etwas (angeblich) nicht können:

> *„Sie können aber doch nicht ..."*
> *„Das können Sie mir nicht erzählen!"*

Auch hier formiert sich Widerstand: Und ob ich kann!

Das unpersönliche „man" gehört ebenfalls zu den Triggern:

> *„Man darf aber natürlich nicht ..."*

Wer ist „man"? Ich nicht!

Bei den folgenden Sätzen muss man ein äußerst gelassener Mensch sein, um sich nicht aufzuregen:

> *„Was Sie da sagen, stimmt so natürlich nicht."*
> *„Da haben Sie mich wohl nicht richtig verstanden ..."*
> *„Ich habe Ihnen ja eben schon erklärt ..."*
> *„Sie irren sich, wenn Sie denken ..."*
> *„Wenn Sie mal ganz ehrlich sind ..."*

Diese Aussagen wirken ziemlich nervig, oder? Also: Bitte abgewöhnen oder wenigstens weitgehend vermeiden!

> *What shouldn't I do?*

- You can also pose the open question constructively, or formulate a constructive question as a follow-up to the analysing question: *"Based on your experience, what would you do differently now?"* And now your discussion partner can't simply be negative any more – now he has to be constructive.

4.3 Triggers (Provocative Formulations)

Just as there are positive formulations with the corresponding effect, there are also words and idioms that have a noticeably negative effect on us. It makes sense that these kinds of provocative words or phrases have no place in small talk. Check the effect that the following sentences have on you:

> *"But you have to admit …"*
> *"Surely you must agree!"*
> *"You'll have to excuse me, but …"*

Generally, the words "must" or "have to" trigger a counter-reaction: must I really …, and resistance is pre-programmed.

It's similar when someone tells us that we (allegedly) can't do something:

> *"But you just can't …"*
> *"You can't tell me that!"*

Here, too, resistance is formed: oh yes, I can!

The impersonal word "one" is also one of these triggers:

> *"Naturally, one can't …"*

Who's "one"? Not me!

In the following sentences, you would need to be an extremely easy-going person to avoid getting upset:

> *"What you're saying there is not actually true."*
> *"Then you just didn't understand me correctly …"*
> *"I just explained to you …"*
> *"You're wrong if you think …"*
> *"If you're really honest …"*

These statements are pretty irritating, aren't they? Therefore, break the habit of using them or at least avoid them as much as possible!

5 Wie kann ich über die Körpersprache einen guten Eindruck machen?

Körpersprache verstehen und nutzen

Der erste Eindruck, den Sie auf jemanden machen oder den Sie von jemandem gewinnen, entsteht durch das gesprochene Wort, d.h. durch das, was Sie sagen, und durch die Körpersprache, also wie Sie es sagen (Körperhaltung, Mimik, Gestik, Stimme und Tonfall).

Wie hoch, schätzen Sie, ist der Anteil der Körpersprache an diesem ersten Eindruck? _____ %

Lagen Sie richtig? Tatsächlich hat der amerikanische Psychologe Albert Mehrabian in den 1970er-Jahren die These aufgestellt, dass sich 93 % des ersten Eindrucks, den wir von anderen Menschen haben oder auf diese machen, über die Körpersprache übermitteln. Mehr dazu lesen Sie im folgenden Kasten.

> ✓ **Die Bedeutung der Körpersprache**
>
> Stolze 55 % des ersten Eindrucks entstehen über Haltung, Gestik und Mimik:
> - Wie steht, geht und sitzt jemand? Offen oder verschlossen, aufrecht oder gebückt? Macht er sich groß oder eher klein?
> - Welche Gestik zeigt er oder sie: ruhig, ausladend, vielleicht hektisch?
> - Und auch die Mimik spricht Bände: Schaut jemand ernst, lächelt er, wirkt das Gesicht ausdruckslos?
>
> Immerhin noch 38 % des ersten Eindrucks resultieren aus Stimme und Tonfall:
> - Wie ist das Redetempo?
> - Betont jemand ausdrucksvoll oder redet er eher monoton?
> - Spricht er mit tiefer oder eher hoher Stimme?
> - Ist die Stimme barsch oder weich?
> - Wie ist die Lautstärke?
>
> Nur 7 % des ersten Eindrucks dagegen entstehen durch das gesprochene Wort – d.h., die Worte selbst, die Sie zu Beginn eines Gespräches wählen, sind gar nicht so entscheidend. Der Gesichtsausdruck (möglichst freundlich und interessiert), der Händedruck (kurz, trocken und fest), die Haltung (aufrecht und offen) und die Tonlage (ausdrucksvoll) dagegen sind es sehr! Nach diesem ersten Eindruck wird dann natürlich das gesprochene Wort wieder wichtiger – allerdings ist es schwer, gegen einen mäßigen oder sogar katastrophalen ersten Eindruck anzureden …

5 How can I make a good impression with my body language?

Understanding and Using Body Language

The first impression that you make on someone or that you get from someone arises through the spoken word, i.e., through what is said, and through the body language, meaning how it's said (physical posture, facial expression, gestures, voice and inflection).

Make an estimate as to what degree of this first impression consists of body language: _____ %

Were you right? In fact, the American psychologist Albert Mehrabian proposed the theory in the 1970s that 93 % of the first impression that we make on or get from other people is conveyed through body language. There's more to read about this in the following box.

> **The Significance of Body Language** ✓
>
> A healthy 55 % of the first impression comes from posture, gestures and facial expressions:
> - How does someone stand, walk and sit? Do they do so openly or closed, straight or hunched over? Do they make themselves large or small?
> - What kind of gestures do they make: calm, sweeping, perhaps hectic?
> - And facial expressions also speak volumes: do they look serious, are they smiling, does the face seem expressionless?
>
> In any case, 38 % of the first impression still results from the voice and inflection:
> - What is the speaking tempo?
> - Does someone emphasise their phrases expressively, or do they tend instead to speak in a more monotonous voice?
> - Do they tend to speak with a higher or lower voice?
> - Is the voice gruffy or soft?
> - How's the volume?
>
> In contrast, only 7 % of the first impression results from the spoken word – i.e., the actual words you choose at the beginning of a conversation aren't really so decisive. The facial expression (as friendly and interested as possible), handshake (short, dry and firm), posture (upright and open) and the tone of voice (expressive) on the other hand are downright essential! After this initial impression, of course, the spoken word begins to take on more significance again – but it's still hard to "outtalk" a mediocre or even catastrophic first impression …

Unsere Körpersprache ist also weit mehr als nur ein Begleitprodukt für die gesprochene Sprache; sie übertrifft diese sogar oft an Genauigkeit und Ausdruckskraft.

> *„Herr Meyer, wie schön, Sie hier zu treffen! Wie geht es Ihnen – gut sehen Sie aus!"*

Diese Small-Talk-Eröffnung bedarf der passenden Körpersprache, um überzeugend zu sein: eine offene Körperhaltung, ein herzliches Lächeln, eine zur Begrüßung ausgestreckte Hand und natürlich eine entsprechende Stimmlage und Betonung.

Werden hingegen dieselben Sätze mit unbewegtem Gesicht, monotoner Stimme, den Händen in den Hosentaschen und mit abgewandtem Blick geäußert, ist Herrn Meyer klar: Da will jemand krampfhaft höflich sein und freut sich in Wahrheit kein bisschen, ihn zu sehen.

Wenn Sie also nicht sagen, was Sie meinen, etwa weil Sie höflich sein möchten und deswegen eine Lüge äußern, dann wird Ihre Körpersprache Sie mit ziemlicher Sicherheit verraten – es sei denn, Sie sind ein guter Schauspieler. Diese inkongruenten Botschaften, in denen sich Körpersprache und Sprache widersprechen, verringern unsere Glaubwürdigkeit, die ein wertvolles Gut in der zwischenmenschlichen Kommunikation ist.

Aber nicht nur die eigene Körpersprache ist bei Gesprächen im Allgemeinen und beim Small Talk im Besonderen wichtig:

> *Wenn Sie auch auf die Körpersprache Ihres Gesprächspartners achten, hilft Ihnen das, ihn besser zu verstehen.*

Allerdings sollten Sie körpersprachliche Signale, die Sie wahrnehmen, überprüfen, z.B. durch Nachfragen (*„Ich sehe, Sie runzeln die Stirn. Sind Sie anderer Meinung?"*). Einzelne Signale wie etwa verschränkte Arme sagen in der Regel nur wenig aus. Erst in Kombination mit anderen Signalen (z.B. kein Blickkontakt mehr, abgewandte Körperhaltung) kann man verschränkte Arme als Abweisung oder Desinteresse interpretieren. In Verbindung mit Blickkontakt und einem interessierten Gesichtsausdruck dagegen sind die verschränkten Arme schlicht und einfach eine Aufmerksamkeitshaltung – verschlossen ist da gar nichts.

Meistens liegen wir mit unserer Deutung von Körpersprache richtig. Die wesentlichen mimischen Ausdrucksformen, also grundlegende Emotionen wie Freude, Trauer, Ekel oder Angst, gelten als

> *Make a good impression with the body language*

So our body language is subsequently far more than just an accompaniment to the spoken language; frequently, it even surpasses our speech in precision and expressiveness.

> *"Mr Moore, how nice to see you here! How are you — you're looking well!"*

This small talk opener requires the corresponding body language in order to be convincing: an open posture, an affectionate smile, a hand extended in greeting, and of course, the appropriate tone of voice and inflection.

If, on the other hand, the same sentences are spoken with an unmoving face, a monotonous voice, hands stuffed into their pockets and a wandering gaze, then Mr Moore will know that someone is simply making a stiff, insincere attempt to sound polite and that they're in fact not happy to see him at all.

So when you don't say what you really mean, perhaps because you want to be polite and accordingly permit yourself a "little white lie", your body language is nonetheless pretty certain to betray your true feelings – that is, unless you're a good actor. These conflicting messages in which the body language and the spoken word contradict one another reduce our trustworthiness, a valuable commodity in interpersonal communication.

But it's not just our own body language that's of special importance in discussions in general, and in small talk in particular:

When you observe the body language of your discussion partners, it will help you to understand them better.

However, you should verify body language signals that you catch; for example, by asking (*"Your furrowed brow seems to indicate that you may have another opinion?"*). Individual signals, such as crossed arms, generally have little to say. It's only in combination with other signals (no more eye contact, uninviting physical posture, for example) that one can interpret crossed arms as rejection or a lack of interest. In contrast, combined with eye contact and an interested facial expression, crossed arms simply signify an attentive posture – there's nothing closed here.

Our interpretations of body language are usually accurate. The essential facial expression forms, consisting of fundamental emotions like joy, sadness, disgust or fear, are considered to be innate

angeboren, und die dazugehörigen Gesichtsbewegungen sind in allen Kulturen, bei beiden Geschlechtern und in jedem Lebensalter weitgehend identisch.

> *Durch dieses verbindende Erbe ist eine Grundverständigung aller Menschen möglich – über alle kulturellen oder geschlechtlichen Grenzen hinweg.*

Ob sich jemand freut, mit Ihnen Small Talk zu halten, oder ob er sich weit weg wünscht, können Sie ihm meist am Gesicht ablesen.

Während die grundlegenden mimischen Ausdrucksformen also angeboren sind, wird ein anderer Teil der Körpersprache – nämlich Haltung, Gestik und Stimme sowie Tonfall – im Umgang mit den Mitmenschen übernommen bzw. anerzogen. Hier gibt es dann entsprechende Unterschiede: zwischen Kulturkreisen, Generationen und Geschlechtern.

- Vergleichen Sie einmal die typische Gestik eines Nordeuropäers mit der eines Südeuropäers: Während der Erste kaum beobachtbare Gesten zeigt, die Arme meist dicht am Körper hält oder die Hände gleich in die Taschen steckt, gestikuliert der Südeuropäer mit weit ausholenden und ausdrucksstarken Arm- und Handbewegungen.
- Und auch die Körpersprache von Männern und Frauen – selbst wenn sie gleichaltrig sind und im gleichen Kulturkreis geprägt – unterscheidet sich beträchtlich: Wo ein Mann eher breitbeinig sitzt, schlägt die Frau die Beine übereinander oder setzt sie sittsam eng nebeneinander.

Körpersprache beim Small Talk – was wirkt sympathisch, was wirkt unsympathisch? Darum geht es im Folgenden.

5.1 Körperhaltung

Darauf sollten Sie bei Ihrer Körperhaltung achten:
- Eine offene, aufrechte, entspannte und dem Gegenüber zugewandte Haltung bringt Sympathiepunkte, sie strahlt Sicherheit und Vertrauen (in sich und den anderen) aus. Jemand, der so steht, geht und sitzt, wirkt souverän und interessiert.
- Eine geschwollene Brust dagegen wirkt tatsächlich aufgeblasen, während das Gegenteil (hängende Schultern und eingezogener Kopf) vermuten lässt, dass hier jemand eine schwere Last zu tragen hat und gestresst oder unsicher ist.

and the corresponding facial movements are for the most part identical in all cultures, in both sexes and at all ages.

> *This unifying inheritance makes basic communication possible between all people– beyond all cultural or sexual borders.*

Whether someone is happy to make small talk with you or whether they wish they were somewhere else can usually be read from their face.

While the fundamental facial expression forms are innate, another part of body language – consisting of posture, gestures, the voice and inflection – is taken on board or acquired through our dealings with others. And here is where we find corresponding differences between cultural circles, generations and sexes.

- Briefly compare the typical gestures of a Northern European with those of a Southern European: while the former makes scarcely any observable gestures and generally holds his or her arms close to the body, or sticks the hands straight into the pockets, the Southern European makes flamboyant gestures with broad-sweeping, expressive arm and hand movements.
- And there are considerable differences in the body language of men and women – even when they are roughly the same age and come from the same cultural circles: while men tend to sit with their knees apart, women are more likely to cross their legs or sit with their knees demurely close together.

Body language in small talk – what makes a congenial impression, and what does the opposite? That's the subject of the following section.

5.1 Physical Posture

Here's what you should observe in your physical posture:

- An open, upright, relaxed posture facing your conversation partner scores you sympathy points and radiates confidence and trust (in both yourself and your partner). Someone who stands, walks and sits in this way appears competent and interested.
- In contrast, a swelled chest actually makes an impression of self-importance, while the opposite (slumped shoulders with the head drawn in) conveys a sense that someone here has quite a load to bear and is under stress or lacking in confidence.

- Der in den Nacken gelegte Kopf zeigt eine distanzierte Haltung und kann arrogant wirken. Ein leicht nach vorn gebeugter Kopf signalisiert dagegen Interesse und Neugier.
- Stehen Sie mit beiden Beinen fest auf dem Boden – das zeigt und fördert eine gewisse Standfestigkeit. Wippen Sie nicht mit den Füßen – das wirkt nervös und macht auch Ihre Gesprächspartner nervös.

Ist Ihre Körperhaltung aufrecht, locker und offen?

Testen Sie es vor einem Ganzkörperspiegel aus: Betrachten Sie sich von vorn und von der Seite. Lassen Sie sich ggf. von einem vertrauten Menschen in eine aufrechte Körperhaltung bringen.

Und wenn man nicht steht, sondern sitzt?
- Das Sitzen auf der Stuhlkante mit vorgebeugtem Oberkörper, die Füße in Schrittstellung, zeigt, dass jemand offensichtlich „auf dem Sprung" ist, nicht bleiben möchte – diese Sitzhaltung signalisiert Unsicherheit oder Angst.
- Auch die um einen Stuhl geschlungenen oder sehr eng übereinandergelegten Beine drücken Anspannung und Unsicherheit aus.
- Eine Sitzhaltung mit gestreckten oder auch gespreizten Beinen dagegen demonstriert Vertraulichkeit und (Nach-)Lässigkeit – und ist damit zumindest bei offiziellen Anlässen absolut fehl am Platz.

Ja, und wie sitzt man nun richtig? – Sympathisch wirkt eine offene, leicht vorgeneigte, also dem Gesprächspartner zugeneigte Sitzhaltung – so zeigt man sich interessiert.

5.2 Distanzzonen

„Zwischenmenschliche Beziehungen sind ‚mit Abstand' die besten."
Gerhard Uhlenbruck (*1929), dt. Aphoristiker, Immunbiologe und Hochschullehrer

Viele häufig benutzte Redewendungen zeigen deutlich, wie positive Körpersprache aussehen sollte: jemanden mit „offenen Armen" empfangen, „Zuneigung" zeigen, jemanden „eines Blickes würdigen". Auch, was wir nicht tun sollten, spiegeln zahlreiche Redewendungen wider: jemandem „zu nahe treten", ihm oder ihr „auf die Füße treten" oder „auf die Pelle rücken". Kommt Ihnen folgende Situation bekannt vor?

> Make a good impression with the body language

- A raised chin demonstrates a distanced demeanour, and can seem arrogant. When the head is tilted slightly forward, however, this displays interest and curiosity.
- Stand with both feet firmly on the ground – this demonstrates and promotes a certain degree of stability. Don't teeter on your feet – this emits an impression of nervousness and also makes your discussion partner nervous.

> **Is your physical posture upright, relaxed and open?**
>
> *Test yourself in front of a full-length mirror: observe yourself from the front and from the side. If need be, let someone you trust help adjust you into an upright physical posture.*

And what if you're sitting and not standing?
- Sitting on the edge of your chair with your body leaning forward and your feet in a stepping position signalises that you are obviously "practically out of the door", that you don't want to stay – this seating posture signalises insecurity or fear.
- Legs wrapped around a chair leg or tightly crossed over one another express tension and insecurity.
- In contrast, a seating posture with the legs stretched out or spread apart demonstrates familiarity and nonchalance (or worse yet, negligence) – and as such, is absolutely out of place, at least at official functions or events.

OK, so how do I sit correctly? – An open seating posture, leaning slightly forward and toward the discussion partner, demonstrates that one is interested.

5.2 Distance Zones

"Interpersonal relationships are 'by far' the best."
   Gerhard Uhlenbruck (*1929), German aphorist, immunologist and university professor

Many frequently used sayings clearly demonstrate what positive body language looks like: receiving someone with "open arms", or "smile and the world smiles with you". And what we shouldn't do is also reflected in numerous sayings: not "crowding someone" or not "stepping on someone's toes", for instance. Does the following situation sound familiar to you?

Über Körpersprache einen guten Eindruck machen

> *Sie unterhalten sich auf einer Feier mit jemandem, den Sie eben erst kennen gelernt haben. Dieser Ihnen eigentlich fremde Mensch kommt Ihnen Ihrem Empfinden nach viel zu nahe, sodass Sie sich bedrängt fühlen. Ihre prompte Reaktion: Sie weichen einen Schritt nach hinten aus. Das ist Ihrem Gesprächspartner anscheinend zu viel Distanz – er verringert den Abstand, indem er Ihnen folgt: ein Schritt nach vorn. Sie ziehen sich weiter zurück. Nützt bloß nichts – Ihr Gegenüber, das offensichtlich Nähe schätzt, rückt auf ...*

Unangenehm, nicht wahr? Was aber können Sie tun, wenn Ihnen jemand zu nahe kommt?

Am besten nicht ausweichen, sondern eher auf Abschreckung setzen: Halten Sie Blickkontakt, gucken Sie dabei aber nicht zu freundlich, knipsen Sie Ihr gewinnendes Lächeln mal kurz aus. Heben Sie den Kopf etwas an – Sie wissen ja, das wirkt etwas distanziert und schafft so die hier sehr erwünschte Distanz. Setzen Sie Ihre Hände und Arme ein und gestikulieren Sie ruhig etwas raumgreifender als sonst in Richtung Ihres Gegenübers – auch das schafft den benötigten Platz. Und wenn gar nichts mehr geht, beenden Sie das Gespräch höflich. (Wie das geht? Mehr dazu in Kapitel 9.)

Eigentlich ist es ganz einfach zu vermeiden, dass sich jemand bedrängt fühlt. Zwar ist das Bedürfnis nach Nähe und Distanz tatsächlich von Mensch zu Mensch und auch je nach Kulturkreis unterschiedlich, es gibt aber Mindestabstände, die Sie unbedingt einhalten sollten.

Generell gilt: Halten Sie lieber etwas zu viel als zu wenig Abstand, Ihr Gegenüber kann die Distanz ja verringern, wenn er oder sie das möchte (vorausgesetzt natürlich, Sie lassen das zu).

Je sensibler Sie selbst für diese Abstandszonen werden, umso eher werden Sie merken, wann Sie anderen im wahrsten Sinne des Wortes „auf die Füße treten". Um diese Sensibilität zu trainieren, machen Sie folgende Übung:

Übung

Lassen Sie einen Ihnen sehr vertrauten Menschen langsam auf Sie zugehen. Sobald Sie merken, dass Ihnen der Abstand zu gering wird, sagen Sie „Stopp" und schätzen oder messen diesen Anstand aus. Wiederholen Sie die Übung dann mit einem guten Bekannten – wie groß ist der Mindestabstand diesmal?
Wie viel Distanz hätte Ihr Übungspartner am liebsten? Entsprechen die Abstände in etwa den beschriebenen Distanzzonen – oder mögen Sie oder Ihr Übungspartner mehr Distanz bzw. mehr Nähe als die meisten anderen Menschen?

Make a good impression with the body language

> *You're talking to someone that you've just met at a party. This person, actually a stranger, is coming a little too close for your comfort, making you feel crowded in. Your prompt reaction: you take a step backwards. For your discussion partner, this is apparently too much distance – so he closes the gap by following you and taking a step forward. You back up further, but it does no good – your conversation partner, who seems to appreciate close quarters, steps in further ...*

Unpleasant, isn't it? But what can you do when someone comes too close to you?

The best thing is not to retreat. Instead, go for deterrence: maintain eye contact, but don't look too friendly, and give your winning smile a quick coffee break. Raise your head a little – you know that this has a somewhat distancing effect, giving you the distance you want here. Use your arms and hands to gesticulate in the direction of your conversation partner in a way that uses a little more room than you normally would – this will also give you more of the space you need. And if none of that works then end the conversation politely (How does that work? More on the subject in Chapter 9.)

It's actually very easy to avoid giving someone the feeling that you're crowding them. Sure, the need for closeness and distance is different from person to person and even from one cultural circle to another, but there are in fact minimum distances that one should definitely maintain.

Generally, the following applies: it's better to keep a little too much distance than a little too little! Your conversation partner can close the gap if he or she wants to (that is of course, if you allow it).

The more sensitive you become to these distance zones, the quicker you will notice when someone is quite literally "stepping on your toes". To train this sensitivity try the following exercise:

Exercise

Have a person you trust completely approach you slowly. As soon as you notice that the distance is too small for you, say "Stop" and then estimate or measure this distance.

Then repeat the exercise with a trusted acquaintance – how great is the minimum distance this time?

How much distance would your exercise partner prefer? Do the distances correspond roughly with the distance zones described above – or do you and your exercise partner prefer more distance or less distance than most other people?

Distanzzonen

Die Intimzone

... reicht vom direkten Körperkontakt bis zu einer Distanz von ca. 60 cm, also etwa einer Armlänge. In diese Zone lassen wir freiwillig nur Menschen, denen wir vertrauen und die uns (im wörtlichen Sinn) nahe stehen, also den oder die Partner/-in, Verwandte, enge Freunde, oder aber Menschen, die aufgrund ihres Berufes eine „Sondergenehmigung" haben, wie etwa Ärzte und Friseure.

> *Eine Missachtung dieser Intimzone ist letztlich nichts anderes als eine (wenn auch vielleicht unbeabsichtigte) Missachtung der Person.*

Sorgen Sie also dafür, dass Sie Ihrem Gesprächspartner nicht „auf die Pelle rücken", sondern ihm oder ihr den benötigten Freiraum lassen. Jeder fehlende Zentimeter Distanz wird als unangenehm empfunden – und dass sich dies kontraproduktiv auf den Small Talk auswirken wird, ist sicher. Eine Verletzung der Intimzone produziert nämlich beim Gegenüber Stress und das damit verbundene typische Verhalten: Angriff oder Flucht. Das Gespräch wird dann zunehmend aggressiv geführt oder Ihr Gegenüber verdrückt sich, so schnell er oder sie es kann.

Die persönliche Zone oder Dialogzone

... hat einen Radius von ca. 60 bis 120 cm. Das entspricht in etwa der Distanz, die beim Händeschütteln erreicht wird. Diese Zone ist ideal für den Small Talk mit Personen, die Ihnen nicht völlig fremd sind, also mit Bekannten, Kollegen, vertrauten Kunden – im Grunde mit all jenen Menschen, mit denen Sie ein entspanntes, wenn auch nicht vertrautes Verhältnis verbindet.

Die soziale Zone oder Respektzone

... lässt dem Gegenüber noch etwas mehr Raum, nämlich etwa 120 bis 200 cm. Sie ist die Zone für oberflächliche soziale Kontakte, für Kontakte mit Personen, die in der Hierarchie über uns stehen, und für alle Menschen, die Sie nur flüchtig kennen oder gerade erst kennen gelernt haben.

Distance Zones

The Intimate Zone

... extends from direct physical contact to a distance of around 60 cm, or some 2 feet, more or less an arm's length. We only voluntarily allow people within this zone that we trust and who (quite literally) are close to us, i.e., our love interest, relatives, close friends, or people who have "special permission" due to their profession, such as doctors or hair stylists.

> *Disregard for this intimate zone is ultimately nothing more than disregard (if perhaps unintentional) for the person.*

So make sure that you're not "cramping" your discussion partner. Instead, leave him or her the free space they need. Every inch too close results in more discomfort – and this is sure to have a counterproductive effect on the small talk. A violation of the intimate zone produces stress for the other person, as well as producing the typical behaviour associated with stress: attack or escape. The course of the conversation will either become increasingly aggressive, or your conversation partner will flee as quickly as they can.

The Personal Zone or Dialogue Zone

... has a radius of some 60 to 120 cm, or around 2–4 feet. This corresponds roughly with the distance achieved in a handshake. This zone is ideal for small talk with persons who are not complete strangers, such as acquaintances, colleagues, trusted clients – basically, for anyone you have a relaxed, but not intimate, relationship with.

The Social Zone or Respect Zone

... consisting of some 120 to 200 cm, or roughly 4 to 6 feet, leaves a little more space for the conversation partner. This is the zone for cursory social contacts, for contacts with persons who are above us in the hierarchy and for everyone that you know only fleetingly or have just met.

5.3 Gestik

Wir reden mit unseren Händen, sie gehören zu unseren wichtigsten Kommunikationsmitteln: Wir begreifen etwas, wir zeigen, berühren, beschreiben, nehmen und geben. Das Spektrum der Gesten ist entsprechend breit gefächert.

- Unterstreichen Sie, was Sie sagen, mit natürlicher Gestik – gestikulieren Sie nicht zu hastig.

> *Die Gesten beginnen idealerweise etwa eine Handbreit über dem Nabel und öffnen sich zum Gesprächspartner hin.*

- Gestikulieren Sie mit sich zum Gegenüber öffnenden Händen: Das sind Gesten, die im Allgemeinen angenehm wirken. Das Zeigen der Handinnenflächen weckt Vertrauen und lädt zum Austausch ein: Da hat jemand offensichtlich nichts zu verbergen, nichts „in der Hinterhand". Es versteht sich von selbst, dass Hände weder in die Taschen noch auf den Rücken gehören.
- Abweisend wirken Hände, die nicht zu sehen sind, ebenso wie die zudeckende Hand, die nur den Handrücken zeigt und so auf dem Tisch oder, noch schlimmer, unter dem Tisch, auf den Beinen oder auf den Stuhllehnen liegt. Das vermittelt den Eindruck, man hätte etwas zu verbergen.
- So genannte ikonische Gesten, die parallel zum Gesprochenen erfolgen und die Inhalte bildlich darstellen, wirken besonders ausdrucksstark.
- Alle Dominanzgesten dagegen wie etwa der hochgereckte Zeigefinger lösen beim Gegenüber negative Gefühle aus.
- Verlegenheitsgesten wie das Zupfen an der Kleidung oder an den Haaren zeigen, dass jemand unsicher ist.
- Gesten, mit denen wir andere Menschen berühren, haben beim Small Talk in unserem Kulturkreis nichts zu suchen:

> *Berührungen verletzen in dieser Situation die Intimzone des Gegenübers.*

5.4 Mimik

Welche Mimik wirkt sympathisch? – Ganz einfach: Das freundliche und interessierte Gesicht. Und das entsteht durch Blickkontakt, eine Mimik, die das vom Gesprächspartner Erzählte spiegelt, und ein echtes Lächeln. Lächeln sollten Sie aber natürlich nur da, wo es passt.

Make a good impression with the body language

5.3 Gestures

We talk with our hands, and they are among our most important tools of communication: we "get" something, we show, touch, describe, take and give. Accordingly, the range of gestures is very broad.

- Underline what you're saying with natural gestures – don't gesticulate too hastily.

   Gestures ideally begin about a hand's width above the navel and open out toward the discussion partner.

- Gesticulate with your hands opened outward toward the conversation partner. Gestures like this generally make a positive impression. Showing the palms awakens trust and serves as an invitation for exchange: here's someone who clearly has nothing to hide, there's nothing "backhanded" going on. It goes without saying that the hands don't belong in the pockets or behind the back.
- Hands that can't be seen have a dismissive effect, as do hands only showing from the top, for instance resting on a table, or worse, concealed under the table resting on the legs or armrests. This conveys the impression that one has something to hide.
- So-called iconic gestures conducted simultaneously with what's being said and depicting it pictorially have a particularly strong expressive effect.
- In contrast, all dominance gestures, such as the raised forefinger, release negative feelings in the conversation partner.
- Bashfulness gestures, such as playing with one's clothes or hair, show a lack of confidence.
- Gestures involving touching other people are not appropriate for small talk in our cultural circle.

   Touching in this situation violates the conversation partner's intimate zone.

5.4 Facial Expressions

Which facial expressions have a personable effect? – That's easy: the friendly, interested face. And this comes from eye contact, a facial expression that reflects what the discussion partner is saying and a genuine smile. Of course, you should only smile where it's appropriate.

Negativ dagegen wirken z.B.
- die gerümpfte Nase als Zeichen von Ablehnung (Hier stinkt es jemandem!),
- zusammengepresste Lippen, die ein gewisses Misstrauen signalisieren (Das nehme ich nicht auf/an!),
- nach unten gezogene Mundwinkel (Wie bitter das Leben doch ist ...) und
- zusammengebissene Zähne (Anspannung pur!).

Wie aber hält man richtig Blickkontakt? – Wenn Ihr Blick abschweift, während Ihr Gegenüber spricht, signalisiert das im günstigsten Fall (also wenn Ihr Blick nur ganz kurz abschweift), dass Sie versuchen, das Gehörte einzuordnen.

> *Längere Phasen des Wegschauens können dagegen Desinteresse, Unkonzentriertheit, Langeweile, Abneigung bedeuten – und das macht garantiert nicht sympathisch.*

Allerdings gibt es unterschiedliche Arten, den anderen anzuschauen – und nicht jede davon ist für den Small Talk zu empfehlen:
- **Ein intensiver Blick mit gerader Sehlinie und angespannter Nackenmuskulatur** ist eine Fixierung des Gegenübers, ein Kräftemessen, das sich auf eine Konfrontation zubewegen kann. Damit ist es für Small Talk ungeeignet.
- **Ein tiefer Blick mit entspannter Augen- und Nackenmuskulatur** signalisiert Verständnis, Zuneigung, Liebe – und das geht im Small Talk ein bisschen zu weit.
- **Ein nach oben gerichteter Blick** wirkt, als suchten Sie Beistand von oben, und kann als Zeichen von Ungeduld (*„Herr, steh mir bei!"*) interpretiert werden. Er macht Sie bei Ihrem Small-Talk-Partner wahrscheinlich nicht beliebt.
- **Ein zu Boden gerichteter Blick** lässt sich als Zeichen von Vorsicht oder Unsicherheit deuten, ein niedergeschlagener Blick gar als Demuts- und Unterwerfungsgeste.
- **Geschlossene Augen** sollten Sie beim Small Talk vermeiden – sie könnten auf Müdigkeit hindeuten.
- **Weit geöffnete Augen** hingegen vermitteln Überraschung oder den Wunsch nach mehr Information.
- **Zusammengekniffene Augen** vermitteln den Eindruck, dass Sie eine Vertiefung des Gesagten wünschen, und drücken manchmal auch eine gewisse Skepsis aus.

> *Make a good impression with the body language*

A negative effect is created by
- a wrinkled nose as a sign of rejection (Something here stinks!),
- lips pressed together, signalising a certain mistrust (I don't swallow that!),
- corners of the mouth turned downwards (Life is bitter …) and
- clenched teeth (Pure tension!).

What's the right way to maintain eye contact? – If your gaze wanders while your conversation partner is speaking, then in the best case (i.e., if your gaze diverts briefly) this signalises that you're trying to "get straight" what's being said.

> *On the other hand, longer phases of looking away could signify disinterest, a lack of concentration, boredom or disfavour – and this definitely doesn't have a personable effect.*

In any case, there are different ways of looking at someone else – and not all of them are recommended for small talk:
- An intensive gaze straight into the eyes with tensed neck muscles represents a "fixation" on the other person, a test of strength that can approach a confrontation. This makes it unsuitable for small talk.
- A deep gaze with relaxed eyes and neck muscles signals understanding, affection, love – and that's a little too much for small talk.
- A look focused upwards gives the impression that you're looking for support from above, and can also be interpreted as a sign of impatience (*"Lord, help me!"*). This is not likely to make you very popular with your small talk partner.
- A gaze down toward the ground can be interpreted as a sign of insecurity, while a defeated look can even be taken as a gesture of meekness or submission.
- You should avoid closed eyes in small talk – they could signal fatigue.
- In contrast, wide-open eyes convey surprise or the desire for more information.
- Squinted eyes indicate that you would like what's been said to be probed more deeply, and sometimes they also convey a degree of scepticism.

✓ Tipps für den Blickkontakt

- Der perfekte Blickkontakt im Gespräch ist der „N-N-Kontakt": Ihre Nase und Ihr Nabel sind auf einer Linie dem Gegenüber zugewandt.

- Sprechen Sie mit mehreren Menschen, wenden Sie sich immer demjenigen zu, der spricht bzw. zu dem Sie sprechen.

- Nur Augenkontakt zu halten, womöglich über die Schulter, reicht nicht aus – es sollte Zuwendung im wahrsten Sinne des Wortes sein.

- Um Blickkontakt zu halten, müssen Ihre Augen nicht ununterbrochen die Pupillen des Gesprächspartners fixieren – lockerer Kontakt zum Gesichtsfeld genügt.

5.5 Stimme und Tonfall

Wir nehmen in Gesprächen bei unserem Gegenüber in Bezug auf Stimme und Tonfall Folgendes wahr:
- den Klang der Stimme,
- die Artikulation,
- das Sprechtempo,
- die Betonung,
- die Lautstärke,
- den Dialekt (sofern vorhanden),
- die Atmung.

Auf der Grundlage dieser Eindrücke bilden wir unsere Meinung – teils unbewusst, teils bewusst.

Was kann man tun, um auch in diesem Bereich der Körpersprache sympathisch zu wirken?

Die meisten von uns hören gern Menschen zu, die lebhaft betonen, deutlich artikulieren, eine weiche, volle und nicht zu hohe Stimme haben und die in einer angenehmen Lautstärke sprechen, also weder brüllen noch so leise sprechen, dass man dauernd nachfragen muss.

- Achten Sie als Erstes auf Ihre Atmung, atmen Sie tief und gleichmäßig – das verbessert Stimmvolumen und Resonanz und macht die Stimme meist auch etwas tiefer. Wer zu schnell und zu flach atmet, dem bleibt im wahrsten Sinn des Wortes „die Luft weg" – dadurch klingt die Stimme gepresst und wenig ausdrucksstark.

Make a good impression with the body language

> **Tips for Eye Contact** ✓
>
> - Perfect eye contact in a discussion is known as "N-N-Contact": your nose and your navel are focused in one line on the conversation partner.
>
> - If you are speaking to a number of people, then always look at who is speaking or who you are speaking to.
>
> - Maintaining eye contact "over the shoulder", so to speak, is not enough – you should face your partner fully.
>
> - In order to maintain eye contact, it's not necessary for your eyes to be fixed on the discussion partners' pupils without interruption – relaxed contact with the facial area is sufficient.

5.5 Voice and Inflection

In regard to voice and its inflection, we perceive the following in conversation:
- the sound of the voice,
- articulation,
- speaking tempo,
- word stress,
- volume,
- dialect or accent (when present),
- and breathing.

We form our opinion, partially conscious and partially unconscious, on the basis of these impressions.

What can one do in order to make a congenial impression in this area of body language as well?

Most of us like to listen to people who have a lively manner of intonation in their speech, who articulate clearly, who have a soft, full voice that's not overly high-pitched and who speak at a pleasant volume that's not too loud and gruff, but also not so quiet that we constantly have to ask them to repeat themselves.

- Pay attention first of all to your breathing. Breathe deeply and evenly – this improves the volume and resonance of your voice, and it generally makes the voice a little deeper. People who breathe flatly and too quickly quite literally can't catch their breath – this reduces the voice's expressive quality and makes it sound forced.

Über Körpersprache einen guten Eindruck machen

- Wie schnell bzw. langsam, wie laut oder leise Sie sprechen sollten, hängt vor allem von Ihrem Gesprächspartner ab: Ist er oder sie ein extrovertierter Mensch und redet entsprechend laut und lebhaft, sollten Sie nicht allzu leise sprechen. Umgekehrt empfinden leise und schüchterne Menschen einen temperamentvollen Gesprächspartner oft als anstrengend. Versuchen Sie Ihr Redetempo und Ihre Intensität also Ihrem Gegenüber anzugleichen.
- Artikulieren Sie sauber und betonen Sie, was Sie sagen – etwa durch wechselnde Lautstärke und Pausen.
- Sprechen Sie deutlich, ohne Anfangs- und Endsilben zu verschlucken.

> **Deutliches Artikulieren können Sie trainieren, indem Sie folgende Zungenbrecher aufsagen:**
>
> *Zwischen zwei spitzen Steinen sitzen zwei zischende Schlangen, lauernd auf zwei zwitschernde Spätzchen.*
>
> *Hinter dichtem Fichtendickicht picken dicke Finken tüchtig.*
>
> *Der Potsdamer Postkutscher putzt den Potsdamer Postkutschenkasten.*
>
> *Ein tschechischer Regisseur inszenierte ein französisches Stück – ein französischer Regisseur inszenierte ein tschechisches Stück.*

Ihre Gedanken steuern Stimme und Tonfall

Was immer Sie über Ihren Gesprächspartner denken – Ihre Körpersprache spiegelt es meist deutlich wider. Ihr Empfinden steuert dabei auch Ihre Stimme und Ihren Tonfall.

> *Versuchen Sie daher, in schwierigen Situationen negative Gedanken („Was für eine Nervensäge!", „Mir ist soooo langweilig ...") zu stoppen, ansonsten laufen Sie Gefahr, Ihre Gedanken bei Ihrem nächsten Redebeitrag ungewollt zu verraten.*

Wie stark Stimme und Tonfall eine Aussage bestimmen, können Sie mit der folgenden Übung ausprobieren:

> Make a good impression with the body language

- How quickly or slowly and how loudly or quietly you should speak depends primarily on your discussion partner: if he or she is an extroverted person who therefore speaks in a loud and lively voice, then you shouldn't speak too quietly. Logically enough, quiet, shy persons often find a lively discussion partner hard work. So try to adapt your speaking tempo and your intensity to the person you're speaking with.
- **Articulate** clearly and **emphasise** what you're saying by changing volume and inserting pauses.
- Speak clearly, without "swallowing" beginning and ending syllables.

You can train clear articulation by repeating the following tongue-twisters:

A big black bug bit a big black bear, made the big black bear bleed blood.

Sally sells seashells by the seashore.

Peter Piper picked a peck of pickled peppers.

A Czech director staged a French piece. A French director staged a Czech piece.

Your thoughts steer your voice and intonation

Whatever you think about your discussion partner is usually clearly reflected by your body language, and it also controls your voice and intonation.

> *So in difficult situations ("What a pest!", "I'm so bored …") try to put a halt to negative thoughts. Otherwise, you run the risk of unintentionally exposing your thoughts with your next contribution to the conversation.*

You can test how much the voice and intonation affect a particular statement in the following exercise:

Über Körpersprache einen guten Eindruck machen

> Sprechen Sie den folgenden Satz mit der beschriebenen Stimmlage und Betonung laut aus und überlegen Sie, welche Wirkung Sie damit erzielen.
>
> *Übungssatz: „Sie möchten also diesen Anzug umtauschen?"*
>
> *Sprechen Sie den Satz …*
> 1. *mit monotoner, flacher Stimme.*
> 2. *langsam und mit tiefer Stimme.*
> 3. *in einer hohen Stimmlage und mit deutlicher Betonung.*
> 4. *abgehackt und mit sehr lauter Stimme.*
> 5. *langsam und mit hoher Stimme.*

Auflösung:
1. Aussage: Langeweile (Mir ist erstens langweilig und zweitens sowieso alles egal.)
2. Aussage: Genervtheit (Das ist mir alles zu viel – ich möchte einfach meine Ruhe haben.)
3. Aussage: Interesse, Anteilnahme (Kein Problem – das mache ich doch gern!)
4. Aussage: Ungeduld (Sie nerven mich!)
5. Aussage: Ungläubigkeit (Wie bitte? Das kann ja wohl nicht Ihr Ernst sein!)

5.6 Wie viel Körpersprache ist eigentlich gut?

Kann man an seiner Ausstrahlung arbeiten? – In der Tat, das geht. Lernen durch Angucken und (in Maßen) auch Nachahmen heißt das Rezept. Zu diesem Zweck gilt es zunächst zu ermitteln, was Menschen mit positiver Ausstrahlung eigentlich auszeichnet: Es sind vor allem ihr Selbstbewusstsein, ihre Emotionalität, ihre Aufgeschlossenheit und ihre Originalität.

- Machen Sie sich bewusst, wovon Ihre Gesprächspartner bei Ihnen profitieren können: Sind Sie ein interessanter Gesprächspartner, weil Sie z.B. eine schnelle Auffassungsgabe, Humor oder Wortwitz haben, oder dank Ihrer aufmerksamen Art zuzuhören, Ihrer Sensibilität, Ihres Einfühlungsvermögens? Eigene Stärken zu erkennen (und weiterzuentwickeln) ist die Basis eines gesunden Selbstbewusstseins und einer positiven Ausstrahlung.
- Zeigen Sie sich als guter Sender: Stehen Sie zu Ihren Emotionen. Welchen Gesprächspartner finden Sie selbst interessanter: den kühlen, unbeteiligten oder den lebhaften, begeisterungsfähigen?
- Reflektieren Sie Ihre Körpersprache, schauen Sie sich in einem Ganzkörperspiegel an: Wie stehen Sie da, wie bewegen Sie sich,

Make a good impression with the body language

> Repeat the following sentence with the tone of voice and stress described below and think about the impression you make in each case.

Exercise sentence: "So you'd like to exchange this suit?"

Repeat the sentence …
1. *with a flat, monotonous voice*
2. *slowly and with a deep voice*
3. *in a high tone of voice and with clear stress and emphasis*
4. *broken up and with a very loud voice*
5. *slowly and with a high voice*

Solution:
1. *Impression: boredom (First of all, I'm bored; and secondly, I don't really care anyway.)*
2. *Impression: irritation (That's all too much for me – I just want to be left alone.)*
3. *Impression: interest, empathy (No problem – I'll be happy to take care of that for you!)*
4. *Impression: impatience (You're getting on my nerves!)*
5. *Impression: incredulity (What? You must be kidding!)*

5.6 How much body language is actually good?

Is it possible to work on one's own charisma? – In fact, yes, it is. And the recipe for this is learning by watching and imitating (to a sensible degree). Doing this initially requires assessing what distinguishes people with positive charisma, and this consists primarily of their confidence, their emotionality, their openness and their originality.

- Be aware of how your discussion partner can profit from you: are you an interesting discussion partner because, for instance, you have a quick grasp of things, a great sense of humour or wordplay, or perhaps because of your attentive manner of listening, your sensitivity, or your capacity to empathise? Recognising your own strengths (and developing them further) is the basis for a sensible level of self-confidence and positive charisma.
- Show yourself to be a good communicator, and don't be afraid to show your emotions. What kind of discussion partner do you find more interesting: the cool, distant type or the lively person who has the capacity to get caught up in the conversation?
- Think about your body language and look at yourself in a full-length mirror: how do you stand, how do you move and what's your facial expression like? Smile instead of wrinkling up your

wie ist Ihr Gesichtsausdruck? Lächeln Sie, statt die Stirn zu runzeln, und lassen Sie die Arme locker hängen, statt sie fest vor der Brust zu verschränken.
- Kommunizieren Sie emotional und dialogorientiert: Hören Sie konzentriert zu, stellen Sie interessierte Fragen, äußern Sie (ehrlich gemeinte) Anerkennung und Komplimente.
- Zerbrechen Sie sich nicht darüber den Kopf, was andere über Sie denken, und passen Sie sich nicht permanent an. Versuchen Sie, einen eigenen Stil zu entwickeln.
- Warten Sie nicht, bis man auf Sie zugeht – wagen Sie den ersten Schritt. Im nächsten Kapitel erfahren Sie, wie das geht.

6 Wie beginne ich den Small Talk?

Kontakte knüpfen

„Beisammen sind wir, fanget an!"
Johann Wolfgang von Goethe (1749–1832)

Wie komme ich mit jemandem in Kontakt, der mir fremd ist? – Es gibt mehrere Möglichkeiten, den Small Talk zu eröffnen und Kontakte zu knüpfen – auf jeden Fall sollten Sie nicht darauf warten, dass der andere den ersten Schritt tut.

Viele Menschen haben eine Scheu davor, Wildfremde anzusprechen. Diese anfängliche Hemmschwelle ist ganz natürlich, aber sie wird durch häufiges Überschreiten immer niedriger: Übung macht auch hier den Meister.

Um mit Fremden in Kontakt zu kommen, können Sie z.B. so vorgehen:

Offene Körpersprache
Im ersten Schritt sollten Sie Ihre Körpersprache auf „offen und freundlich" programmieren: Bewegen Sie sich so im Raum.

Lockerer Blickkontakt
Nun sind lockerer Blickkontakt (ca. drei Sekunden lang), ein nettes Lächeln und ein leichtes Kopfnicken ein guter Anfang.

Der erste Satz
Wenn der andere Ihren Blick und vielleicht auch Ihr Lächeln erwidert, ist es Zeit für Ihren ersten Satz, der gar nicht besonders originell sein muss – schließlich wollen Sie ja nicht, dass Ihrem anvisierten Gesprächspartner die Luft wegbleibt, sondern dass er ohne große

forehead and relax your arms at your sides instead of folding them in front of your chest.
- Communicate emotionally and in a way that's dialogue-oriented: listen attentively, ask interesting questions and express (genuine) recognition and compliments.
- Don't worry too much about what others think about you, and don't permanently adapt your behaviour to fit the others. Try to develop your own style.
- Don't wait until someone approaches you – instead, dare to take the first step. You'll find out how to do that in the next chapter.

6 How do I start small talk?

Making contact

"We are all together, so let's begin!"
  Johann Wolfgang von Goethe (1749–1832)

How do I establish contact with a stranger? – There are several possibilities to open small talk and make contact – in any case, you shouldn't wait for the other person to take the first step.

Many people are shy about speaking to a complete stranger. This initial barrier of reluctance is natural, but it increasingly dissipates by breaking through it frequently: here as in other areas of life practice makes perfect.

Here are some examples of how you can make contact with strangers:

Open Body Language
The first step is to programme your body language for "open and friendly" and to move accordingly within the particular space.

Relaxed Eye Contact
Now relaxed eye contact (approximately three seconds long), a nice smile and a slight nod of the head are a good start.

The First Sentence
If the other person returns your look and perhaps even your smile, then it's time for your first sentence; and it doesn't even have to be particularly original – after all, you're not looking to leave your prospective partner speechless. Instead, you want him or her to be able

intellektuelle Verrenkungen sofort antworten kann. Gefragt ist also etwas eher Schlichtes – etwa in dieser Art:

> *„Guten Abend! Woher kennen Sie denn unseren Gastgeber?"*

Nachdem Ihr Gegenüber geantwortet hat, sind Sie wieder am Ball und erzählen ein bisschen von sich, z.B.:

> *„Ich bin übrigens Elke Wegener, eine Kollegin von Jochen, wir arbeiten jetzt seit acht Jahren zusammen."*

Wem das zu locker ist, der kann sich zunächst vorstellen und dann den Small Talk eröffnen:

> *„Hallo, ich bin Andreas Wiebe. Haben Sie schon mal an so einem Telefontraining teilgenommen?"*

Wenn Sie sich mit Namen vorstellen, nennen Sie am besten immer Vor- und Zunamen. Nur der Vorname kann je nach Anlass zu lässig wirken, nur der Nachname zu förmlich.

Für viele berufliche Situationen eignet sich ein etwas ausführlicherer Gesprächseinstieg mit Begrüßung, Höflichkeitsfloskel („*Wie geht es Ihnen?*", „*Schön, Sie zu treffen.*") und Vorstellung:

> *„Guten Morgen! Schön, dass wir uns kennen lernen – ich bin Frau Mettmann aus der Vertriebsabteilung der Lüttkemeyer GmbH."*

Sie können Ihrem Gegenüber darüber hinaus Anknüpfungspunkte für den weiteren Dialog geben, indem Sie eine Frage anhängen oder etwas zum speziellen Anlass sagen:

> *„Sind Sie auch schon so gespannt auf den ersten Referenten?"*
> *„Ich bin das erste Mal für unser Unternehmen hier – die Ankündigung für diese Tagung klang sehr interessant."*

Was tun, wenn man auf Ablehnung stößt? – Dass Ihr Gegenüber auf eine höfliche Vorstellung oder Frage unhöflicherweise nur einsilbig oder gar nicht antwortet, kommt selten vor – und sollte es tatsächlich mal passieren, betrachten Sie das nicht als Ihr Problem: Wenn er oder sie wüsste, welche Chance auf ein angenehmes Gespräch er oder sie sich da verbaut hat! Wirklich Pech gehabt.

How do I start small talk?

to answer you immediately without a great deal of intellectual effort. So try something fairly simple – maybe along these lines:

> "Hello! So where do you know our host from?"

After your conversation partner has answered, it's your turn again and time for you to tell a little about yourself, for example:

> "By the way, I'm Tracy Weber, a colleague of Dave's. We've been working together now for eight years."

If that's too casual for some of you, then you can introduce yourself first and then start the small talk:

> "Hello, I'm Tom Cooper. Have you ever done a telephone training session like this before?"

When you introduce yourself by name, it's best to always give both your first and last name. Only giving your first name can seem a little too casual depending on the occasion, while only the last name can seem too formal.

Many professional situations are suited for a more extensive conversation starter, with a greeting, a polite comment (*"How are you?"*, *"It's nice to meet you."*) and an introduction:

> "Good morning! I'm glad to meet you – I'm Ms Brandon from the Sales Department at Luther Ltd."

You can additionally give your conversation partner cues for the continued dialogue by tacking on a question or by saying something about the respective special occasion:

> "Are you also looking forward to the first speaker?"
> "I'm here for our company for the first time – the announcement for this seminar sounded very interesting."

What do you do if you encounter rejection? – It's seldom that your conversation partner will impolitely only give a one-word answer or no answer at all to a polite introduction or question. Should this happen anyway, don't look at it as your problem: if they only knew what a chance they just blew for an enjoyable chat ... Oh well, tough luck!

Aber im Ernst: Natürlich neigen wir dazu, solche Momente der Ablehnung persönlich zu nehmen und uns davon entmutigen zu lassen. Gehen Sie nicht gleich vom schlechtesten aller Fälle aus, nämlich davon, dass der andere Sie nicht sympathisch findet. Schließlich wissen Sie nicht, was in dem betreffenden Menschen vorgegangen ist: Vielleicht ist er einfach nur schüchtern und hat deshalb weggeguckt. Oder er hat gerade den Kopf voll mit Problemen und ist schlecht gelaunt.

Und was mache ich, wenn sich alle Leute schon kennen und in Grüppchen zusammenstehen? – Das ist tatsächlich etwas komplizierter als der Kontakt mit Einzelpersonen – die ja vielleicht dankbar sind, dass jemand sie anspricht. Schauen Sie sich die verschiedenen Gruppen zunächst mal an, schlendern Sie durch den Raum.

Falls Sie wahrnehmen, dass ein paar Leute die Köpfe zusammengesteckt haben, sehen Sie von einer Kontaktaufnahme ab. Hier hat man offensichtlich etwas Vertrauliches zu besprechen – es wäre unhöflich, da zu stören.

Wenn die Menschen locker nebeneinander stehen und sich in normaler Lautstärke unterhalten, sieht es schon besser für Sie aus. Jetzt können Sie ...

- auf die Gruppe zugehen, sich vorstellen, reihum die Hand geben und ein Thema Ihrer Wahl anschneiden. Den Gedanken allein finden Sie schon gruselig? Zugegeben – diese Methode ist nichts für zurückhaltende Naturen. Denn damit sie überzeugend wirkt, müssen Sie sehr locker und selbstbewusst auftreten. Es besteht auch die Gefahr, dass dieses Vorgehen als störend bis aufdringlich wahrgenommen wird. Sie müssen also gut abwägen, wie sicher Sie sich fühlen und wie die Gruppe auf Sie wirkt.
- sich zur Gruppe stellen und erst einmal zuhören, über was gerade gesprochen wird. Sobald sich Ihnen eine Gelegenheit bietet, sich in das Gespräch einzuklinken, ohne unhöflich zu sein, sagen Sie etwas oder Sie stellen eine Frage:

> *„Ich höre gerade, dass Sie sich über den Aufbau einer Kunden-Datenbank unterhalten. Haben Sie damit bisher gute Erfahrungen gemacht? Wir planen so etwas in unserem Betrieb nämlich auch."*

Schon besser. Und wenn Sie, bevor Sie etwas sagen, mit einzelnen Gruppenmitgliedern schon nonverbalen Kontakt aufgenommen und ein paar kurze (natürlich zustimmende) Bemerkungen gemacht haben, wirkt diese Art der Kontaktaufnahme noch besser.

How do I start small talk?

But seriously, it's natural for us at such times to take the momentary rejection personally and to let it get us down. Don't assume the worst-case scenario that the other person just instinctively didn't like you. After all, you don't know what was going through their mind at the time. Perhaps they're just shy and that's why they looked away. Or maybe they're going through some problems and are just in a bad mood.

And what do I do when all the other people already know each other and have gathered into cliques? – This is indeed a little more complicated than making contact with an individual person who may well even be thankful that someone has spoken to them. First, have a look at the different groups by wandering through the room a little.

In situations where you can see that a few people are "putting their heads together", then don't interrupt. When it's obvious that people are speaking about something confidential, it would be impolite to disturb them.

If a group is standing together in a relaxed fashion and speaking at a normal volume level, then things look better for you. Now you can ...

- approach the group, introduce yourself, offer your hand all around and then open a topic of your choice. The very thought of this makes you uneasy? Admittedly, this method is not for reserved personalities, because for it to be convincing, you have to be very relaxed and self-confident. There is also the risk that proceeding this way can be perceived as anything from disruptive to pushy. So be sure and check your "confidence pulse" as well as how the group reacts to you.
- join in the group and listen first to what's being discussed. As soon as the opportunity presents itself for you to contribute to the conversation without being impolite, say something or ask a question:

> *"It sounds like you're talking about building up a client databank. What's your experience been like with that up to now? I'm asking because we're also planning the same kind of thing in our company."*

That's better. And before you say something, if you've managed to already establish non-verbal contact with a few group members and have made a couple of short comments (in the affirmative, of course), then this means of making contact works even better.

Wie beginne ich den Small Talk?

Der Einsatz von Eisbrechern

Ganz gleich, ob Sie einzelne Menschen oder Gruppen ansprechen: „Eisbrecher" erleichtern die Kontaktaufnahme.

Eisbrecher sind einfache Floskeln, mit denen etwas sehr Offensichtliches und Unstrittiges angesprochen wird.

Die inhaltliche Aussage ist also im Grunde nicht wichtig, die Formulierung schlicht. Da die meisten dieser Eisbrecher beim Small Talk zum Standardrepertoire gehören, kann man sie leicht verwenden, und es fällt auch nicht schwer, auf sie zu reagieren. Originalität – das brauchen wir hier nicht. Oft reicht es sogar, einen Eisbrecher in den Raum zu werfen – irgendjemand reagiert bestimmt. Und wenn tatsächlich mal niemand reagiert? Dann ist das auch nicht schlimm: Es entsteht keine peinliche Situation, weil Eisbrecher fast wie ein Selbstgespräch wirken.

> „Das ist ja wieder eine Kälte heute!"
> „Interessante Architektur, dieses Gebäude."

Möchten Sie doch lieber den direkten Dialog? Dann suchen Sie den Blickkontakt zu jemand Bestimmtem und hängen Sie einfach noch eine Frage an die Floskel:

> „Jetzt brauche ich erst mal einen starken Kaffee – Sie auch?"
> „Eine tolle Veranstaltung, nicht wahr?"

Übung

Das können Sie auch: Überlegen Sie sich drei Beispiele für Eisbrecher-Floskeln (mit oder ohne angehängte Frage), die Sie im beruflichen Small Talk einsetzen können. Schreiben Sie sie dabei nicht nur hin, sondern sprechen Sie sie laut aus: So merken Sie am besten, ob der Satz nicht zu künstlich, zu „gewollt" klingt.

1. _____

2. _____

3. _____

How do I start small talk?

Using Ice Breakers

Regardless of whether you are addressing individuals or groups, "ice breakers" ease the process of making contact.

> *Ice breakers are simple phrases used to talk about something that is very obvious and uncontroversial.*

So the content of the statement is basically not really important, while its formulation is short and to the point. Since most ice breakers are part of the standard repertoire of small talk, they are easy to use and it's not difficult to respond to them. Originality is not what's needed here. It's often enough just to toss an ice breaker into the room – somebody's sure to react. And what do you do in the unlikely event that no one does react? No harm done here either; there's no embarrassing situation, because ice breakers work almost like talking to oneself.

> "Boy, it's cold again today!"
> "This building's architecture is certainly interesting."

You prefer a direct dialogue instead? Then look for eye contact with someone in particular and tack a question onto your friendly comment:

> "I'd really like a strong coffee – you, too?"
> "Great event, don't you think?"

Exercise

You can also do this: think up three ice-breaking phrases (with or without a question at the end) that you can use in your professional small talk. And don't just write them down; say them out loud. This is the best way to make sure a particular sentence doesn't sound too artificial.

1. _____

2. _____

3. _____

Persönliche Anrede

Mit Namen angesprochen zu werden, wirkt positiv. Versuchen Sie daher, sich den Namen Ihres Gegenübers zu merken.

Sie haben den Namen nicht verstanden? – Dann fragen Sie höflich nach – das muss Ihnen nicht unangenehm sein. Peinlich wird es erst, wenn Sie den Gesprächspartner mit einem falsch verstandenen Namen ansprechen.

Sie können sich Namen nur schlecht merken? – Dann probieren Sie folgende Merkhilfen aus:
- Visualisieren Sie: Stellen Sie sich vor Ihrem geistigen Auge ein zum Namen passendes Bild vor. Das klappt gut bei gegenständlichen Namen wie Jäger, Dickmann, Vogel oder Hundt.
- Bilden Sie Eselsbrücken („Frau Hesse" wie der Dichter Hermann Hesse oder wie das Bundesland, nur ohne „n").
- Lassen Sie sich ausgefallene Namen buchstabieren.
- Fragen Sie nach der Herkunft („*Ist das ein typischer Name hier in Bayern?*").

Ihnen fällt der Name einer Person nicht ein, mit der Sie erst kürzlich zu tun hatten? – Keine Panik:

- Geben Sie es einfach zu:

> *„Ich weiß Ihren Namen leider nicht mehr, ich habe so ein schlechtes Namensgedächtnis. Helfen Sie mir?"*

- Um dem anderen zu zeigen, dass Sie sich erinnern, können Sie einen Aspekt Ihres letzten Treffens aufgreifen:

> *„Ach ja, wir haben uns ja erst im April gesehen – Sie wollten damals in den Osterurlaub fahren."*

- Sie umgehen die direkte Anrede und warten, ob sich jemand zu Ihnen gesellt, der Ihr Gegenüber kennt und eventuell mit Namen begrüßt. Diese Methode ist allerdings etwas riskant: Möchten Sie etwa eine dritte Person ins Gespräch einbeziehen, könnte es sein, dass Sie Ihren ersten Gesprächspartner vorstellen müssen – und dann geraten Sie natürlich ins Rudern, wenn Sie den Namen nicht mehr wissen.

> How do I start small talk?

Personal Greeting

Being addressed by name has a positive effect, so try to remember the name of your conversation partner.

You didn't understand the name? – Then ask the person politely to repeat it. There's no reason for this to be embarrassing for you. On the other hand, addressing your partner with an incorrectly understood name can be very embarrassing.

You have a hard time remembering names? – Then try the following memory aids:
- Visualising: imagine a picture in your mind's eye that fits with the name. This works well with easily understood names like Hunter, Armstrong, Baker or Fisher.
- Form memory hooks ("Ms Carter", like ex-president Jimmy Carter or the brand name Cartier, without the "i").
- Have unusual names spelled out for you.
- Ask about the origin of the name (*"Collier? Is that a French or English name?"*).

You can't remember the name of someone you recently met? – Don't panic:

- Just admit it:

> *"I'm sorry, your name has momentarily slipped my mind. That happens to me all the time, I'm afraid. Could you please tell me again?"*

- To show the other person that you remember them, you can mention something about your last meeting:

> *"Oh right! We met just last April – you were looking forward to a trip in the spring."*

- You initially avoid speaking directly to the person and wait to see if someone joins you who knows the conversation partner and greets them by name. This method is a little risky, however: if you want to include a third person in the conversation, you may find yourself having to introduce your initial discussion partner – and that can of course be awkward if you can't remember the name.

7 Worüber spreche ich – und worüber besser nicht?

Geeignete und ungeeignete Themen beim Small Talk

„Das ist die Kunst des Gesprächs: alles zu berühren und nichts zu vertiefen." Oscar Wilde (1854–1900), irisch-englischer Schriftsteller

Welches Thema fällt Ihnen spontan ein, wenn Sie an Small Talk denken? Richtig: das Wetter! Und in der Tat ist das nicht nur ein beliebtes Thema, sondern es entspricht auch den Regeln des Small Talks: Das Thema Wetter ...

- ist kaum konfliktträchtig (die meisten Menschen haben die gleichen Vorstellungen von schönem und schlechtem Wetter),
- kann niemanden verletzen,
- können Sie gegenüber jedem ansprechen, ohne ihn oder sie intellektuell zu überfordern,
- ist tagesaktuell: Wetter hat man schließlich immer.

Welche Themen sind darüber hinaus denkbar? Nun, falls Sie Ihren Gesprächspartner kennen, wissen Sie wahrscheinlich, welche Themen ihn interessieren. Falls Sie Ihr Gegenüber jedoch nicht kennen, liegt die Kunst des Small Talks darin, die Gesprächsthemen herauszufinden, die den anderen interessieren.

> **Für Small Talk eignen sich generell alle Themen, die ...**
>
> - kein bestimmtes Vorwissen, intellektuelles Niveau oder ausgeprägte Bildung voraussetzen,
> - sich im Leben möglichst vieler Menschen wiederfinden,
> - nicht konfliktträchtig oder allzu düster sind,
> - niemandem unangenehm aufstoßen,
> - angenehm und unterhaltsam aufbereitet werden können.

Natürlich kann es trotzdem vorkommen, dass das eine oder andere prinzipiell geeignete Thema mal auf Abneigung oder Desinteresse stößt. Beobachten Sie daher immer die verbalen und nonverbalen Reaktionen Ihres Gesprächspartners: Wirkt er noch interessiert, hält er Blickkontakt? Ist der Gesichtsausdruck freundlich?

Ganz gleich, welches Thema Sie wählen: Um den Einstieg zu finden, haben Sie immer zwei Möglichkeiten:

- Sie erzählen ein bisschen von sich und beziehen dann Ihren Gesprächspartner über Fragen ein. Diese Variante eignet sich für diejenigen, denen das Erzählen leichtfällt.

7 What do I talk about – and what do I avoid?

Suitable and unsuitable topics for small talk

"Conversation should touch everything, but should concentrate itself on nothing." Oscar Wilde (1854–1900), Irish-English author

What topic pops into your mind spontaneously when you think of small talk? Right: the weather! And as a matter of fact, it's not just a popular subject; it also conforms to the rules of small talk: weather as a topic …
- is scarcely controversial (most people have the same ideas about good and bad weather),
- can't offend anyone,
- can be brought up in front of anybody without overwhelming their intellectual capabilities,
- is in fact topical, because we all have weather all the time.

What other topics can you imagine as being suitable? Well, if you already know your discussion partner, then you probably know what subjects interest them. But in the event that you're not already acquainted with your conversation partner, the art of small talk consists of finding out what topics of discussion the other person is indeed interested in.

> **For small talk, all topics are generally suitable that …**
> - don't require specific prior knowledge, great intellectual ability or an extensive education,
> - are relevant in the lives of most people,
> - are not controversial or too bleak,
> - don't offend anyone,
> - can be presented in a pleasant, entertaining way.

Naturally, it's possible that this or the other generally suitable topic can still be met with reluctance or disinterest, so always observe the verbal and non-verbal reactions of your discussion partner: do they still seem interested and are they maintaining eye contact? Is the facial expression friendly?

Regardless of which subject you choose, you always have two possibilities to find your entry:
- You can tell a little about yourself and then integrate your discussion partner by using questions. This approach is suited for people who find it easy to talk to others.

- Sie beginnen gleich mit einer Frage, auf die Ihr Gegenüber etwas zu erzählen hat.

Auf den folgenden Seiten finden Sie eine Auswahl an Themen, die sich für Small Talk eignen.

Ergänzen Sie die Liste mit eigenen Themen, über die Sie gemäß den Small-Talk-Regeln sprechen könnten.

7.1 Small-Talk-Themen von A bis Z

Anreise

Bei allen Anlässen, die nicht gerade vor der Haustür stattfinden, ist dies ein gut geeigneter Einstieg in den Small Talk: Wie und womit ist man hergekommen, hat man das Hotel / den Tagungsort gut gefunden ... Sie kennen ja den alten Spruch: Wer eine Reise tut, hat was zu erzählen.

Mögliche Einstiegsfragen:

> *„Und wie war Ihre Anreise?"*
> *„Haben Sie unser Firmengebäude gut gefunden?"*
> *„Sind Sie mit der Bahn oder dem Auto angereist?"*

Berufliches

Über berufliche Themen kann man unter Kollegen und mit Chefs fast immer sprechen. Allerdings: Wenn Sie Menschen aus dem beruflichen Umfeld bei privaten Anlässen treffen, gibt es bessere Themen als den Job.

Wichtig: Sprechen Sie keine kritischen Punkte an, sondern eher harmlose Dinge, auf die der andere gern eingehen wird. Gut geeignete Themen für den Small Talk sind z.B. Weiterbildungen, Fachbücher, die Sie gelesen haben, Fragen nach dem beruflichen Hintergrund und Alltag des Gegenübers.

Mögliche Einstiegsfragen:

> *„Ich habe gehört, Sie sind im Marketing. Das ist sicher eine sehr spannende Tätigkeit?"*
> *„Wie kommt ihr denn mit dem neuen EDV-Programm klar?"*
> *„Sie waren doch letztes Wochenende auf dem Vertriebsseminar – welche Punkte fanden Sie denn am interessantesten?"*

What do I talk about – and what do I avoid?

- You start off with a question that sets your conversation partner up to talk about something.

In the pages that follow, you'll find a selection of topics that are appropriate for small talk.

Supplement the list with topics of your own that you can talk about in accordance with the rules of small talk.

7.1 An Extensive List of Small Talk Topics

The Journey

For all occasions or events taking place somewhere away from home, this is a well-suited small talk opener: how and by what means of transport did the other person arrive; did they find the hotel / event location easily … It really is a truism that "people who travel have stories to tell".

Possible opening questions:

> *"So, how was your trip?"*
> *"Did you find our offices easily?"*
> *"Did you come by train or car?"*

Job

With co-workers and bosses, one can almost always talk about job-related topics. But when you meet people from your work environment at private occasions, there are better things to talk about than the job.

Important: don't talk about critical matters, but instead about harmless things that the other person will eagerly discuss. Appropriate subjects for small talk include training measures, field-related books or literature that you have read, questions about one's professional background and the other person's day-to-day.

Possible opening questions:

> *"I heard that you're in marketing. Isn't that an exciting field?"*
> *"How do you get on with the new DP program?"*
> *"You were at the sales seminar last weekend – what were the most interesting points for you?"*

Worüber spreche ich – und worüber besser nicht?

Computer
Das ist vor allem in beruflichen Small-Talk-Situationen ein geeignetes Thema; im privaten Bereich sprechen Sie es entweder nur bei Interessierten an oder aber Sie halten es allgemein.

Mögliche Einstiegsfragen:

> *„Mit welchem Programm machen Sie in Ihrer Firma die Terminplanung?"*
> *„Erinnern Sie sich noch an Ihren ersten Rechner?"*
> *„Demnächst soll es ja wieder Schnäppchen-PC's beim Discounter geben. Was halten Sie denn davon?"*

Dichter und Denker
Lesen Sie gern? Haben Sie den begründeten Verdacht, dass es Ihrem Gegenüber ähnlich geht? Dann sind Bücher und Schriftsteller ein gutes Thema.

Mögliche Einstiegsfragen:

> *„Was ist Ihr Lieblingsbuch?"*
> *„Ich kenne jemanden, der liest immer zuerst das Ende eines Buches – erst dann entscheidet er, ob sich das ganze Buch lohnt. Wie finden Sie das?"*
> *„Haben Sie schon mal ein Hörbuch ausprobiert?"*

Einkaufen
Nicht nur für Frauen ein geeignetes Thema! Auch Männer kaufen ein. Und da bieten sich unzählige Themenfacetten an: etwa was man kürzlich in Sachen Kundenservice erlebt hat, was man erst neulich gekauft hat oder demnächst kaufen möchte ...

Mögliche Einstiegsfragen:

> *„Geht Ihr Mann eigentlich gern einkaufen?"*
> *„Waren Sie schon mal in einem Designer-Outlet?"*
> *„Ich erlebe es beim Einkaufen immer häufiger, dass die Menschen beim Preis zu handeln versuchen – wie finden Sie das?"*

Film und Fernsehen
Sprechen Sie über Filme im Kino oder Fernsehen (*„Haben Sie letzten Sonntag den Tatort gesehen?"*) oder über sonstige Sendungen. Achten Sie aber darauf, dass das gewählte Thema zur „Zielperson" passt: Das Bekenntnis, ein Fan von Rosamunde-Pilcher-Verfilmungen zu sein, kann unter Umständen zu einem unerwünschten Image führen.

What do I talk about – and what do I avoid?

Computer
This is a suitable topic above all in professional small talk situations; in private situations, it's a topic either for people specifically interested in the subject or as a general topic of conversation.

Possible opening questions:

> *"What program do you use in your company for appointment planning?"*
> *"Can you still remember your first computer?"*
> *"I hear that the discount chains are going to have bargain-priced PC's again soon. What do you think about that?"*

Poets and Thinkers
Are you an avid reader? Are you pretty sure that your conversation partner is, too? Then books and authors are a good topic.

Possible opening questions:

> *"What's your favourite book?"*
> *"I know someone who always reads the end of a book first – then he decides whether or not it's worth reading. How do you feel about that?"*
> *"Have you tried an audio book before?"*

Shopping
This topic is not just appropriate for women! Men go shopping as well. And this offers a world of topic possibilities, such as recent experiences involving customer service, for instance, or recent and/or upcoming or planned purchases …

Possible opening questions:

> *"Does your husband actually like to go shopping?"*
> *"Have you ever been to a designer outlet?"*
> *"I find more and more that people are increasingly trying to haggle over the price when shopping – how do you feel about that?"*

Film and TV
You can talk about cinema films or television shows or productions (*"Did you see the match on TV last Sunday?"*). But be sure that your subject choice fits the personality of your conversation partner: under certain circumstances, for instance, admitting to being a fan of old Joan Collins films can lead to an image problem!

Mögliche Einstiegsfragen:

> „Haben Sie schon den neuen Kinofilm XYZ gesehen?"
> „Was schauen Sie sich denn im Fernsehen am liebsten an?"
> „Haben Sie eine/-n Lieblingsschauspieler/-in?"

Gastgeber/-in

Gastgeber kann eine Person, bei geschäftlichen Veranstaltungen auch ein Unternehmen sein. Das Thema eignet sich gut, um Kontakte mit einem Unbekannten zu knüpfen – und um mehr über den Gastgeber zu erfahren.

Mögliche Einstiegsfragen:

> „Woher kennen Sie denn die Beckers?"
> „Die Eckhardt AG soll ja jedes Jahr diese Hausmesse veranstalten. Waren Sie schon mal hier?"
> „Kennen Sie Herrn Jürgens schon länger?"

Hobbys

Die meisten Menschen haben mindestens ein Hobby – geeignet als Small-Talk-Thema ist sowohl das eigene wie das des Gegenübers. Wenn Sie letzteres schon kennen, können Sie es direkt ansprechen:

> „Sie sollen ja einen fantastischen Garten haben."

Ansonsten sind eher allgemein gehaltene Fragen gut:

> „Was machen Sie denn, um abends abzuschalten?"
> „Sie haben ja einen sehr stressigen Beruf. Bleibt Ihnen denn noch Zeit für Hobbys?"

Wenn Sie über Ihr eigenes Hobby sprechen möchten, achten Sie auf die Reaktionen Ihres Gesprächspartners. Ein Eishockeyfan findet womöglich ausführliche Beschreibungen Ihrer Yoga-Abende zum Gähnen, die Hobbypianistin kann eventuell nur wenig mit Schilderungen eines Motorrad-Rennens anfangen. Sehr ungewöhnliche Hobbys haben immer zudem auch ein gewisses Potenzial, andere zu verstören:

> „Ich halte in meiner Wohnung mehrere Schlangen und Mini-Alligatoren."

> *What do I talk about – and what do I avoid?*

Possible opening questions:

> "Have you already seen the new movie 'XYZ'?"
> "What are your favourite kinds of TV shows?"
> "Do you have a favourite actor/actress?"

Host

A host can be a person, or at business-related events, a company. This topic is well-suited for making contact with people you don't know – and for finding out more about the host.

Possible opening questions:

> "Where do you know the Beckers from?"
> "I heard that Eagle Ltd puts on this company convention every year. Have you been here before?"
> "Have you known Mr Taylor for a long time?"

Hobbies

Most people have at least one hobby – and both yours and your conversation partner's are suitable for small talk. If you already know what your partner's hobby is, then you can mention it directly:

> "You're rumoured to have a magnificent garden."

Otherwise, more generalised questions are probably more appropriate:

> "What do you do then to wind down in the evenings?"
> "You've got a pretty stressful job. Does it leave you any time for hobbies?"

If you want to talk about your own hobby, then pay attention to your discussion partner's reaction. An ice hockey fan is likely to find extensive descriptions of a yoga evening fairly boring, while an amateur pianist might not be able to relate all too well to a conversation about motorcycle racing. And very unusual hobbies also have the added potential of making others uncomfortable:

> "I have several snakes and mini alligators as pets at home."

Worüber spreche ich – und worüber besser nicht?

Internet
Ein mittlerweile alltagstaugliches und Small-Talk-geeignetes Thema – vorausgesetzt, Sie gehen nicht zu sehr in technische Details. Tauschen Sie Erfahrungen aus: über gute Internet-Shops, Reisebüros, Suchmaschinen etc.

Mögliche Einstiegsfragen:

> *„Wofür nutzen Sie denn das Internet hauptsächlich?"*
> *„Haben Sie auch schon mal etwas bei E-Bay ersteigert?"*

Kind und Kegel
Wenn Sie mit Menschen sprechen, die Sie kennen, sind Fragen nach dem Befinden von Familienmitgliedern immer ein guter und persönlicher Einstieg. Allerdings sollten Sie dafür die aktuelle Familiensituation Ihres Gesprächspartners kennen. Die Frage *„Und was macht Ihre Frau?"*, kurz nachdem Ihr Gegenüber von derselben verlassen wurde, wäre eher unangebracht.

Mögliche Einstiegsfragen:

> *„Wie geht es Ihrer Frau?"*
> *„Ich habe gehört, Ihr Vater ist jetzt in Rente gegangen. Wie geht es ihm denn?"*
> *„Geht Ihre Jüngste schon zur Schule?"*

Lob
„Lob ist eine gewaltige Antriebskraft, dessen Zauber seine Wirkung nie verfehlt." (Andor Foldes, amerik.-ungar. Pianist, 1913–1992)

Stimmt. Wichtig dabei: Damit das Lob glaubwürdig klingt, muss es ernst gemeint sein. Und es sollte eher beiläufig und zwanglos daherkommen, denn übertriebenes Schmeicheln (*„Was sehen Sie heute wieder zauberhaft aus, Frau Winter!"*) wirkt meist aufgesetzt und kommt daher nicht gut an. Auch anzügliche Komplimente über das Aussehen, die Figur etc. sind absolut verboten.

Ein weiterer Hinweis:

> *Verknüpfen Sie ein Lob nicht mit einer direkt anschließenden Bitte – diese Form der Manipulation wird sehr schnell durchschaut.*

Mögliche Einstiegsfragen:

Internet

This has become an everyday topic that's certainly suitable for small talk – providing you don't delve too deeply into technical details. Talk about your experiences with good internet shops, travel sites, search engines, etc.

Possible opening questions:

> *"What do you use the internet for primarily?"*
> *"Have you ever bought or sold anything on E-Bay?"*

Family Life

When you're talking with people you already know, asking about family members is always a good, personal opener. However, make sure that you know your discussion partner's current family situation. The question, *"And how's your wife?"*, shortly after the two have separated would hardly be appropriate.

Possible opening questions:

> *"How's your wife, then?"*
> *"I heard that your father recently retired. How's he getting along?"*
> *"Is your youngest child already in school?"*

Praise

"Praise is a potent force, a candle in a dark room. It is magic, and I marvel that it always works." (Andor Foldes, American-Hungarian pianist, 1913–1992)

That's right. But for praise to sound believable, it's important that it's genuine. And it should be given in a way that's more casual and spontaneous, because exaggerated flattery (*"You're looking fabulous today as usual, Ms Winter!"*) generally sounds somewhat disingenuous and subsequently leaves a negative impression. And "racy" compliments about a person's appearance, figure, etc. are an absolute no-no.

One more tip:

> *Never combine praise followed immediately by a request – this form of manipulation is very easy to see through.*

Possible opening questions:

> *Worüber spreche ich – und worüber besser nicht?*

> *„Sie sehen so erholt aus – waren Sie im Urlaub?"*
> *„Ich habe gehört, du machst jetzt eine nebenberufliche Weiterbildung zur Personalkauffrau – das finde ich toll, so viel Energie und Disziplin."*
> *„Darf ich Sie mal etwas fragen? Sie haben so eine schöne Uhr/ Tasche/etc. – wo bekommt man so etwas?"*

Musik

Gibt es Menschen, die überhaupt keine Musik hören? Wohl nur wenige. Musik ist also ein gutes Small-Talk-Thema, immer vorausgesetzt, Sie bereiten es „zielgruppenspezifisch" auf: Gegenüber einem pensionierten Oberstudienrat über das letzte Robbie-Williams-Konzert zu schwärmen, zielt mit großer Wahrscheinlichkeit ins Leere. Sprechen Sie über die jeweilige Lieblingsmusik oder über Instrumente, die Sie oder Ihr Gegenüber spielen bzw. gern gelernt hätten, fragen Sie nach guten CDs.

Mögliche Einstiegsfragen:

> *„Interessante Hintergrundmusik hier im Restaurant – was hören Sie denn gern?"*
> *„Ich war vor Kurzem das erste Mal in der Oper – sind Sie ein Klassik-Fan?"*
> *„Werden Sie das neue Musical hier in der Stadt besuchen?"*

Nachrichten

Das aktuelle Tagesgeschehen hält immer gute Small-Talk-Themen bereit. Meiden sollten Sie jedoch Themen, die sehr kontrovers oder schockierend sind. Gut geeignet sind hingegen interessante Artikel, die Sie gelesen haben, oder unterhaltsame Begebenheiten, die durch die Presse gegangen sind.

Mögliche Einstiegsfragen:

> *„Ich habe heute im Radio gehört, dass ein Dreijähriger bei E-Bay ein Auto ersteigert hat, als seine Mutter kurz aus dem Zimmer gegangen ist – wie finden Sie das?"*
> *„Haben Sie gestern im Lokalteil die Bilder von dem geplanten Schwimmbadumbau gesehen?"*

Orte

Geeignet sind ...
- der Wohn- oder Geburtsort,
- der Veranstaltungsort,

What do I talk about – and what do I avoid?

> "You're looking fit – were you on holiday?"
> "I heard that you're studying in your spare time to be a Human Resources Manager – I think it's great that you've got so much energy and discipline."
> "Can I ask you a question? That's a beautiful watch/bag/etc. – where did you get it?"

Music

Is there anyone who doesn't listen to music at all? Not many. So music makes a good small talk topic, providing you always "know your audience": raving to a retired schoolteacher about a recent Robbie Williams concert is unlikely to win you a standing ovation! Talk about one another's favourite music or about instruments that you play or would like to have learned, or ask about good CDs.

Possible opening questions:

> "Interesting background music here in the restaurant – what kind of music do you like to listen to?"
> "Recently I was in the opera for the first time – are you a fan of the classics?"
> "Will you be going to the new musical here in the city?"

The News

The daily news is always brimming with good small talk topics. But you should avoid subjects that are very controversial or shocking. But interesting articles that you've read or entertaining items from the press are well-suited conversational topics.

Possible opening questions:

> "Today I heard on the radio that a three-year-old bought a car on E-Bay when his mother left the room for a minute – what do you think about that?"
> "Did you see the pictures of the planned swimming pool renovations in the local paper yesterday?"

Places

Suitable places are ...
- places of residence or birth,
- the event location,

- ein Ort, an dem Sie häufig geschäftlich zu tun haben,
- ein Ort, den Sie lieben ...

Tauschen Sie Erinnerungen, Hintergrundwissen und Insidertipps aus. Mögliche Einstiegsfragen:

> „Kommen Sie auch aus Köln?"
> „Kennen Sie sich hier in München aus?"
> „Ich fliege demnächst zum ersten Mal geschäftlich nach New York – waren Sie schon einmal in den USA?"

Personen des öffentlichen Lebens

Ein bisschen Klatsch ist völlig okay – man sollte allerdings nicht bösartig über andere herziehen. Die neue Frisur einer bekannten Adligen, die Hochzeit eines Filmstars und die nach 30 Tagen erfolgte Scheidung – das sind nicht nur für „Gala"- und „Bunte"-Leser schöne Themen.

Mögliche Einstiegsfragen:

> „Was halten Sie denn von dem Wirbel um Günter Grass?"
> „Wie finden Sie die Thesen von Eva Herman?"
> „Der Ulrich Wickert geht ja jetzt in Rente – ich habe ihn immer ganz gern gesehen. Und Sie?"

Restaurants und Essen

Gespräche rund ums Thema Essen sind ein Leichtes – erst recht natürlich, wenn die Gelegenheit (Kantine, Geschäftsessen, Buffet) es auch noch nahelegt.

Sprechen Sie über Restaurants, tauschen Sie Tipps und Empfehlungen aus. Und für diejenigen, die nicht nur gern essen, sondern auch gern kochen: Tauschen Sie Kochrezepte aus oder Tipps, wo man exotische Zutaten bekommt.

Mögliche Einstiegsfragen:

> „Waren Sie schon bei dem neuen Italiener?"
> „Ich habe vor Kurzem einen Kurs für thailändische Küche besucht – kochen Sie auch gern?"
> „Oh, es gibt Lasagne – das hab ich schon als Kind gern gegessen. Was mögen Sie denn am liebsten?"

Sport

Sie sind begeisterter Sportfan – aktiv oder passiv? Dann testen Sie aus, ob Ihr Gesprächspartner das Thema auch spannend findet.

What do I talk about – and what do I avoid?

- a place that you visit frequently on business,
- a place that you love …

Trade memories, background knowledge and insider tips.
Possible opening questions:

> *"Are you also from Birmingham?"*
> *"Do you know your way around here in Munich?"*
> *"I'm going to New York on business for the first time soon – have you ever been there?"*

Public Figures

A little gossip is completely OK – however, one should avoid talking badly about others. A royal family member's new hairstyle, a film star's wedding and subsequent divorce after 30 days – these aren't just fun topics for boulevard press readers.

Possible opening questions:

> *"What do you think about all the furore surrounding Tom Cruise?"*
> *"Do you think Prince Harry will marry?"*
> *"I keep hearing that Jack Nicholson is going to retire – I always loved his movies. How about you?"*

Restaurants and Eating

It's easy to talk about the subject of eating – above all when the occasion (cafeteria, business meal, buffet) puts it right in front of you, so to speak.

Talk about restaurants and exchange tips and recommendations. And for those who don't just like to eat, but also like to cook: trade recipes or tips about where one can get exotic ingredients.

Possible opening questions:

> *"Have you been to that new Italian place yet?"*
> *"I recently took a course in Thai cooking – do you also like to cook?"*
> *"Oh, great, lasagne – I've loved that since I was a child. What's your favourite dish?"*

Sport

You're an avid sports fan, either active or passive? Then check out whether your discussion partner is also interested in the subject.

Worüber spreche ich – und worüber besser nicht?

Mögliche Einstiegsfragen:

> „Ich habe gehört, Sie sind ein Fußballkenner. Glauben Sie, dass der BVB irgendwann noch mal an alte Erfolgszeiten anknüpfen kann?"
> „Machen Sie regelmäßig Sport?"
> „Bei mir im Bekanntenkreis sind momentan alle wild auf Nordic Walking. Haben Sie das schon mal ausprobiert?"

Tiere

Auch ein Thema für den Small Talk, vor allem, wenn Sie wissen, dass Ihr Gesprächspartner tierlieb oder sogar Tierbesitzer ist.

Mögliche Einstiegsfragen:

> „Wie geht es Ihrem Pferd?"
> „Ich habe gehört, Sie haben einen Hund – welche Rasse denn?"
> „Ein Aquarium wie hier in der Eingangshalle soll ja sehr beruhigend wirken – finden Sie das auch?"

Urlaub

Hier bieten sich zahllose Möglichkeiten für ein Gespräch. Sie können Ihren geplanten oder den zurückliegenden Urlaub erwähnen oder den, den Sie schon immer mal machen wollten – und daran beispielsweise eine Frage über den Urlaub Ihres Gegenübers anknüpfen.

Mögliche Einstiegsfragen:

> „Waren Sie diesen Sommer schon im Urlaub?"
> „Wir wollen demnächst nach Schweden. Waren Sie da schon mal?"
> „Wie sähe Ihr Traumurlaub aus?"

Verkehr

Vom Thema Verkehr ist jeder auf irgendeine Weise betroffen: Sprechen Sie beispielsweise Parkplatzprobleme oder Staus an, aber auch Verkehrsmittel wie Bahn, Flugzeug und Auto.

Mögliche Einstiegsfragen:

> „Haben Sie auch in dem Stau auf der A1 gestanden?"
> „Fahren Sie öfter mit der Bahn?"
> „Ich habe gesehen, Sie fahren ein Cabrio. Das ist auch ein Traum von mir – sind Sie zufrieden damit?"

> *What do I talk about – and what do I avoid?*

Possible opening questions:

> *"I've heard that you know a lot about motor racing. Do you think that Schumacher will really retire, or will the roar of the crowd lure him back?"*
> *"Do your exercise regularly?"*
> *"All of my friends are crazy about Nordic Walking at the moment. Have you ever tried that?"*

Animals

This is also a small talk topic, especially if you know that your discussion partner is an animal lover or even an owner.

Possible opening questions:

> *"How's your horse?"*
> *"I heard you have a dog – what breed is it?"*
> *"An aquarium like the one here in the foyer is supposed to have a very calming effect – do you think it does?"*

Holidays

This topic offers an endless supply of possibilities for a chat. You can mention your upcoming or a past holiday, or perhaps your dream holiday – and then link it with a question about your conversation partner's holiday.

Possible opening questions:

> *"Were you already on holiday this summer?"*
> *"We want to go to Sweden soon. Have you ever been there?"*
> *"What would be your dream holiday?"*

Transport

Everyone is affected in one way or another by the subject of transport: for example, mention parking problems or traffic jams, but also means of transport such as rail travel, air travel and cars.

Possible opening questions:

> *"Did you also get stuck in the traffic jam on the way here?"*
> *"Do you travel by train frequently?"*
> *"I saw that you drive a convertible. That's always been a dream of mine – do you enjoy it?"*

Wetter

Alle reden über das Wetter – und Sie am besten auch. Wenig originell? Stimmt, aber darauf kommt es auch nicht an, es ist ja meist bloß der Aufhänger für ein Gespräch.

Mögliche Einstiegsfragen:

> „Allmählich wird diese Hitzewelle ja schon ein bisschen anstrengend, nicht wahr?"
> „So ein Herbsttag wie heute – das gefällt mir fast besser als der Sommer. Welches ist denn Ihre Lieblingsjahreszeit?"
> „Man glaubt kaum, in Deutschland zu sein bei diesen Temperaturen – mögen Sie diese Wärme?"

Ziele, Wünsche, Träume

Von konkreten über vage bis hin zu utopischen Zukunftsplänen – über viele davon können Sie reden: Ihre beruflichen Ziele für die nächsten Jahre, der Wunsch, den Flugschein zu machen, Ihr Traumhaus – und ebenso natürlich über die Ziele, Wünsche und Träume Ihres Gegenübers. Dabei sollten Sie natürlich ein feines Gespür dafür haben, welche Themen Sie besser aussparen, weil sie zu persönlich sein und Fettnäpfchen bereithalten könnten.

Mögliche Einstiegsfragen:

> „Ich will im neuen Jahr endlich das Rauchen aufgeben – wie haben Sie es damals geschafft?"
> „Ich würde gern noch Klavierspielen lernen – glauben Sie, das kann man auch noch als Erwachsener?"
> „Was war eigentlich Ihr Wunschberuf als Kind?"

7.2 Themenwechsel, bitte!

Natürlich müssen Sie nicht bei einem Thema bleiben – die meisten Gespräche bieten diverse Anknüpfungspunkte, um von einem Thema zum nächsten zu mäandern. So eignet sich etwa ein Einstieg mit dem Thema Wetter, um zum Thema Urlaub weiterzudriften, vom Urlaub kann man dann auf Hobbys kommen usw.

> *Indem Sie hin und wieder das Thema wechseln, verhindern Sie, dass der Small Talk langweilig wird.*

Außerdem können Sie ein Thema elegant wechseln, falls Sie merken, dass es auf Desinteresse oder Ablehnung stößt.

> *What do I talk about – and what do I avoid?*

Weather

Everybody talks about the weather – and you should, too. Not very original? That's true, but that's not the point; generally, it's just an opener for a conversation.

Possible opening questions:

> *"Slowly but surely, this heat wave is beginning to get old, isn't it?"*
> *"A beautiful autumn day today – I like that almost better than summer. What's your favourite season?"*
> *"You'd hardly think we're in Europe with these temperatures – do you like the heat?"*

Goals, Wishes, Dreams

Future plans spanning the spectrum from vague to firm to utopian – many of these are great topics for discussion: your career goals for the coming years, the wish to get a pilot's licence, your dream house – and naturally, equal time for your conversation partner's future aims as well. Of course, you should be highly sensitive to which topics are better left unmentioned because they might be too personal and could leave you with your foot in your mouth!

Possible opening questions:

> *"I want to finally stop smoking in the New Year – how did you manage that?"*
> *"I'd love to learn to play the piano – do you think things like that are still possible for adults?"*
> *"What was your dream job when you were a child?"*

7.2 Can we change the subject, please!

Of course, you don't have to stick to only one topic – most conversations provide a number of possibilities to link one subject to the next. For example, opening a talk on the subject of the weather can lead to the topic of holidays, and from holidays it's only a short jump to hobbies, and so on.

> *By changing the subject from time to time, you prevent the small talk from becoming tedious.*

In addition, you can smoothly change the subject if you begin to notice disinterest or reluctance.

Worüber spreche ich – und worüber besser nicht?

Ein Beispiel
Auf einer Fachmesse unterhält sich Herr Gernoth am Kaffeestand mit einer Kundin, Frau Wittler, die er bislang nur dem Namen nach kannte. Ausgangspunkt beim Small Talk ist die Frage nach der Anreise:

- Herr Gernoth: „Sie kommen ja auch von weiter her. Haben Sie denn Ihr Hotel und die Messehalle gut gefunden?"
- Frau Wittler: „Ja, danke – seit ich mein Navigationssystem habe, ist Autofahren wirklich stressfrei für mich."
- Herr Gernoth: „Das habe ich schon von vielen gehört. In meinem nächsten Auto werde ich wohl auch eins haben. Bis dahin lasse ich mir im Internet einen Routenplan erstellen, wenn ich den Weg nicht kenne."
- Frau Wittler: „Was haben wir früher eigentlich ohne Internet gemacht? Ich bestelle mittlerweile schon meine Bücher, meine Kleidung, DVDs und was nicht alles im Netz! Mein Arbeitstag ist häufig so lang, da reichen selbst die erweiterten Ladenöffnungszeiten oft nicht."

Stellen Sie sich vor, Sie sind Herr Gernoth: Wie könnten Sie jetzt das Gespräch weiterführen?
Überlegen Sie sich mindestens drei Themen, mit denen Sie an das Gesagte anknüpfen können, und formulieren Sie einen entsprechenden Satz bzw. eine entsprechende Frage:

Thema 1: _____
Satz/Frage: _____

Thema 2: _____
Satz/Frage: _____

Thema 3: _____
Satz/Frage: _____

Mögliche Lösungen:
- *Sie können den angesprochenen langen Arbeitstag aufnehmen, indem Sie fragen, was der andere beruflich macht. Sie können auch erzählen, dass es bei Ihnen ähnlich aussieht, und fragen, wie Ihr Gegenüber mit der Situation umgeht. Von da aus kann man dann z.B. den nächsten Schritt in Richtung persönliches Stress- oder Zeitmanagement machen.*
- *Auch das Thema Internet eignet sich zu einer Vertiefung: Wie sind z.B. Ihre Erfahrungen mit Internet-Shops? Fragen Sie nach und/oder berichten Sie Ihrerseits von besonders empfehlenswerten Internetadressen.*
- *Ihr Gesprächspartner hat Bücher oder DVDs angesprochen – gehen Sie darauf ein, fragen Sie, was sich in dem Bereich anzuschaffen*

What do I talk about – and what do I avoid?

Here's an example
At a trade fair, Mr Gernoth is talking at the coffee stand with a client, Ms Whistler, who he has previously only known by name, but not in person. The starting point for this small talk chat is a question about the journey:

- Mr Gernoth: "You also had a long trip. Did you find the hotel and convention centre easily enough?"
- Ms Whistler: "Yes, thanks – since I've had my navigation system, driving has really become stress-free for me."
- Mr Gernoth: "I've heard that from a lot of people. I'm going to make sure I have one too in my next car. For now, I always get a route plan from the internet if I don't know the way."
- Ms Whistler: "How did we ever manage before without the internet? These days, I order my books, my clothes, DVDs and heaven knows what else online! My workday is often so long that I'm just too tired to go shopping afterwards."

Now imagine that you are Mr Gernoth: How could you continue the conversation now?
Think up at least three topics with which you could pick up on what's just been said, and then formulate a suitable sentence or question for each of them:

Topic 1: _____
Sentence/Question: _____

Topic 2: _____
Sentence/Question: _____

Topic 3: _____
Sentence/Question: _____

Possible solutions:
- You could pick up on the long **workday** that was mentioned by asking what the other person's profession is or what their job entails. You can also explain that the situation is similar for yourself, and then ask how your conversation partner deals with it. From that point, you can move on to the subject of personal stress or time management, for example.
- The **internet** is also a topic that can be discussed more extensively: for instance, what kind of experience have you had shopping online? Inquire about and/or mention websites you know about that are worthy of special recommendation.
- Your discussion partner mentioned **books** and **DVDs** – pick up on this and ask what titles are worth buying – and talk about what you've recently read or seen yourself that you liked.

lohnt – und erzählen Sie, was Sie kürzlich gelesen oder gesehen haben und Ihnen besonders gut gefallen hat.
- Und auch das Thema **Ladenöffnungszeiten** gibt etwas her: Macht z.B. eine komplette Freigabe der Öffnungszeiten oder der verkaufsoffene Sonntag Sinn? Wie sieht Ihr Gesprächspartner das?

7.3 Tabu-Themen von A bis Z

„Die ganze Kunst des Redens besteht darin, zu wissen, was man nicht sagen darf." George Canning (1770–1827), brit. Politiker

Es gibt Themen, die Sie beim Small Talk in den meisten Fällen meiden sollten, weil sie zu konfliktträchtig, zu peinlich oder zu nervig sind.

Arbeitsplatzinterna

> „Mal ganz unter uns …"
> „Das ist jetzt natürlich vertraulich, aber …"
> „Erzählen Sie es nicht weiter, aber bei uns …"

Berufliches eignet sich meist gut für Small Talk, **bestimmte Dinge aber müssen außen vor bleiben**: Geschichten über Kunden, auch wenn sie noch so witzig sind, gehören dazu; und Interna über Arbeitsbedingungen, Gehälter, neue Produkte oder Fehler der Unternehmensführung sind ebenfalls tabu. Auch fachliche Diskussionen oder gar Streitgespräche sind ungeeignet, wie der nächste Punkt verdeutlicht.

Belehrungen, Verbesserungen und Rechthaberei
… sind unerwünscht beim Small Talk (und nicht nur da …):

> „Das ist interessant, was Sie da erzählen, allerdings sollten Sie wissen, dass …"
> „Sie kennen sich da wahrscheinlich nicht so aus, aber …"
> „Nun, das stimmt so natürlich nicht, tatsächlich sieht es so aus, dass …"

So macht man sich keine Freunde. Darüber hinaus geht es beim Small Talk (anders als bei einem Fachgespräch) ja weitaus weniger um die Sachebene als um die **Beziehungsebene** – und der schadet Besserwisserei enorm.

> *What do I talk about – and what do I avoid?*

- And the subject of *shop opening hours* is also a matter of particular interest for German discussion partners: for example, does it make sense to have special "Shopping Sundays" or to deregulate opening hours completely? What's your conversation partner's opinion?

7.3 The Entire Spectrum of Taboo Topics

"The entire art of speaking consists of knowing what one may not say." George Canning (1770–1827), British politician

There are topics that are better avoided in most small talk situations, because they are too controversial, too embarrassing or too annoying.

Internal Workplace Matters

> *"Between you and me …"*
> *"This is of course confidential, but …"*
> *"Don't tell anyone else, but we're …"*

The job is usually a good small talk subject, but certain things are simply no-go areas: these include stories about clients, even if they're genuinely funny, as well as internal matters of working conditions, wages, new products or company management mistakes. Technical discussions also, and even arguments are inappropriate, as is illustrated in the following section.

Admonishments, Corrections and "Knowing-It-All"

… are not what you want in small talk (and not only there …):

> *"What you're saying is interesting, but you should know that …"*
> *"You probably don't know so much about the subject, but …"*
> *"Well, that's not really true, of course. The fact is that …"*

That's no way to make friends. Additionally, the issue in small talk (in contrast to a technical discussion) has much less to do with the factual level than with the relationship level – and being a "know-it-all" does untold damage at this level.

Worüber spreche ich – und worüber besser nicht?

Dramen und Desaster
... eignen sich nicht für Small Talk, weil sie dem Gespräch einen eher düsteren Anklang verleihen – die Gesprächsatmosphäre kann darunter leiden.

> „Ja, das Wetter ist wirklich sehr schön, so warm – aber wenn man sich die neuesten Klimamodelle anschaut, kommen noch schlimme Zeiten auf uns zu. Alles vom Menschen selbst verschuldet – CO_2-Ausstoß und so."

Unter Umständen hält man Sie nach so einer Äußerung für einen Schwarzseher – und das ist sicherlich nicht der Eindruck, den Sie hinterlassen möchten.

Ehe-/Familienprobleme
... sind kein Small-Talk-Thema – es sei denn, es sind lustige Anekdoten über kleine Probleme.

Geld
... gehört (zumindest in Deutschland) nicht ins Themenrepertoire des Small Talks, ganz gleich ob Sie viel oder wenig davon haben. Prahlereien sind dementsprechend einfach nur peinlich. Und Jammern, dass es allen anderen viel besser geht als einem selbst („*In unserer Berufssparte sind wir einfach alle unterbezahlt.*"), ist auch nicht besser.

> *Ebenso verbieten sich Fragen nach der finanziellen Situation des anderen:*

> „Als Arzt verdienen Sie doch bestimmt gut – wie viel ist es denn so im Jahr?"

Geldprobleme bespricht man am besten mit dem Kundenberater der Bank – aber nicht beim Small Talk.

-ismen
Alles, was auf -ismus endet, ist kein ideales, weil konfliktträchtiges Thema: Sozialismus, Kommunismus, Kapitalismus, Katholizismus, Feminismus – alles zweifellos spannend. Zu spannend für Small Talk, denn i.d.R. kennen Sie die Moral- und Wertvorstellungen Ihres Gesprächspartners nicht oder wissen nur wenig darüber. Und das erhöht die Fettnäpfchengefahr enorm.

What do I talk about – and what do I avoid?

Dramas and Disasters
... are not appropriate for small talk, because they tend to give the conversation a bleak tone – and the conversational atmosphere can suffer as a result.

> *"Yes, the weather really is lovely, very warm – but if you look at the latest climate models, we're in for some nasty times ahead. All caused by people – CO_2 emissions and all that."*

Under certain circumstances, a statement like this could paint you as a doomsayer – and this is surely not the impression you want to make.

Marital/Family Problems
... are not small talk topics – unless they consist of witty anecdotes about small problems.

Money
... is not included (at least in Western society) in the repertoire of small talk topics, regardless of whether you have a lot of it or a little. Accordingly, boasting is just embarrassing. And moaning that everyone else is better off than oneself (*"In our profession, we're all simply overworked and underpaid."*) is no better.

Equally taboo are questions about the other person's financial situation:

> *"As a doctor, I'll bet you earn a lot of money – how much is it then roughly on an annual basis?"*

Financial problems are ideally discussed with your bank's customer service representatives – but not in small talk.

-isms
Everything that ends with "-ism" is not an ideal topic, due to the generally inherent controversial nature: socialism, communism, capitalism, Catholicism, feminism – all doubtless enthralling subjects, but a little too "hot" for small talk, because as a rule, you're not familiar (or familiar enough) with your discussion partner's moral concepts or value system. And this raises the "open-mouth/insert-foot" danger significantly.

Krankheiten
Stellen Sie sich vor, Sie sind bei einem Geschäftsessen und Ihr Tischnachbar erzählt Ihnen beim zweiten Gang von seiner kürzlich erfolgten Leistenbruch-Operation – und zwar in allen (blutigen) Einzelheiten. Das möchten Sie bestimmt nicht hören.

Auch Gratiskonsultationen bei zufällig anwesenden Ärzten, denen man ausführlich die eigene Krankengeschichte darlegt und von denen man dann womöglich Therapievorschläge erwartet, sind unbedingt zu vermeiden. (Das Gleiche gilt natürlich auch für Rechtsanwälte, Steuerberater etc.)

Lästern und Meckern
Kritisches, Spöttisches oder gar Herabsetzendes zu äußern – worüber auch immer – hinterlässt keinen guten Eindruck, selbst dann nicht, wenn Sie recht haben. Harmloser Klatsch und Tratsch gehört in einem gewissen Maß zum Small Talk, Lästern hingegen nur maximal in homöopathischen Dosen. Es kann anfangs witzig und sogar verbindend wirken, gemeinsam festzustellen, wie merkwürdig jemand aussieht – irgendwann aber kommt garantiert der Punkt, an dem Sie sich fragen, was diese Lästerzunge gegenüber Dritten wohl über Sie erzählen wird. Und genau das ist der Punkt, an dem der vorher rege sprudelnde Quell des Small Talks plötzlich versiegt.

Negatives
Die schlechte Geschäftslage in Ihrer Branche, die nervigen Kollegen, die Jugend von heute, der allgemeine Sittenverfall – all das sind keine Small-Talk-Themen. Es ist zwar möglich, dass man auf jemanden trifft, der alles ähnlich schwarz sieht und mit dem man sich prächtig darüber austauschen kann, wie schlecht die Welt ist. Den meisten Menschen gehen Berufspessimisten aber ziemlich auf die Nerven.

Politik
... ist ein äußerst spannendes Thema – aber leider unter Umständen geeignet, einen hitzigen Streit zu entfachen. Warum Sie wen gewählt haben, was Sie von der Gesundheitsreform halten, was Sie tun würden, um Deutschland wieder nach vorn zu bringen – diskutieren Sie es in Ihrem Freundeskreis, aber machen Sie es nicht zum Small-Talk-Thema.

Religion
Hier gilt das Gleiche wie für Politik – meiden Sie Themen, bei denen es um persönliche Weltanschauungen geht und bei denen Sie die Werte Ihres Gegenübers nicht ganz genau kennen.

> What do I talk about – and what do I avoid?

Illnesses
Imagine you're at a business dinner and as the second course arrives, the person sitting next to you begins to tell you about his recent hernia operation – in (bloody) detail. Surely, that's not what you want to hear.

And "free" consultations with physicians who happen to be present, in which one lays out his or her own medical history and then longingly awaits therapy recommendations, are absolutely forbidden. (The same applies as well for lawyers, tax consultants, etc.)

Derision and Complaining
Critical, derisive or disparaging statements – regardless of the subject matter – don't make a good impression, even when you're right. A little harmless gossip in moderation has its place in small talk; derision, on the other hand, only in miniscule doses. It can initially be funny and even have a somewhat bonding effect to note how odd someone looks – but at some point, you're certain to start asking yourself what these backbiters are saying to others about you. And that is precisely the point when the small talk, previously flowing freely, suddenly dries up.

Negative Topics
The bad state of business affairs in your industry, the annoying co-workers, the "youth of today", general moral decay – none of these are topics for small talk. While it's possible that one might meet someone else who has just as bleak a view of things, opening up the opportunity to enjoy talking about how rotten the world is, the fact is that most people see "professional pessimists" as a pain!

Politics
... is an extremely gripping topic – but it's also unfortunately loaded with the potential to unleash a heated argument. Why you voted for a particular candidate, your views on health care reform, what you would do to put your country back on its feet – discuss these things within your circle of friends. But avoid politics as a small talk topic.

Religion
The same applies here as to politics – avoid topics revolving around personal world views and where you're not certain of the other person's value system.

Zügeln Sie also in Small-Talk-Situationen Ihr möglicherweise vorhandenes Sendungsbewusstsein – es gibt bessere Gelegenheiten, Menschen zu überzeugen.

Sexualität
Egal, ob es um Erfahrungen, Probleme oder gar Witze geht – nichts aus dem Bereich der Sexualität passt ins Repertoire der Small-Talk-Themen.

Tiefschürfendes
Monologe oder Diskussionen über den Sinn des Lebens, philosophische Gedanken über den Tod – in vertrauter Runde mit Freunden gern, nicht beim Small Talk.

Witze
Natürlich könnten Sie beim Small Talk Ihren Lieblingswitz erzählen, nur: Sind Sie ganz sicher, dass Ihr Gesprächspartner die gleiche Humor-Frequenz hat wie Sie? Wird er die gleichen Dinge lustig finden wie Sie? Wenn auch nur der Hauch eines Zweifels besteht, dann lassen Sie es besser sein. Generell absolut verboten – nicht nur beim Small Talk – sind diskriminierende und sexistische Witze, Anzüglichkeiten und Zoten.

Zynismus, Sarkasmus, selbst Ironie
... ist meist nicht zum Lachen, sondern ungefähr so ätzend wie Salzsäure und oft so verletzend wie ein Hundebiss. Einzige Ausnahme ist die hohe Kunstform der sanften Selbstironie – und das heißt nicht Selbstherabsetzung!

> **Keine Regel ohne Ausnahme!**
>
> Es gibt einige Situationen, in denen ein paar der Tabu-Themen ausnahmsweise erlaubt sind:
> - Machen Sie einen Krankenbesuch, werden Sie kaum umhinkönnen, über Krankheiten zu sprechen.
> - Nehmen Sie an einer entsprechenden Fachveranstaltung teil, sind Politik, Geschäftsprobleme etc. möglicherweise genau die richtigen Themen für Small Talk.
>
> Wann immer Sie sich nicht ganz sicher sind, ob das Thema geeignet ist: **Halten Sie sich einfach ein bisschen zurück.** Beziehen Sie keine extremen Standpunkte, formulieren Sie zurückhaltend und fragen Sie wertneutral nach der Meinung des anderen. Gehen Sie nicht zu sehr ins Detail.

What do I talk about – and what do I avoid?

So in small talk situations, rein in any sense of mission you might have – there are other, better opportunities to persuade others of your views.

Sexuality
Regardless of whether the subject is experiences, problems or even jokes – nothing from the realm of sexuality is appropriate for the repertoire of small talk topics.

Profound Matters
Monologues or discussions about the meaning of life, philosophical views or death may make sense in intimate discussions with friends, but not in small talk.

Jokes
Of course, you can tell your favourite joke in small talk, but are you absolutely sure that your discussion partner's humour is on the same frequency as yours? Will they find the same things funny that you do? If there is even a shadow of doubt, you're better off just leaving it. And innuendo, along with sexist, discriminatory and obscene jokes, is absolutely out of bounds – and not just in small talk.

Cynicism, Sarcasm and even Irony
... are usually not funny. On the contrary, they're generally as caustic as sulphuric acid and as hurtful as a dog bite. The only exception is the high art of self-deprecating irony – and this doesn't mean self-belittlement!

> **No rule without an exception!** ✓
>
> There are some situations in which a few "taboo" topics are permissible:
> - If you're visiting someone who is ill, you'll hardly be able to get around the subject of illnesses.
> - If you are participating in a professional event, or a seminar, etc., then politics, business problems, etc. may well be just the right topics for small talk.
>
> Whenever you're not absolutely sure whether the topic is appropriate, simply hold back a little. Don't take any extreme stands, formulate what you say in a reserved manner and ask about the opinion of the other person in a way that is "value-neutral". Don't go into extensive detail.

8 Small Talk als Karrierefaktor

Manche Stimmen behaupten, Small Talker wüssten nicht, worum es im Leben geht, und verschwendeten kostbare Arbeitszeit mit dem Reden übers Wetter und andere „Nicht-Themen". Ist das wirklich so?

Kommt ganz darauf an, was Ihre Ziele sind: Wollen Sie Kontakte knüpfen, neue Menschen kennen lernen und sich selbst „ins Gespräch bringen", auch (aber nicht nur), um Karriere zu machen? Dann führt kein Weg am Small Talk vorbei.

Small Talk im Job dient der Beziehungspflege. Diese Vernetzung sichert nach Ansicht von Experten den Arbeitsplatz und fördert das berufliche Weiterkommen:

> *Small Talk ist also weit mehr als nette Plauderei. Er ist tatsächlich ein Karrierefaktor.*

Mit Small Talk können Sie in einem kurzen, scheinbar belanglosen Gespräch am Kopierer, in der Kantine oder im Fahrstuhl etwas dafür tun, dass man sich positiv an Sie erinnert.

Und Gelegenheiten zum Small Talk gibt es in Ihrem Arbeitsalltag reichlich. Manchmal können Sie entscheiden, ob Sie Small Talk machen möchten oder nicht: Wenn Sie z.B. mit Kollegen im Aufzug stehen und nur zwei Stockwerke mitfahren, müssen Sie nicht unbedingt ein Gespräch beginnen oder sich an einem beteiligen. Allerdings: Den Blickkontakt – eine elementare Höflichkeitsgeste – zu verweigern, stattdessen zu Boden zu schauen, muffig ein paar Silben durch zusammengebissene Zähne zu pressen, wirkt abweisend und unfreundlich. Wer dem Small Talk am frühen Morgen nicht gewachsen ist, der kann im Aufzug auch mal den Mund halten (oder die Treppe nehmen ...). Ein freundlicher Gruß und ein Lächeln sollten es aber in jedem Fall sein.

Es gibt allerdings zahlreiche Situationen, in denen Sie Small Talk machen sollten oder sogar müssen, weil es von Ihnen erwartet wird – z.B. auf einer Betriebsfeier oder bei einem Geschäftsessen, aber auch beim täglichen Gang in die Kantine.

Für die meisten Situationen – ob beruflich oder privat – gilt das, was generell für Small Talk gilt: Einstieg, Themenwahl, Anwendung der verschiedenen Gesprächstechniken.

In speziellen beruflichen Situationen sind allerdings noch ein paar zusätzliche Dinge zu beachten.

8 Small Talk as a Career Factor

Some say that "small talkers" have no idea what's important in life and that they waste valuable working time talking about the weather and other "non-subjects". Is this really true?

It depends entirely on what your goals are. Do you want to make contacts, meet new people and get yourself "into the discussion" in order to advance (not just) your career? Then there's no avoiding small talk.

Small talk on the job helps you maintain and look after relationships. According to experts, such networking secures jobs and promotes professional advancement:

> *Small talk is therefore much, much more than just "pleasant chat". It is a genuine career factor.*

Small talk can contribute to making people remember you positively in a brief, apparently trivial chat at the copier, in the cafeteria or in the lift.

And there is a wealth of opportunities to make small talk during the average workday. Sometimes you can decide if you want to engage in small talk or not: for example, if you're standing in the lift with colleagues and only going up two floors, then you don't necessarily have to start or get involved in a conversation. But avoiding the elementary gesture of courtesy, namely eye contact, and staring instead at the floor, pressing a couple of syllables through clenched teeth comes off as cold and unfriendly. Those who aren't up to small talk early in the morning can remain silent in the lift (or take the stairs ...), but a friendly greeting and a smile cost nothing and should be manageable in any case.

There are, however, numerous situations where you should or even have to make small talk, simply because it's expected of you – for example, at a company party or business dinner, but also in your daily trip to the cafeteria.

For most situations – professional or private – the same rules apply that generally apply for small talk: opener, choice of topic and application of the various conversation techniques.

In special professional situations, however, there are a couple of other things to observe.

8.1 Small Talk mit Vorgesetzten

„Im Zusammensein mit einem Mann von Rang und Würden gibt es drei Verstöße: Reden, ehe er dich angesprochen hat – das ist vorlaut; nicht reden, wenn er dich angesprochen hat – das ist verschlagen; reden, ohne dabei seine Miene zu beobachten – das ist blind."
Konfuzius (551–479 v. Chr.), chin. Philosoph

Das, was Konfuzius sagt, gilt mit Einschränkungen auch heute noch: Blickkontakt halten – ja, unbedingt. Antworten, wenn der Vorgesetzte Sie anspricht – auch das. Aber:

> *Sie müssen heutzutage nicht mehr warten, bis der Chef Sie anspricht. Sie dürfen die Initiative ergreifen, ohne dass man Sie für vorlaut hält.*

Die Frage ist: Traut man sich das? Abhängig vom Führungsstil Ihres Vorgesetzten ist die Hemmschwelle, den Small Talk zu eröffnen, niedrig bis sehr, sehr hoch. Wenn Sie Vorgesetzte haben, die Sie respektieren, vielleicht sogar mögen, ist es recht einfach. Mit sehr autoritären Chefs hingegen spricht man am liebsten so wenig wie möglich. Bei bestimmten Gelegenheiten (Betriebsfest, Geschäftsessen) können Sie dem aber nicht aus dem Weg gehen. Und dann ist es hilfreich, wenn man vorbereitet ist.

Warum muss ich überhaupt Small Talk mit Vorgesetzten machen? – Wenn Sie wollen, dass Ihr Chef Sie kennt und sich positiv an Sie erinnert, dann sollten Sie die Chance nutzen.

Natürlich ist ein solcher Small Talk nie die lockere, unbefangene Plauderei, die er unter Gleichrangigen wäre. Und auch wenn die Vorgesetzten noch so nett und freundlich sind: Das Abhängigkeitsverhältnis lässt sich nicht leugnen. Für Sie bedeutet das, dass Sie Ihre Small-Talk-Themen besonders sorgfältig auswählen sollten. Sie wissen ja, dass sich heikle Themen nicht für Small Talk eignen. Dementsprechend sind Gespräche über anstehende Personalentlassungen, sinkende Aktienkurse etc. schon mal tabu.

Treffen Sie Chef oder Chefin im alltäglichen Arbeitsumfeld, …

… können Sie z.B. über ein Projekt sprechen, an dem Ihr Chef beteiligt war oder das er initiiert hat. Das kann eine abgeschlossene Renovierung oder Umgestaltung von Büroräumen ebenso sein wie eine geplante Schulung. Über ehrliche und echte Anerkennung freut sich jeder – auch ein Vorgesetzter.

8.1 Small Talk with Superiors

"In the company of a man of rank and dignity, there are three offences: speaking before he has spoken to you – this is impertinent; not speaking when he has spoken to you – this is devious; and speaking without observing his face – this is blind."
  Confucius (551–479 B.C.), Chinese philosopher

What Confucius said still applies in large part today: maintaining eye contact – yes, absolutely. Answering when addressed by the supervisor – this, too.

> *But these days, you don't have to wait until your boss has spoken to you first. You can take the initiative without making the impression that you are impertinent.*

The question is, are you confident enough to do that? Depending upon your boss's management style, the inhibition to opening a small talk conversation varies from low to very, very high. When you have superiors that you respect, perhaps even like, then it's quite easy. With very authoritarian bosses on the other hand, the tendency to speak with them is as little as possible. However, in certain situations (company parties, business dinners), there's no getting around it. And then it's helpful to be prepared.

Why do I have to engage in small talk with my superiors at all? – If you want your boss to know you and remember you in a positive light, then you should take advantage of the opportunity.

Naturally, a small talk situation of this type is never the casual, relaxed chat that it would be with those of equal rank. And even if your superiors are cordial and friendly, there's no denying the dependent nature of the relationship. For you, this means that you must select your small talk topics with special care. You are, of course, aware that controversial topics are inappropriate for small talk. Accordingly, discussions about upcoming redundancies, falling stock values, etc. are taboo.

If you meet your boss in your daily work environment, ...

… you could talk about a project that your boss was involved in or has initiated. This can be anything from a completed renovation of the office space to a planned training programme. Everyone likes to hear an honest, genuine compliment – even a superior.

Beschreiben Sie dabei konkret, was Sie gut finden und warum. Das unterscheidet ein Lob von Schmeichelei. **Schmeicheln** ist i.d.R. wenig konkret, nicht unbedingt ehrlich gemeint und meist auch noch übertrieben – etwa so:

> *„Ich finde ja, dass Sie immer und absolut zum Wohle der Belegschaft handeln, das finde ich einfach super!"*

Ehrliche Anerkennung hört sich hingegen z.B. so an:

> *„Ich habe gehört, dass Sie eine Seminarreihe zum Thema ‚Besprechungen effizient moderieren' planen. Das finde ich gut, wir verbringen wirklich viel Zeit in Sitzungen, und es wäre schön, da ein paar Tipps an die Hand zu bekommen."*

Sie können auch sich selbst oder Ihre Abteilung loben, aber bitte möglichst unaufdringlich. Beschreiben Sie die positive Leistung (*„Wir haben unser Projekt Alpha übrigens vorgestern plangemäß abgeschlossen."*), aber bewerten Sie sie nicht selbst (also nicht: *„Wir haben das echt toll gemacht, wir sind exakt im Zeitplan geblieben."*).

Treffen Sie Chef oder Chefin im nichtalltäglich beruflichen Umfeld, ...

... z.B. auf Betriebsfeiern, Geschäftsessen, sollten Sie nur dann über berufliche Themen sprechen, wenn Ihr Vorgesetzter diese anschneidet. Reden Sie eher über allgemeine Themen wie das Essen, den Wein, die Musik und was das Umfeld und die Gelegenheit so hergeben, und zwar positiv.

Treffen Sie Chef oder Chefin im privaten Umfeld, weil Sie sich in der Freizeit über den Weg laufen, ...

... sprechen Sie nicht über Berufliches. Hier funktionieren die üblichen Small-Talk-Themen wie Wetter & Co. Kennen Sie Interessen Ihres Vorgesetzten? Dann können Sie diese, falls sie nicht zu privat sind, ansprechen.

8.2 Small Talk mit Kolleginnen und Kollegen

Hier ist Small Talk einfach, weil Sie unter Ihresgleichen sind; oft kennt man sich schon lange und weiß, welche Themen man anschneiden kann. Alle Regeln, die auch sonst für Small Talk gelten, sind uneingeschränkt anzuwenden.

In doing so, be specific about what you appreciate and why. This distinguishes praise from flattery. **Flattery** is generally less specific, not necessarily genuine and also usually exaggerated – something like this:

> *"I think you always act on behalf of the good of the entire staff, and that's really great!"*

In contrast, a genuine compliment sounds more like this, for example:

> *"I heard that you're planning a seminar series on 'Efficiently Moderating Discussions'. I like that; we spend a lot of time in meetings, and it would be a good thing to get a couple of tips."*

You can also praise yourself or your department, but make sure in doing so that you avoid seeming pushy as much as possible. Describe the positive performance (*"Incidentally, we completed our Alpha Project the day before yesterday as planned."*), but don't assess yourself (meaning not, *"We really did a great job, and we finished right on schedule."*).

If you meet your boss in professional situations that are not part of the normal day-to-day, ...

... for example, at company parties or business meals, then you should only talk about job-related topics if your superior has already opened the subject. Talk instead about more general topics such as the meal, the wine, the music and things associated with the surroundings and the occasion, and do so in a positive manner.

If you meet your boss in private circumstances, for instance, running into each other during your free time, ...

... then don't talk about job-related matters. Such situations are best served by the accustomed small talk topics, like the weather and so on. Do you know what your superior's interests are? Then you can mention these if they're not too private.

8.2 Small Talk with Colleagues

Small talk is easy here because you're with "birds of a feather"; often, you've known each other for a good while and you know what topics are appropriate. All of the rules that otherwise apply for small talk also apply without restriction here.

Small Talk mit neuen Kolleginnen und Kollegen

Machen Sie es der oder dem Neuen leicht: Beziehen Sie ihn oder sie ins Gespräch ein, wenn Sie sich mit anderen Kollegen unterhalten, stellen Sie Eisbrecherfragen. Da die Neuen den Kommunikationsstil Ihres Unternehmens noch nicht kennen, sollten Sie vorsichtig mit Insiderwitzen und ironischen Bemerkungen sein. Stellen Sie keine allzu persönlichen Fragen und meiden Sie Themen, die zu heftigen Diskussionen führen könnten. Kenne und schätze ich jemanden erst mal, vertrage ich es auch, dass sie oder er anderer Meinung ist. Gleich zu Beginn eines neuen Kontaktes erschweren oder verhindern solche Meinungsverschiedenheiten das weitere Kennenlernen.

Was tun, wenn ich selbst neu im Unternehmen bin?

Gerade, wenn Sie neu in einem Unternehmen sind, müssen Sie Kontakte knüpfen – und das funktioniert natürlich nicht, indem man sich in seinem Bürosessel zurücklehnt und darauf wartet, dass die anderen kommen. Umgekehrt ist es aber auch nicht ratsam, gleich loszugaloppieren und jeden anzusprechen.

> *Halten Sie sich in den ersten Wochen etwas zurück und versuchen Sie, durch Beobachten ein Gefühl für die Unternehmenskultur zu entwickeln.*

Gibt es ungeschriebene Kommunikationsregeln, bestimmte Rituale auch beim Small Talk? Spricht man sich mit Nach- oder Vornamen an? Duzen sich vielleicht alle? Ist der Kommunikationsstil sehr förmlich oder eher locker?

8.3 Small Talk mit Kundinnen und Kunden

Kunden lassen sich in ihrem Kommunikationsverhalten in verschiedene Typen einteilen: Wie erkenne ich, welcher Typ mein Gegenüber ist, und wie gestalte ich dementsprechend den Small Talk?

Der extrovertierte Kunde

… hat meist ein selbstbewusstes und emotionales Auftreten, ist freundlich, humorvoll, gesellig, lebhaft, manchmal etwas unbeherrscht. Direkte Kommunikation (Gespräche, Besprechungen, Geschäftsessen) werden der indirekten Kommunikation (Briefe, E-Mails) vorgezogen. Die Körpersprache zeigt schnelle und ausdrucksstarke Gestik, lebhafte Mimik; er spricht eher schnell und betont.

Small Talk with New Colleagues

Make it easy for the new employee: include them in a conversation you're holding with other colleagues and pose questions that break the ice. Since the new person is not yet familiar with the communication style in your company, be careful with "insider jokes" and ironic comments. Don't ask any questions that are overly personal and avoid subjects that could lead to heavy discussions. If I already know and appreciate someone, then I can deal with him or her having an opinion that's different from mine about something. But such differences of opinion right at the beginning of a new contact can make getting better acquainted with one another more difficult, or even block it altogether.

What do I do if I'm the new person in the company?

Especially when you're the new person in a company, you've got to make contacts – and of course, this won't work by sitting back in your office chair and waiting for others to come to you. On the other hand, it's also not recommended to take off and start talking to everybody.

> *Hold off a little during the first few weeks and try to observe and get a feel for the company culture.*

Are there unwritten rules of communication or certain rituals, even in small talk? Do people address each other by the first or last name? Is the style of communication more formal or casual?

8.3 Small Talk with Customers

Customers can be divided into a variety of types in their communication conduct. How do I recognise which type my conversation partner is and how do I arrange the small talk accordingly?

The extroverted customer

... usually makes an emotional and self-confident impression; they're friendly, humorous, gregarious, lively and sometimes a little uncontrolled. Direct communication (discussions, meetings, business meals) is preferred over indirect communication (letters, e-mails). Their body language consists of rapid, expressive gestures, lively facial expressions, and they tend to speak quickly and with pronounced speech emphasis.

Was Sie tun sollten: Nehmen Sie sich Zeit für diese Kunden: Zeit für Small Talk und Zeit für das Geschäftsgespräch. Geben Sie Ihrem Gegenüber Raum, sich auszudrücken, überlassen Sie ihm den größeren Gesprächsanteil und hören Sie zu. Halten Sie dabei direkten Blickkontakt und spiegeln Sie die Emotionen des anderen. Wenn Sie selbst etwas erzählen, konzentrieren Sie sich eher auf das Allgemeine als auf Details – wenn der Extrovertierte mehr wissen will, wird er sich schon melden.

Der sachlich-nüchterne Kunde

... ist recht reserviert und kann Gefühle nur schlecht ausdrücken. Seine Sprache ist i.d.R. sehr präzise, die Körpersprache dagegen wenig aussagekräftig. Dieser Kundentyp ist eher auf Fakten als auf Gefühle konzentriert – und schätzt Small Talk nur begrenzt.

Was Sie tun sollten: Bleiben Sie eher formell, was Sprache und Umgang angeht. Small Talk ja, aber nicht zu ausführlich und nur über allgemeine, keine persönlichen Themen. Sprechen Sie nicht zu schnell oder zu laut, bleiben Sie höflich und sachlich – bitte kein Enthusiasmus.

Der (an-)treibende Kunde

... hat es immer eilig. Er tritt selbstbewusst auf, denkt und handelt ergebnisorientiert. Typisch für die Körpersprache sind schnelle, zielgerichtete Bewegungen, eine recht laute Stimme, hohes Sprechtempo und direkter Blickkontakt. Effizienz ist das Wichtigste – und allzu ausführlicher Small Talk ist für diesen Kundentyp uneffizient.

Was Sie tun sollten: Erscheinen Sie pünktlich und gut vorbereitet zum Geschäftstermin und kommen Sie ohne große Umschweife zur Sache. Beschränken Sie den Small Talk zu Gesprächsbeginn auf das aus Höflichkeit Notwendige: Begrüßung, Frage nach dem Befinden oder der Anreise, Abwarten der Antwort – und das war's auch schon. Zum Gesprächsende das gleiche: Ein bis zwei nette Sätze zum Abschluss, Verabschiedung – Ende. Halten Sie währenddessen direkten Blickkontakt, sprechen Sie eher schnell (ungefähr so schnell wie Ihr Gegenüber), drücken Sie sich präzise und knapp aus.

Der zurückhaltende Kunde

... ist freundlich, meist geduldig, entspannt und eher ruhig. Körpersprachlich sind eine freundliche Mimik, lockerer Blickkontakt und ein ruhiger, sanfter Tonfall typisch.

Was Sie tun sollten: Small Talk ist wichtig, um die Gesprächsatmosphäre angenehm und entspannt zu gestalten. Halten Sie

What you should do: take time for these customers; time both for small talk and for business talk. Give your conversation partner room to express themselves, leave them the largest speaking part of the conversation and simply listen. Keep direct eye contact in the process and reflect their emotions. When you explain something yourself, concentrate more on generalities than on details – if the extrovert wants to know more, they'll let you know!

The businesslike-down-to-earth customer

... is quite reserved and not very adept at expressing feelings. Their speech is generally very precise, while their body language is less expressive in contrast. This type of customer is likely to be more focused on facts than on emotions and to have a limited appreciation of small talk.

What you should do: as a rule, be more formal in regard to language and your behaviour. Small talk yes, but not so extensive and only about general topics, not any personal matters. Don't speak too fast or too loud and stay courteous and factual – no enthusiasm, please!

The impelling customer

... is always in a hurry. They are self-confident and act in a results-oriented fashion. Typical body language characteristics are quick, targeted movements, a rather loud voice, rapid speech tempo and direct eye contact. Efficiency is the most important thing – and small talk which is too comprehensive is a waste of time for this type of customer.

What you should do: be punctual and well-prepared for business meetings, and get to the point without any extensive detours. Limit your small talk to the beginning of the discussion and to what courtesy dictates: greetings, asking how they are or how the journey was – and that's it already. The same goes for the end of the discussion: one or two courteous concluding phrases, farewell – the end. Maintain direct eye contact while doing so, don't speak too slowly (approximately as quickly as your conversation partner) and express yourself briefly and precisely.

The reserved customer

... is friendly, usually patient, relaxed and tends to be rather quiet. Body language is typically characterised by a friendly facial expression, relaxed eye contact and a calm, soft tone of voice.

What you should do: small talk is important for creating a pleasant, relaxed discussion atmosphere. Maintain relaxed eye contact,

lockeren Blickkontakt, sprechen Sie ruhig und in sanftem Tonfall. Achten Sie auf einen ausgewogenen Gesprächsanteil, stellen Sie interessierte Fragen. Vermeiden Sie alles, was Ihr Gegenüber unter Druck setzen könnte.

8.4 Small Talk bei Geschäftsessen

„Ein Arbeitsessen bietet den Vorteil, dass man unangenehme Fragen mit lang anhaltendem Kauen beantworten kann."
Arno Sölter (1911–1987), dt. Volkswirtschaftler

Der Name Geschäftsessen ist etwas irreführend: Es ist ja keineswegs so, als spräche man während des Essens die ganze Zeit über Geschäfte.

> *Ziel eines solchen Essens ist die Kontaktanbahnung oder -pflege.*

Über das eigentlich geplante Geschäft wird oft erst beim Dessert oder sogar noch später bei einer weiteren Besprechung entschieden. Und das heißt: Viel Zeit und Raum für Small Talk – es sei denn, der Kunde selbst drängt.

Im Idealfall konnten Sie sich auf dieses Essen vorbereiten und wissen schon etwas über Ihren Gesprächspartner: Woher kommt er, hatte er eine längere Anreise, ist er zum ersten Mal hier, wie gefällt ihm das Hotel, die Stadt – das sind schon mal einige Themen zur Gesprächseröffnung. Vielleicht kennen Sie auch ein paar Fakten aus dem Leben Ihres Gesprächspartners: Ausbildung, Auslandsaufenthalte, kürzlich erfolgte Beförderungen. Oder Sie haben im Vorfeld schon etwas über private Interessen, Hobbys etc. erfahren ... All das sind geeignete Small-Talk-Themen.

Zeigen Sie Interesse, stellen Sie interessierte Fragen, hören Sie zu. Achten Sie dabei darauf, dass der Kunde sich immer wohl fühlt.

8.5 Small Talk bei Feiern und Events

Betriebsfeiern und -ausflüge, Jubiläen, Messen, Kongresse – all das sind keine alltäglichen Small-Talk-Situationen. Und genau das macht sie so spannend: Schließlich ist das mal etwas anderes als die Gespräche am Fotokopierer und in der Kantine.

Für Feiern aller Art gelten die üblichen Small-Talk- und Benimm-Regeln – und an die erinnert man sich leichter und wendet sie gekonnter an, wenn der Alkoholspiegel niedrig ist. Gehen Sie also einigermaßen nüchtern an die Sache heran. Rechnen Sie aber damit, dass andere dies nicht immer tun. Small Talk mit angeheiterten Kol-

speaking calmly and with a soft intonation. Make sure you share the conversation time equally between the two of you, and pose interesting questions. Avoid anything that could put your conversation partner under pressure.

8.4 Small Talk at Business Meals

"A business meal offers the advantage that one can answer unpleasant questions with sustained chewing."
Arno Sölter (1911–1987), German economist

The name "business meal" is somewhat misleading, since it's definitely not the case that the only topic of discussion throughout the entire meal is business.

> *The aim of such a meal is the initiation or maintenance of the contact.*

Often, the decision about the specific envisioned business venture is actually made at dessert, or even later in a continued discussion. And this means lots of time and space for small talk – unless the customer is in a hurry.

In the ideal case, you can prepare for this meal and you already know a little something about your discussion partner: where are they from, did they have a long trip, are they here for the first time, how do they like the hotel, the city, etc. – these are already a few opening topics for the conversation. Maybe you also know a few facts about the life of your discussion partner: education, foreign assignments, recent promotions. Or perhaps you've learnt something in advance about their private interests, hobbies, etc. These are all suitable small talk topics.

Show interest, ask interested questions and listen. Make sure in the process that the customer always feels comfortable.

8.5 Small Talk at Parties and Events

Company parties and excursions, anniversaries, conventions, conferences, etc. – these are not daily small talk situations. And this is precisely what makes them so exciting. After all, these are situations that are different from the odd chat at the copier and in the cafeteria.

For parties of all kinds, the accustomed rules of small talk and behaviour apply – and these are more easily and readily remembered at low levels of alcohol consumption. So approach the situation somewhat "soberly". But don't necessarily count on others do-

legen, Kunden oder gar Vorgesetzten erfordert viel Geduld und Feingefühl.

Bei Messen, Kongressen und ähnlichen Fachveranstaltungen gilt ebenfalls alles, was bisher zum Thema Small Talk gesagt wurde. Bereiten Sie sich ruhig ein bisschen vor: Wer wird teilnehmen, wo können Sie etwas darüber erfahren? Wer von diesen Menschen könnte für Sie ein interessanter Kontakt sein? Wo und wann bekommen Sie ihn oder sie zu fassen? Welche Themen könnten ihn oder sie interessieren, womit können Sie ihn/sie locken?

8.6 Small Talk in Vorstellungsgesprächen

Wie die meisten Gespräche beginnt auch das Vorstellungsgespräch mit Small Talk. Da wird man aus dem Foyer abgeholt oder in einen Besprechungsraum gebeten, und kaum hat man sich vorgestellt und die Hände geschüttelt, kommt eine Frage wie: *„Haben Sie gut hergefunden?"* Die Antwort *„Kein Problem"* wäre jetzt entschieden zu kurz. Noch schlimmer wäre es allerdings, eine Klage über die mangelhafte Beschilderung, den katastrophalen Berufsverkehr o.Ä. anzustimmen.

Natürlich soll Small Talk zu Beginn des Vorstellungsgespräches vor allem die Atmosphäre lockern, den Bewerbern die Nervosität nehmen. Man erwartet aber schon hier – bei aller Nervosität – von dem Bewerber, dass er in der Lage ist, den Ball aufzunehmen und zumindest in einem ganzen, freundlichen Satz zu antworten:

> *„Ja, vielen Dank. Ich kenne Hamburg ganz gut, ich war schon öfter hier."*

Daraus kann sich dann ein kurzes Gespräch entwickeln.

Wichtig: Der Small Talk zu Beginn des Bewerbungsgespräches bleibt ein zeitlich begrenzter Einstieg – sobald der Bewerber Platz genommen hat, vielleicht noch ein Getränk angeboten wurde, beginnt i.d.R. das eigentliche Gespräch. Erzählen Sie also nicht zu viel und stellen Sie nicht zu viele Fragen.

Was immer Sie auf Standarderöffnungen wie die oben erwähnte Frage nach der Anreise sagen:

Achten Sie darauf, dass Sie es positiv formulieren.

Auch wenn die Anfahrt noch so verzwickt und die Skizze der Sekretärin völlig unübersichtlich war: Sie haben alles problemlos gefunden, und die Sekretärin hatte Ihnen ja netterweise auch eine Anfahrtsbeschreibung gemailt.

ing the same; small talk with tipsy co-workers, clients or even superiors requires a great deal of patience and sensitivity.

At conventions, conferences and similar job-related events, everything equally applies that has previously been said on the subject of small talk. Go ahead and prepare a little: who's participating, where can I find out more about that? Which of these people could be an interesting contact for you? Where and when will you encounter them? What subjects could be of interest to them; how can you "hook" them?

8.6 Small Talk in Job Interviews

Just as with most conversations, the job interview also begins with small talk. You are picked up from the reception area or asked into a conference room, and hot on the heels of the introduction and handshake comes a question like, *"Did you find us easily?"*. Answering with *"No problem"* would definitely be too short here. But it would be even worse to complain about the lack of road signs, the catastrophic rush hour traffic or similar things.

Naturally, small talk at the beginning of a job interview is intended to loosen up the atmosphere a little and quieten the nerves of the applicant. But even with all the attendant nerves, it is still expected of the applicant that they are capable of picking up the ball and at least answering in a complete, friendly sentence:

> *"Yes, thank you. I've been to the city several times, so I know my way around reasonably well."*

This can develop into a brief chat.

Important: small talk at the start of a job interview is a brief opener – as soon as the applicant has taken a seat and perhaps been offered something to drink, the actual interview usually begins. So don't talk too much and avoid asking too many questions.

Whatever you say in response to standard openers, such as the above question about your journey:

Make sure you formulate your answer positively.

Even if the drive was like a maze and the secretary's directions were completely unintelligible: you found everything without any problems and the secretary was even nice enough to mail you directions, OK?

9 Small Talk im Ausland

Die spinnen, die Römer? Andere Länder, andere Sitten!

9.1 Small Talk mit ausländischen Kunden

Wir leben im Zeitalter der viel beschworenen Globalisierung. Da mag sich manch einer fragen, ob es sich überhaupt noch lohnt, über kulturelle Unterschiede in der Kommunikation im Allgemeinen und im Small Talk im Besonderen nachzudenken, wo doch immer wieder die Rede davon ist, dass diese Unterschiede verschwinden und wir uns immer stärker aneinander angleichen.

Tatsächlich ist es so, dass nicht nur trotz, sondern vielleicht sogar wegen der fortschreitenden Globalisierung kulturelle Unterschiede auch weiterhin wahrgenommen und gepflegt werden. Und das heißt:

> *Wenn wir – egal ob im Ausland oder in Deutschland – mit Geschäftspartnern und Kunden aus anderen Ländern erfolgreich kommunizieren wollen, brauchen wir interkulturelle Kompetenz.*

Wer beruflich mit Menschen aus anderen Ländern und Kulturen zu tun hat, braucht zunächst einmal eine gewisse „Cultural Awareness", also das Wissen um Geschichte, Kultur, religiöse und moralische Wertvorstellungen eines Landes, bestimmte Denk- und Verhaltensmuster und (Kommunikations-)Rituale. Cultural Awareness hilft dabei, sensibel für das eigene Verhalten zu werden und es so an die jeweiligen Gegebenheiten anzupassen, dass konfliktreiche Situationen vermieden werden können.

In einem Umfeld, das nicht das eigene ist und dessen kulturspezifische Regeln man nicht kennt, fühlt man sich verloren. Und dann ist man mit seinem gewohnten Verhalten schnell in ein Fettnäpfchen gestolpert. Der Geschäftspartner zeigt dann im besten Fall Irritation, im schlimmsten Fall ist der geschäftliche Kontakt so belastet, dass er abgebrochen wird.

Natürlich reicht es nicht allein aus, bestimmte Spielregeln zum Thema Etikette oder Kommunikation zu kennen und beim eigenen Verhalten zu berücksichtigen – aber es hilft schon mal sehr.

Eine wirklich gelungene interkulturelle Kommunikation braucht als Grundlage neben der Kenntnis unterschiedlicher Verhaltensregeln auch Offenheit, Toleranz und Anpassungsbereitschaft. Das bedeutet jedoch nicht, die eigene kulturelle Prägung, die eigenen Werte und die eigene Identität völlig aus den Augen zu verlieren.

9 Small Talk Abroad

**Are the Romans really nuts?
Other countries, other customs!**

9.1 Small Talk with Foreign Customers

We live in the age of the much-proclaimed globalisation. So some might ask if it really makes sense to consider cultural differences in communication generally, and particularly in small talk, when we're constantly hearing how these differences are disappearing and we're becoming ever more similar.

In actual fact, the situation is such that not only despite, but perhaps even because of increasing globalisation, cultural differences continue to be acknowledged and cultivated.

> *And this means that regardless of whether we're abroad or at home, if we want to successfully communicate with business partners and customers from other countries, we need intercultural competence.*

Anyone who has professional dealings with people from other countries and cultures initially needs a certain amount of "cultural awareness", or in other words, knowledge about the history, culture, religious and moral value systems of the particular country and its specific patterns of thinking and behaviour, as well as its communication rituals. Cultural awareness helps to become sensitive to one's own behaviour and adapt it to the respective circumstances in order to be able to avoid situations where conflict could arise.

In an environment that's unaccustomed and where you don't know the applicable cultural-related rules, you'll feel lost. And then it's easy to stumble into a situation where you can quickly find your foot in your mouth! In the best case, your business partner is likely to show mild irritation, while in the worst case, the business contact can subsequently suffer so much that it is broken off.

Of course, it's not enough by itself to simply know certain rules of etiquette or communication and to observe these in one's own behaviour – but it certainly helps a lot.

Genuinely successful intercultural communication needs a basis consisting not only of the knowledge of differing rules of conduct, but also of openness, tolerance and a willingness to adapt. But this doesn't mean losing sight completely of one's own cultural imprint, one's own values and own identity. A thorough copy or imitation of certain patterns of behaviour (assimilation) is not necessary: you

Eine vollständige Kopie oder Nachahmung bestimmter Verhaltensmuster (Assimilation) ist nicht notwendig: Sie müssen nicht spanischer als der Spanier sein. Solche Versuche wirken meist wenig überzeugend, vielleicht sogar anbiedernd und peinlich.

Den goldenen Mittelweg zwischen der Ablehnung fremder Kulturen und ihrer Spielregeln und der Assimilation beschreiben Sie mit dem **integrativen Anpassungsstil**. Das beinhaltet eine bewusste Erweiterung unseres Horizonts, unserer Werte und Einstellungen – und wenn es uns höflich, nützlich, sinnvoll erscheint, können wir unser Auftreten entsprechend anpassen.

Übrigens: Eine übermäßige Kritik am eigenen Herkunftsland (*„Wir Deutschen sind ja leider so ..."*) wird von anderen Nationalitäten eher mit Befremden aufgenommen.

Wie sehen nun solche kulturspezifischen Spielregeln oder Verhaltensmuster aus – speziell für den Bereich, um den es in diesem Buch geht, nämlich für den Small Talk im Berufs- und Geschäftsleben?

Testen Sie zunächst einmal, wie viel Sie über diese Kommunikationsspielregeln bereits wissen:

1. *Ein kräftiger Händedruck gilt auch in asiatischen Ländern als sympathisch.*
   Stimmt ❏   *Stimmt nicht* ❏

2. *Jemanden zu unterbrechen und ins Wort zu fallen, gilt in europäischen Ländern als unhöflich.*
   Stimmt ❏   *Stimmt nicht* ❏

3. *In Polen werden Frauen gern mit Handkuss begrüßt.*
   Stimmt ❏   *Stimmt nicht* ❏

4. *Außer in asiatischen Ländern gilt überall: Häufiger Blickkontakt während des Gesprächs ist interessiert und höflich.*
   Stimmt ❏   *Stimmt nicht* ❏

5. *Ein beliebtes Small-Talk-Thema in Großbritannien ist das Wetter.*
   Stimmt ❏   *Stimmt nicht* ❏

6. *Titel und Hierarchie sind in den Niederlanden nicht so wichtig.*
   Stimmt ❏   *Stimmt nicht* ❏

7. *In Europa wird direkt und offen kommuniziert – Ablehnung wird nicht blumig umschrieben, sondern klar geäußert.*
   Stimmt ❏   *Stimmt nicht* ❏

don't have to be "more Spanish than the Spanish". On the contrary; most such attempts scarcely come off as convincing and might even be seen as sycophantic and embarrassing.

The middle ground between rejection of foreign cultures and their rules of behaviour and total assimilation is taken with the **integrative adaptation style**. This consists of a conscious expansion of our horizons, values and attitudes – and when it appears to us to be polite, beneficial and sensible, we can adapt our conduct accordingly.

By the way, excessive criticism of one's own country or origin (*"Unfortunately, we're just so ..."*) is generally greeted with uneasy surprise by other nationalities.

What are such culture-related rules or patterns of behaviour like – particularly in regard to the subject that's the focus of this book, namely small talk in one's professional and business life?

First test yourself on just how much you already know about these rules of communication:

1. *A firm handshake is also viewed as congenial in Asian countries.*
   True ❑   *False* ❑

2. *Interrupting and cutting others off while they're speaking is seen as impolite in European countries.*
   True ❑   *False* ❑

3. *In Poland, women like to be greeted with a kiss on the hand.*
   True ❑   *False* ❑

4. *With the exception of Asian countries, we can say that everywhere else frequent eye contact during a discussion shows interest and is polite.*
   True ❑   *False* ❑

5. *The weather is a popular small talk topic in Great Britain.*
   True ❑   *False* ❑

6. *Title and hierarchy are not so important in The Netherlands.*
   True ❑   *False* ❑

7. *In Europe, communication is direct and open – reluctance or rejection is not sugar-coated, but is instead expressed clearly.*
   True ❑   *False* ❑

Lösungen:
1. *Stimmt nicht – Händedruck ja, aber nur leicht.*
2. *Stimmt nicht – in südeuropäischen Ländern werden Gespräche und Diskussionen lebhaft geführt, Unterbrechungen sind häufig und völlig akzeptiert. Stumm dabeizusitzen, gilt eher als unhöflich: Man vermutet hinter einem solchen Verhalten nämlich Desinteresse.*
3. *Stimmt – vor allem die ältere Generation praktiziert dies.*
4. *Stimmt nicht – in den arabischen und vielen afrikanischen Ländern gilt beispielsweise Blickkontakt zwischen den Geschlechtern als unhöflich; in Ländern Süd- und Mitteleuropas wird generell weniger Blickkontakt als im übrigen Europa praktiziert.*
5. *Stimmt! Aus gegebenem Anlass ...*
6. *Trotz Monarchie – stimmt.*
7. *Stimmt nicht – so wird z.B. in Frankreich und in Großbritannien eher indirekt kommuniziert, wenn es um Ablehnung geht.*

Alles gewusst? Super! Und wenn nicht, gibt es im Folgenden vielleicht noch ein paar Überraschungen für Sie.

9.2 Landestypische Unterschiede

Nicht nur in Deutschland gelten für den Small Talk bestimmte Regeln, auch in anderen Ländern ist das so. Was die Sache allerdings erschwert (oder spannend macht, je nach Sichtweise), ist, dass so ziemlich jedes Land seine eigenen Regeln hat.

Wer die Regeln nicht kennt, liegt, was sein Verhalten angeht, trotz aller Bemühungen unter Umständen völlig daneben. Und das wiederum kann, wenn es um Geschäfte geht, sehr teuer werden.

Auf was ist also beim Small Talk mit ausländischen Geschäftspartnern und Kunden zu achten?

> *Im Wesentlichen sollten Sie wissen, über was Sie sprechen dürfen (und über was nicht) und – besonders wichtig – auf was Sie bei Ihrer Körpersprache achten sollten.*

Auf den nächsten Seiten finden Sie grundsätzliche Informationen zum Kommunikationsverhalten in verschiedenen Regionen und Ländern der Erde.

Natürlich ist das Kommunikationsverhalten in den beschriebenen Regionen wie etwa Afrika, Asien und den USA alles andere als homogen: Selbst in einzelnen Ländern unterscheidet es sich oft von Bundesstaat zu Bundesstaat. So ist beispielsweise der Kommunikationsstil in den Staaten Neuenglands anders als an der Westküste oder im „Bible Belt" der USA.

Answers:
1. False – handshake yes, but only light.
2. False – in Southern European countries, conversations and discussions are conducted in a lively manner where interruptions are frequent and completely accepted. Sitting in silence is more likely to be seen as impolite, since such conduct is suspected of being a sign of disinterest.
3. True – above all the older generation practices this.
4. False – in Arab and many African countries, for example, eye contact between the sexes is viewed as impolite; in Southern and Central European countries, eye contact is generally exercised less than in the rest of Europe.
5. True! And for good reason ...
6. Despite the Monarchy – this is true.
7. False – for example, in France or Great Britain, reluctance or rejection tend to be communicated indirectly.

Did you know everything? Super! And if not, then the following pages might just hold a few more surprises for you.

9.2 Typical National Differences

It's not just here at home that small talk has certain rules; this is also the case in other countries. What makes this fact interesting (or exciting, depending on the point of view), is that pretty much every country has its own rules.

Those who don't know the rules can, under certain circumstances, end up behaving in a completely inappropriate way, despite all their best intentions and efforts. And when business is the main issue, this can end up being very, very expensive.

So what does one have to pay attention to when engaging in small talk with foreign business partners and customers?

> *Essentially, you should know what you can talk about (and what not) and, of particular importance, what you should observe about your body language.*

In the coming pages, you'll find fundamental information on communication conduct in various regions and countries in the world.

Naturally, communication behaviour in the regions depicted such as Africa, Asia and the USA are anything but uniform: even in the individual countries, behaviour sometimes differs from one national state or region to another. For example: the communication style in America's New England is different from that of the West Coast or in the "Bible Belt".

Grundlegende Regeln für den Small Talk im Ausland

Zunächst einmal hat Small Talk in vielen Ländern eine wesentlich höhere Wertigkeit als in Deutschland, wo er oft genug eher zähneknirschend als Mittel zum Zweck akzeptiert wird.

Die hohe **Sachorientierung** der Deutschen ist vielen anderen Nationalitäten selbst im Geschäftsleben fremd: Auch eine Geschäftsbeziehung gilt z.B. in südeuropäischen, arabischen, asiatischen oder südamerikanischen Ländern als persönliche Beziehung, die man aufbauen und pflegen muss – und die sich eben nicht nur aufgrund von Fakten und Zahlen einstellt.

Damit einher geht, dass man sich mehr Zeit nimmt, um über Dinge zu sprechen, die zunächst einmal nichts mit dem geplanten Geschäft zu tun haben – Small Talk eben! So pflegt und festigt man die bereits bestehende Beziehung oder baut eine neue auf: Man erfährt etwas über den privaten und beruflichen Hintergrund, die Persönlichkeit, Vorlieben und natürlich den sozialen und beruflichen Status des potenziellen Geschäftspartners.

Verbunden ist dieser Small Talk mit bestimmten **landestypischen Ritualen** wie etwa dem Austausch von Geschenken oder gemeinsamen Mahlzeiten. Die diversen Etiketteregeln (die oft auch noch je nach Geschlecht unterschiedlich ausfallen) hier auszuführen, würde den Rahmen dieses Bandes sprengen. Im Literaturverzeichnis finden Sie daher einige Bücher, die sich mit diesem Aspekt ausführlich beschäftigen.

Die ungeschriebenen Gesetze für Inhalte und Themen des Small Talks differieren von Land zu Land ebenso wie die **Kommunikationsregeln**. Ein bekanntes Beispiel betrifft die Körpersprache: Während stetiger Blickkontakt im deutschen Kulturkreis als Zeichen von Interesse und Anteilnahme gilt, finden Japaner längeren und direkten Blickkontakt unangenehm und unhöflich.

Tabu im Small Talk sind in jedem Fall Religion, politische, wirtschaftliche und gesellschaftliche Probleme des jeweiligen Landes oder Körperliches wie Krankheiten oder Sexualität. Bei Witzen ist ebenfalls äußerste Vorsicht geboten.

In vielen Ländern gelten klar formulierte Ablehnung, deutlicher Widerspruch, Kritik (auch sachlich oder konstruktiv formuliert) oder kontrovers geführte Diskussionen als unhöflich – **Harmonie** ist wichtiger. Wenn Sie also anderer Meinung sind als Ihr Gesprächspartner, sollten Sie dies, wenn überhaupt, dann sehr diplomatisch formulieren.

Fundamental Rules for Small Talk Abroad

First of all, in many countries, small talk enjoys a much greater appreciation and value than say, in Germany, where it's often grudgingly accepted as a means to an end, while the **high level of factual orientation** of the Germans is foreign for many other nationalities, even in their business life.

For example, in Southern European, Arab, Asian or South American countries, a business relationship is also viewed as a personal relationship that must be built up and cultivated – and which is by no means based solely on facts and numbers.

This inherently means that one takes more time to talk about things that, in and of themselves, have nothing to do with the planned business – in other words, small talk! This is how one maintains and solidifies already existing relationships or builds up new ones: One discovers something about the private and professional background, the personality, preferences, and of course, the social and professional status of the potential business partner.

This small talk is combined with **certain rituals typical of the respective country**, such as the exchange of gifts or having meals together. To list the diverse rules of etiquette (which are often different according to which sex they apply to) would exceed the limits of this book. For this reason, you'll find a number of books listed in the bibliography that deal extensively with this aspect.

The unwritten laws for the content and topics of small talk differ from country to country, as do the **rules of communication**. One popular example has to do with body language: while constant eye contact is seen in Western cultural circles as a sign of interest and empathy, the Japanese find long, direct eye contact uncomfortable and impolite.

Taboos for any round of small talk include: the subjects of religion, political, economic and societal problems of the country in question, or physical matters such as illnesses or sexuality. And extreme care is to be taken with jokes.

In many countries, clearly formulated rejection, direct contradiction, criticism (even when formulated in a technical or constructive way) or discussions conducted in a controversial manner are seen as impolite – **harmony** is more important. If you are of a different opinion than your discussion partner, then you should formulate your disagreement very diplomatically, if at all.

Selbst im vergleichsweise kleinen Deutschland kennen wir dieses Phänomen. Denken Sie nur an das viel zitierte Nord-Süd-Gefälle: Wir können davon ausgehen, dass ein Bayer und ein Hamburger unterschiedliche Kommunikationsstrategien haben. Und um das Ganze noch weiter zu differenzieren: Der Bayer aus der Großstadt München wird sich, was seinen Kommunikationsstil angeht, von dem Bayern aus einem kleinen Dorf auf dem Land auch noch einmal unterscheiden.

Dennoch gibt es wichtige Gemeinsamkeiten und Ähnlichkeiten im Kommunikationsverhalten der Weltregionen und Nationen, deren Kenntnis Ihnen bei Geschäftskontakten helfen kann.

Afrika
Zeigen Sie Geduld und nehmen Sie sich ausreichend Zeit für den Small Talk. Geeignet sind allgemeine Themen, wie z.B. die Reise, das Land, das Wetter und die Familie. Zu den Tabu-Themen gehören Politik und Menschenrechte.

Sollten Sie aus irgendwelchen Gründen verärgert oder frustriert sein, zeigen Sie das nicht, und vermeiden Sie es, das Gespräch spürbar (z.B. durch Themenwechsel) voranzutreiben. Titel sind wichtig und werden bei der mündlichen ebenso wie bei der schriftlichen Anrede gern und häufig benutzt.

Die Körpersprache: Berührungen – etwa ein langer, kräftiger Händedruck (oft mit beiden Händen) – sind unter Männern üblich, Körperkontakt zwischen den Geschlechtern in der Öffentlichkeit eher nicht. Intensiver, direkter Blickkontakt wird in vielen Ländern als unangenehm empfunden, zwischen den Geschlechtern gilt er oft sogar als sexuell motivierte Kontaktaufnahme. Auch das Berühren älterer Menschen gilt in einigen Ländern Afrikas als unangebracht und unhöflich. Vermeiden Sie Dominanzgesten – deuten Sie also z.B. nicht mit dem Zeigefinger auf Menschen.

Übrigens: Kopfschütteln heißt in Tunesien „vielleicht", ein Nein wird durch ein leichtes Anheben des Kopfes mit vorgerecktem Kinn ausgedrückt.

Arabische Länder
Auch in diesem Kulturraum spielt der Small Talk eine ungleich größere Rolle als in Deutschland. Das Ziel ist der Aufbau und die Festigung von Beziehungen. Nicht nur bei privaten, auch bei Geschäftsbeziehungen ist hier ein persönliches, von Vertrauen geprägtes

We see comparable situations throughout Europe. Just think about the often-mentioned "North-South Divide": we can assume that someone from Hamburg and someone from Bavaria have different communication strategies. And to break it down even further, the Bavarian from the metropolis of Munich will communicate with a different style than the resident of a small village in Bavaria's countryside.

> *Despite all this, there remain important commonalities and similarities in the conduct of communication throughout the world's regions and nations, and knowing about them can help you with your business contacts.*

Africa

Be patient and allow sufficient time for small talk. General topics such as the journey, the country, the weather and the family are suitable. Politics and human rights are among topics to be avoided.

If, for whatever reason, you become annoyed or frustrated, don't show it and avoid noticeably coaxing the discussion along (for example, by changing the subject). Titles are important and are eagerly and frequently used, both in verbal and in written communication.

Body language: touching – for instance, a long, firm handshake (often with both hands) – is customary among men, while public physical contact between the sexes is less common. Intensive, direct eye contact is viewed as annoying in many countries, and between members of the opposite sex it is often even interpreted as a sexually motivated attempt to establish contact. Physical contact with older persons is also seen as inappropriate and impolite in some African countries. Avoid dominance gestures – for example, don't point at people with your forefinger.

And by the way: shaking your head in Tunisia means "maybe", while "no" is expressed by raising the head slightly with the chin protruding.

Arab Countries

In this cultural area as well, small talk plays a comparatively larger role than is customary in the West, and its aim is the development and deepening of relationships. Not only in private, but also in business relationships, a personal, trusting relationship serves as the

Verhältnis die Grundlage. **Nehmen Sie sich also viel Zeit**, bleiben Sie geduldig, bis das eigentliche Geschäftsgespräch beginnt – das ist z.B. bei Geschäftsessen erst nach dem Hauptgericht der Fall.

Wichtig ist, dass Sie den Gesprächspartner schon bei der Gesprächseröffnung mit Namen und ggf. Titel ansprechen, und zwar mit der korrekten Aussprache und Betonung. Es empfiehlt sich, das im Vorfeld zu üben.

Small Talk werden Sie in der Regel unter oder mit Männern halten; Frauen werden von Männern in der Öffentlichkeit nicht angesprochen. Als Gesprächsstoff eignen sich Themen wie Sport (insbesondere landestypische Sportarten), Geschäfte oder gemeinsame Bekannte.

Tabu sind kritische Diskussionen zu den Themen Religion, Politik und Frauen. Auch die bei uns als höflich geltende Erkundigung *„Wie geht es Ihrer Frau?"* ist in arabischen Ländern unüblich bis unerwünscht. Nach den Kindern dagegen dürfen Sie sich ruhig erkundigen.

Stellen Sie keine Fragen, von denen Sie nicht mit Sicherheit sagen können, ob Ihr Gesprächspartner sie beantworten kann, und haken Sie nicht nach, wenn Sie keine oder nur eine ausweichende Antwort bekommen: Unwissenheit zuzugeben, kommt einem Gesichtsverlust gleich. Auch Kritik, Belehrungen oder Ratschläge werden als unangenehm empfunden.

Die Körpersprache: In der arabischen Welt fallen die Distanzzonen – zwischen Männern! – deutlich geringer aus als bei uns: Man steht und sitzt dichter beieinander, Berührungen sind häufiger (so dauert auch der Händedruck zur Begrüßung meist länger als in Deutschland), direkter und langer Blickkontakt ist üblich. Körperliche Nähe ist positiv besetzt, sie drückt Sympathie und Vertrauen aus.

Für **Frauen** gelten andere Verhaltensregeln: Körperkontakt zwischen den Geschlechtern ist in der Öffentlichkeit tabu. Eine arabische Frau wird also nicht per Handschlag begrüßt, es sei denn, sie initiiert es. Auch Blickkontakt wird ihr gegenüber nur sparsam eingesetzt.

Eine gerade, aufrechte Körperhaltung zeigt Stärke und Autorität. Dominanzgesten dagegen, wie etwa mit dem Finger auf eine Person zu deuten, können als Angriff missverstanden werden.

Achten Sie darauf, dass Sie während des Gesprächs Ihre **linke Hand**, die als unrein gilt, nicht einsetzen: Visitenkarten, Geschenke etc. müssen mit der rechten Hand übergeben und angenommen werden. Auch gegessen wird ausschließlich mit rechts. Hände zu verstecken, etwa in den Hosentaschen, gilt als unhöflich.

basis. So take plenty of time and be patient until the actual business discussion begins – in the case of business meals, for example, this comes after the main dish.

It is important for you to already **address the discussion partner by name and, if applicable, also by title** at the opening of the discussion and to do so with the correct pronunciation and intonation. It is recommended that you practise this in advance.

Small talk is generally conducted among or by men; women are not addressed by men in public. Suitable **topics** of conversation include sports (in particular, the national sports of the country in question), business or mutual acquaintances.

Critical discussions on the subjects of religion, politics and women are **out of bounds**. Even the question generally viewed in our society as a polite gesture, *"How is your wife?"*, is unaccustomed or even unwanted in Arab countries. In contrast, asking about the children is completely OK.

Don't pose any questions that you're not certain your discussion partner can answer, and don't attempt to delve any deeper if you receive an evasive answer or even no answer at all: admitting ignorance is comparable to a loss of face. And criticism, admonitions or suggestions are seen as disagreeable conduct.

Body language: in the Arab world, the distance zones between men are much smaller than ours: men stand and sit closer to one another, touching is more frequent (for instance, the greeting handshake usually lasts longer than it does with us in the West) and direct, longer eye contact is normal. Physical closeness is viewed in a positive light, signifying friendship and trust.

Other rules of conduct apply for **women**: physical contact between opposite sexes in public is a no-no. So an Arab woman is not greeted with a handshake, unless she initiates it. And eye contact with your conversation partner is only exercised sparingly.

A **straight, upright posture** demonstrates strength and authority. Dominance gestures on the other hand, such as pointing at someone with the forefinger, can be misinterpreted as an attack.

Make sure during the discussion that you don't use your **left hand**, which is viewed as impure: business cards, gifts, etc., must be handed over and received with the right hand and eating is additionally also conducted only with the right hand. Hiding one's hands, in the pockets, for instance, is seen as impolite.

Wenn Sie mit Geschäftspartnern in einer Runde sitzen, achten Sie außerdem darauf, dass Ihre Schuhsohlen nicht zu sehen sind, das gilt mindestens als grob unhöflich.

Australien

Im Gegensatz zu vielen anderen Ländern wird in Australien ausgesprochen **wenig Wert auf Hierarchien** gelegt. Sie sollten daher bei der Vorstellung (und auch bei den Visitenkarten) auf Titel verzichten. Statt Förmlichkeit und speziellen Ritualen ist eine **ungezwungene, lockere Atmosphäre** wichtig.

Für den Small Talk heißt dies vor allem, dass es unkompliziert zugeht: Es können viele **Themen** angeschnitten werden (z.B. Hobbys, Sport, Sehenswürdigkeiten); direkte und offene Fragen sind ebenso erlaubt wie direkte Meinungsäußerungen – Höflichkeit im Umgang miteinander spielt aber dennoch eine wichtige Rolle. Verpönt sind betonte Selbstdarstellungen (etwa über berufliche Leistungen) und langatmige, umständliche oder negativ formulierte Darstellungen.

Die **Körpersprache** ist so unkompliziert wie die verbale Kommunikation: Direkter Blickkontakt und offene Körpersprache werden als angenehm empfunden.

Beneluxländer

In den **Niederlanden** (sprechen Sie bitte nicht von Holland, das ist eine Provinz der Niederlande) werden – ganz im Sinne der calvinistischen Tradition – Sachlichkeit und Bescheidenheit in der Kommunikation großgeschrieben. Titel und Hierarchien spielen in der mündlichen Kommunikation keine tragende Rolle. Es wird offen kommuniziert; Ablehnung wird allerdings oft freundlich verpackt. Auch die Körpersprache ist ruhig, sachlich und freundlich.

In **Belgien** und **Luxemburg** geht es etwas formeller zu: Mit Höflichkeit, Zurückhaltung und Understatement liegen Sie hier genau richtig.

Frankreich

In Frankreich legt vor allem, aber nicht nur die ältere Generation Wert auf eine **geschliffene und höfliche Rhetorik**: Man kommuniziert indirekt (mit vielen Konjunktiven) und förmlich; direkt geäußerte Kritik wird als unhöflich, ein klares Nein als unelegant und plump empfunden.

Da es eher förmlich zugeht (die Etikette spielt eine große Rolle), spricht man sich in der Regel mit „Sie" an. Sowohl bei der Begrüßung

When you are sitting in a round with business partners, make sure that the soles of your shoes are not visible; this is seen in the best case as grossly impolite.

Australia

In contrast to many other countries, precious little value is attached to hierarchies in Australia. So in your introduction (as well as on your business cards), leave out the title. Instead of formalities and special rituals, a relaxed atmosphere is important here.

In regard to small talk, this means above all that it runs in an uncomplicated manner: many topics can be addressed (for example, hobbies, sports, tourist sights); direct and open questions are allowed, just as direct expressions of opinion – but courtesy in dealing with one another still plays an important role. Demonstrative self-portrayals (about professional achievements, for example) and long-winded, laborious or negatively formulated presentations are frowned upon.

Body language is just as uncomplicated as verbal communication: direct eye contact and open body language are viewed positively.

Benelux Countries

In the Netherlands (please don't say "Holland" – Holland is a province in The Netherlands), objectivity and humility are the golden rules of communication, in keeping with the nation's Calvinist tradition. Titles and hierarchies do not play a major role in verbal communication. Communication is open; however, reluctance or rejection is often wrapped in friendly packaging. Body language is also calm, realistic and friendly.

In Belgium and Luxembourg, things are somewhat more formal: politeness, restraint and understatement can take you a long way here.

France

In France, refined, courteous rhetorical skills are held in high esteem, and not just by the older generation. One communicates indirectly (with many subjunctives) and formally; direct criticism is seen as impolite, and a clear "no" is viewed as gauche and crude.

Since things are more formal here (etiquette plays a large role), one generally addresses others in the formal form: both in greeting and in bidding farewell, you should add a "Monsieur" or "Madame"/

als auch bei der Verabschiedung sollten Sie ein „Monsieur" bzw. „Madame"/„Mademoiselle" hinzufügen (*„Bonjour, Monsieur"*); das Gleiche gilt für kurze Antworten: *„Oui, Madame."* Überhaupt: Französisch-Kenntnisse werden ausgesprochen positiv aufgenommen.

Die Begrüßung erfolgt per Händedruck. Die typisch französische Begrüßung mit – je nach Region zwei bis vier – Wangenküssen („la bise") gibt es nur für Menschen, die man gut kennt.

Beim Small Talk kann neben dem Land, seiner Geschichte und Kultur, Essen und Wein durchaus auch Privates angesprochen werden. Konfliktträchtige Themen sollte man aber unbedingt meiden.

Für Geschäftsessen gilt: Zunächst wird ausgiebig Small Talk gemacht.

> *Geschäftliches wird erst nach dem Hauptgang, nämlich zwischen Dessert und Kaffee, besprochen.*

Trotz aller Höflichkeit und manchmal Förmlichkeit schätzt man in Frankreich ein lebhaftes Gespräch, in dem man sich durchaus gegenseitig ins Wort fallen darf: Eine lebendige und charismatische Persönlichkeit wird weit mehr geschätzt als jemand, der sachlich und nüchtern kommuniziert oder – schlimmer noch – zwar fachlich versiert, aber rhetorisch ungeschickt ist.

Großbritannien

Auch in Großbritannien, dem Geburtsland des Small Talks, kommuniziert man diplomatisch und eher indirekt. Temperamentsausbrüche, Widerspruch, deutlich formulierte Ablehnung und hitzig geführte Diskussionen gelten als unhöflich – ebenso wie allzu intensives Selbstmarketing.

Ratsam ist ein gewisses Understatement. Der häufige Gebrauch von „Unschärfe-Markierern" wie Konjunktiven (*could, would, might*), Verneinungen (*don't you*) oder Entschuldigungen (*sorry*), der in Deutschland als zu vage und unsicher gilt, ist typisch.

Beliebte Small-Talk-Themen sind neben dem Standardthema Wetter vor allem Urlaub, Hobbys (Sport, Garten ...), Land und Leute. Typisch für das höfliche, aber distanzierte Kommunikationsverhalten ist, dass Fragen nach dem Privat- und Familienleben nicht zum Small Talk gehören. Diese Themen kann man erst dann anschneiden, wenn man schon ein etwas vertrauteres Verhältnis zu seinem Gegenüber hat.

Händeschütteln zur Begrüßung ist nur bei offiziellen Anlässen bzw. der ersten Vorstellung üblich; bei allen anderen Gelegenheiten ist es weniger beliebt: Die Briten schätzen Distanz und legen Wert

"Mademoiselle" (*"Bonjour, Monsieur"*); the same applies for brief answers, for example, *"Oui, Madame"*. And in any case, French language skills make a very positive impression.

Greeting is done by handshake. The typical French greeting with two to four kisses on the cheek ("la bise"), depending on the region, only goes for people who one knows well.

In addition to the country itself, its history and culture, cuisine and wine, topics for small talk can certainly include the private sphere, but controversial topics should definitely be avoided.

The rule for business meals is that small talk comes first.

> *Business is discussed after the main dish, between dessert and coffee.*

Despite all the focus in France on civility and even formality, the French still appreciate a lively discussion in which it is fully permissible for the parties participating to interrupt one another: a lively, charismatic personality is far more appreciated than someone who communicates in a factual, sober fashion, or – even worse – someone who is factually well-versed, but rhetorically clumsy.

Great Britain

Even in Great Britain, the motherland of small talk, people communicate diplomatically and somewhat indirectly. Outbursts of temper, contradiction, clearly formulated rejection and hotly conducted discussions are viewed as impolite – as is overly intensive "self-marketing".

A certain degree of understatement is advisable. The frequent use of "blurred markings", such as subjunctives (*could, would, might*), negations (*don't you*) or apologies (*sorry*), that might be perceived in other countries as too vague and uncertain, is typical.

Popular small talk topics, aside from standards like the weather, consist above all of holidays, hobbies (sports, the garden ...), the country and people. It is additionally typical for the civil but somewhat distanced communication behaviour that questions regarding one's private and family life are not included in small talk; these topics may be addressed only after the relationship with the conversation partner has become more familiar.

The handshake is only customary at official functions or the first introduction; it is less popular for all other occasions, as the British appreciate distance and value as little physical contact as possible.

auf möglichst wenig Körperberührungen. Die höfliche Einstiegsfloskel „*How do you do?*" zielt (genau wie das deutsche Äquivalent „*Wie geht es Ihnen?*") nicht auf einen ausführlichen Zustandsbericht des Gesprächspartners ab; als Antwort genügt ein „*How do you do?*". Sehr zu empfehlen ist darüber hinaus der häufige Gebrauch von Höflichkeitspartikeln wie „*sorry*", „*excuse me*", „*please*" oder „*thank you*".

Auch der sprichwörtliche englische Humor spielt in der Kommunikation eine große Rolle.

Ironische und selbstironische Bemerkungen gehören zum Small Talk.

Beweisen Sie Humor und lachen Sie mit – nehmen Sie Ihrerseits aber Rücksicht auf eventuelle Empfindlichkeiten. Bei Witzen über das Königshaus ist z.B. Vorsicht geboten.

Die Körpersprache ist zurückhaltend. Ein höfliches Lächeln und lockerer Blickkontakt sind ebenso typisch wie eine wenig ausgeprägte Gestik und Mimik: Die hochgezogene Augenbraue oder die „stiff upper lip" sind z.B. oft schon das Äußerste, was sich bei einer ablehnenden Haltung in der Körpersprache ausdrückt, und sie zeigen, dass hier jemand „not amused" ist.

Übrigens: Schotten und Waliser sind keine Engländer, sondern allenfalls Briten.

Israel

Generell legt man Wert auf eine lockere, freundliche und nicht allzu förmliche Gesprächsatmosphäre. Small Talk ist zur Gesprächseröffnung wichtig, nach kurzer Zeit kann es aber dann zur Sache gehen. Der Kommunikationsstil ist direkt; Ablehnung kann und sollte höflich und sachlich, aber klar formuliert sein. Ein blumiger und ausweichender Gesprächsstil gilt als eher unvorteilhaft.

Zu den Tabus beim Small Talk zählt neben kritischen Äußerungen über das Land und seine Politik insbesondere das Thema Palästinenser. Aufgrund der deutschen Vergangenheit ist in der Kommunikation mit Israelis generell Feinfühligkeit angesagt – ganz besonders bei Gesprächspartnern der älteren Generation.

Die Körpersprache: Direkter Blickkontakt, eine lebhafte Mimik und Gestik sind üblich, die Distanzzonen sind ähnlich wie in Deutschland.

Small Talk Abroad

The courteous opening phrase, *"How do you do?"*, is not an invitation to explain your current state in detail; the answer *"How do you do?"*, is sufficient. It is also highly recommended to use polite phrases like *"sorry", "excuse me", "please"* or *"thank you"* frequently.

And the renowned English sense of humour plays a large role in communication.

> *Ironic and self-deprecating comments are a part of small talk.*

Show that you've also got a sense of humour and laugh too – but be aware of possible "sore spots". For instance, care is recommended with jokes about the Royal Family.

Body language is restrained. A polite smile and relaxed eye contact are as equally typical as are rather distinctive gestures and facial expressions: the raised eyebrow or the "stiff upper lip", for example, are often the most distinguishable body language expressions of a reluctant posture, and they demonstrate that the person in question is "not amused".

And very important: the Scots and the Welsh are indeed British, but they are not "English", as they will eagerly inform you should you mistakenly confuse these terms!

Israel

Generally, Israelis appreciate a relaxed, friendly discussion atmosphere that's not overly formal. A brief period of small talk is important in opening a discussion, after which talk can turn to the business at hand. The style of communication is direct; rejection or reluctance can and should be polite and factual, but it should be formulated clearly. A flowery, evasive discussion style is likely to be viewed negatively.

There are subjects to be absolutely avoided in small talk, and aside from critical statements about the country and its politics, this also includes in particular the subject of the Palestinians. Due to the unique nature of German history in the 20th century, a great deal of sensitivity is required in communication between Israelis and Germans – particularly in discussions between members of the older generation.

Body language: direct eye contact, lively facial expressions and gestures are normal, and the distance zones are similar to those in the West.

Kanada

Während im französischsprachigen Osten des Landes der frankophone Einfluss auch in der Kommunikation stärker spürbar wird, ist das Kommunikationsverhalten im englischsprachigen Westen typisch angelsächsisch.

Insgesamt ist der Gesprächsstil offen, direkt und locker. Small Talk ist auch hier der Einstieg in Geschäfts- und Verhandlungsgespräche, danach kommt man schnell zum eigentlichen Thema.

Beim Essen dagegen sollte nicht über Geschäftliches gesprochen werden. Geeignete Small-Talk-Themen sind z.B. Sport oder Natur – Privates hält man vom geschäftlichen Bereich eher fern.

Mittelmeerraum

Persönliche, direkte Kommunikation spielt in Italien, Spanien, Griechenland, der Türkei und Portugal eine große Rolle – und ohne Small Talk geht gar nichts. Zu den üblichen Small-Talk-Themen gehört auch Privates; gern unterhält man sich über Familie, Kinder, Essen und Trinken, Kultur etc.

Die Themenbehandlung ist meist emotional und kann durchaus kontrovers erfolgen. Die ausgeprägte Lebhaftigkeit macht sich in der Lautstärke ebenso bemerkbar wie in gegenseitigen Unterbrechungen, die – anders als in Deutschland – nicht als unhöflich gelten. Beteiligen Sie sich ebenso lebhaft an Gesprächen, denn ein sehr introvertiertes Verhalten stößt oft auf Unverständnis.

Wissen über die einzelnen Länder, ihre Kultur und Geschichte, Sprachkenntnisse (auch rudimentäre) werden sehr geschätzt. Lob, Anerkennung und Komplimente werden freigiebig verteilt und ebenso gern entgegengenommen.

Tabu-Themen im Small Talk sind Kritik am Land oder der Politik. Ferner sollten Sie folgende landesspezifischen Besonderheiten beachten:

- In Griechenland ist alles tabu, was mit den schwierigen Beziehungen zur Türkei zu tun hat.
- In Italien meidet man Themen rund um die Mafia.
- In Spanien sollte man nicht über die Sitte des Stierkampfes oder die ETA diskutieren.
- Und für die Türkei gilt: keine Diskussionen über den Islam, die Rolle der Frau oder die Verletzung von Menschenrechten.

In Italien spricht man einander übrigens gern und viel mit Titel an: Auch nicht promovierte Akademiker können Sie ruhig mit „Dottore" ansprechen.

Canada

While the francophone influence is significantly more noticeable in the French-speaking eastern part of the country, including in its communication, the communication behaviour in the English-speaking west is typically Anglo-Saxon.

All in all, the conversational style is open, direct and relaxed. Small talk is also the opener for business and negotiation discussions here, and after the small talk one can quickly get down to business.

In contrast, business should not be discussed during meals. Appropriate small talk topics consist for example of sports or nature – the private life is generally excluded from matters of business.

The Mediterranean Region

Personal, direct communication plays a large role in Italy, Spain, Greece, Turkey and Portugal – and without small talk, absolutely nothing happens. The normal small talk topic repertoire also includes items within the private sphere; there's no hesitation in talking about the family, children, food and drink, culture, etc.

Treatment of the various topics is usually emotional and can certainly be conducted controversially. The distinctive vitality is just as noticeable in the volume level as in the mutual interruptions – which, in contrast to northwestern Europe, are not seen as impolite. You should also participate energetically in discussions, because notably introverted behaviour is often viewed with a lack of understanding.

Knowledge about the individual countries, their cultures and histories, along with language skills (even rudimentary ones) are greatly appreciated. Praise, acknowledgement and compliments are generously distributed and are just as eagerly received.

Small talk taboos include criticism of the respective country or its politics. Furthermore, you should observe the following particularities related to the specific countries:

- In Greece, do not discuss anything related to the difficult relationship with Turkey.
- In Italy, avoid topics related to the Mafia.
- In Spain, one should not discuss the custom of bullfighting or the ETA organisation.
- And for Turkey, avoid discussions on Islam, the role of women or the violation of human rights.

In Italy, it is a popular custom to address each other frequently by title: you can even address academics who actually have no PhD as "Dottore".

Die Körpersprache ist generell ausdrucksstark, sowohl in Bezug auf Mimik und Gestik als auch in Bezug auf Stimme und Tonfall. Die Distanzzonen sind geringer als in Deutschland, Berührungen an Armen und Schultern keine Seltenheit.

Ostasiatische Länder

Eine grundlegende Regel für Kommunikation im asiatischen Raum lautet: Tun Sie alles dafür, dass niemand, weder Sie selbst noch Ihre Gesprächspartner, „das Gesicht verliert", sondern setzen Sie im Gegenteil alles daran, dass die Anwesenden „an Gesicht gewinnen".

Absolute Höflichkeit sowie Kenntnis und Einhaltung der verschiedenen Kommunikationsrituale sind ein Muss.

Wenn Sie anderen Respekt erweisen, wird man auch Ihnen mit Respekt begegnen.

Achten Sie immer auf Hierarchien und begrüßen Sie zuerst die ranghöchste unter den anwesenden Personen. Tauschen Sie gleich zu Beginn Visitenkarten aus. Ihrer Visitenkarte sollten Ihre Position und – falls vorhanden – Ihr Titel zu entnehmen sein, damit die Gesprächspartner Sie richtig einschätzen können. Überreichen Sie Ihre Karte mit beiden Händen und nehmen Sie auch die Karten Ihrer Gesprächspartner mit beiden Händen entgegen. Studieren Sie sie einige Sekunden lang, bevor Sie sie wegstecken (nicht in die Hosentaschen!). Danach wird zunächst Small Talk gemacht, bevor das eigentliche Geschäftsgespräch beginnt.

Für den Small Talk geeignet sind alle unverfänglichen Themen – z.B. Fragen nach der Familie, nach Sehenswürdigkeiten der Region, Komplimente über das Land oder das Unternehmen (jedoch keine persönlichen Komplimente!). Es geht darum, eine angenehme Atmosphäre herzustellen und Gemeinsamkeiten zu betonen.

Kontroverse Themen, Diskussionen oder gar kritische Bemerkungen sind vor allem in der Auftaktphase eines Gespräches unbedingt zu vermeiden. Zeigen Sie Humor, aber reißen Sie keine Witze.

Nehmen Sie sich ausreichend Zeit für Small Talk, drängen Sie nicht zu schnell zum eigentlichen Thema. Vermeiden Sie alles, was zu Gesichtsverlust auf beiden Seiten führen könnte. Dazu gehören beispielsweise kritische, herabsetzende oder ironische Bemerkungen (auch über das eigene Land oder das eigene Unternehmen), bohrende oder zu persönliche Fragen, Ungeduld oder das Zeigen von (negativen) Emotionen.

Tabu sind im Small Talk Sexualität, Religion und Politik; insbesondere in China auch das Thema Menschenrechte.

Body language is generally expressive, both in relation to facial expressions and gestures as well as to the voice and intonation. The distance zones are smaller than in northwestern Europe, and physical contact on the arms and shoulders is not uncommon.

East Asian Countries

A fundamental rule of communication in Asia is to do everything within your power to ensure that neither you nor your discussion partner "lose face"; instead, do your best to make sure that everyone present "wins face", so to speak!

> *Absolute courtesy as well as knowledge of and compliance with the various communication rituals are a must.*

When you show respect to others, they will also treat you with respect.

Always observe hierarchies and greet the person with the highest rank among those present first. Exchange business cards right at the start. Your business card should specify your position and, if applicable, your title so that your discussion partner can correctly assess you. Offer your card with both hands and also make sure to take the cards of your discussion partners with both hands. Study them for a few seconds before you put them away (not in the trouser pockets!). This is followed by small talk before the actual business discussion begins.

All uncontroversial topics are suitable for small talk – for example, questions about the family, regional tourism sights, compliments about the country or the company (but no personal compliments!). The point is to create a pleasant atmosphere and to emphasise common ground.

Controversial topics, discussions or, heaven forbid, critical statements are to be avoided, above all in the initial phase of a discussion. Demonstrate humour, but don't make any jokes.

Take plenty of time for small talk and don't push the actual matter at hand too heavily. Avoid everything that could lead to a loss of face for both sides. For example, this includes critical, derisive or ironic comments (also about one's own country or company), questions that are probing or too personal, impatience or the demonstration of (negative) emotions.

Sexuality, religion and politics are out of bounds for small talk; and in China in particular, also the subject of human rights.

Die Körpersprache: Auch wenn der Händedruck zur Begrüßung in asiatischen Ländern nicht üblich ist, wird er mittlerweile als Geste der Höflichkeit mit westlichen Kunden praktiziert, oft kombiniert mit einer leichten Verbeugung. Drücken Sie aber die Hand, die Ihnen gereicht wird, nur leicht und lassen Sie sich nicht davon in die Irre führen, dass ein solcher weicher Händedruck in Deutschland oft als Zeichen von Schwäche gesehen wird: In Asien ist das anders.

> *Direkter Blickkontakt, vor allem mit Personen von hohem Rang, gilt, wie bereits erwähnt, als unhöflich.*

In Deutschland ist es üblich, das Gesagte durch eine recht lebhafte Körpersprache sowie durch Betonung lebendig zu machen. In asiatischen Ländern hingegen spricht man eher mit gleichmäßiger Modulation und Lautstärke; eine lauter werdende Stimme wird hier als Zeichen von Unbeherrschtheit interpretiert. Auch eine lebhafte Gestik und Mimik empfindet man in Asien als unangenehm. Um Sachverhalte hervorzuheben, wiederholt man sie eher – was wiederum in Deutschland als Zeitverschwendung gilt.

Sie sehen: Hier lauern zahlreiche Fettnäpfchen, derer Sie sich bewusst sein sollten, um sie zu meiden.

Als positiv gelten in Asien ruhige Körpersprache und gerade Sitzhaltung sowie die Einhaltung der vom Gesprächspartner vorgegebenen Distanzzonen.

Aufmerksamkeit (nicht Zustimmung!) wird durch Kopfnicken gezeigt. Lächeln wirkt ebenfalls positiv; wenn Sie allerdings Fremde anlächeln würden, empfände man das etwa in Japan als respektlos. Auch ein offen stehender Mund und lautes Lachen gelten insbesondere in Japan als unschicklich. Wenn Japaner amüsiert sind, lächeln sie oder halten die Hand vor den Mund.

Österreich

Hier gilt: Höflichkeit und Charme (z.B. Handkuss bei der „gnädigen Frau") sind gefragt, der Gebrauch von Titeln (ohne Namen: *„Grüß Gott, Herr Professor"*) ausgeprägt und gern gesehen. Dem Small Talk kommt ein hoher Stellenwert zu, zu den Themen darf durchaus das Privatleben gehören.

Gehen Sie hier aber nicht in allzu persönliche Details, halten Sie das Gespräch an der Oberfläche. Absolut tabu ist die deutsch-österreichische Geschichte. Bleiben Sie in Ihrem Kommunikationsstil verbindlich und höflich, vermeiden Sie alles, was Ihnen als (typisch deutsche) Arroganz oder Überheblichkeit ausgelegt werden könnte.

Small Talk Abroad

Body language: even though the handshake is not customary as a greeting in Asian countries, it is widely practiced meanwhile as a gesture of courtesy with Western customers, often combined with a slight bow. Take the hand offered to you, but only lightly, and don't make the mistake of assuming that such a mild handshake is a sign of weakness, as is so often perceived in the West; in Asia, things are different.

> *Direct eye contact, above all with persons of higher rank, is viewed as impolite, as was mentioned previously.*

In the West, it is customary to enliven what's being said with lively body language and emphasis of speech. In Asian countries on the other hand, one generally speaks with an **even modulation and volume level**; a voice increasing in volume is interpreted as a sign of a lack of control. Lively gestures and facial expressions are also perceived in Asia as unpleasant. In order to emphasise factual matters, it is more customary to repeat them – which is often viewed in the West as a waste of time.

So as you can see, the opportunities for saying the wrong thing here are virtually endless, meaning that you should be aware of them in order to avoid them.

In Asia, there is a positive view of **calm body language** and an **upright seating posture**, as well as compliance with the distance zones prescribed by the discussion partner.

Attention (not agreement!) is demonstrated by nodding the head. Smiling also has a positive effect; however, smiling at a stranger in Japan is perceived as showing a lack of respect. And a hanging, open mouth and loud laughing are seen as unbecoming, particularly in Japan. When the Japanese are amused, they smile or hold their hand in front of their mouth.

Austria

Here, **politeness and charm** (for example, a hand kiss for the "honourable lady") are appreciated, and the **use of titles** (without the name: *"Greetings, Herr Professor"*) is widespread and common. Small talk is a valuable commodity and its topics may certainly include one's private life.

Still, avoid going into great detail in doing so. Instead, keep the conversation at a superficial level. **Under no circumstances** should you mention German-Austrian history. Keep your communication style obliging and polite and avoid anything that can be interpreted as arrogance or haughtiness.

Polen

In Polen schätzt man die Balance zwischen Herzlichkeit und Höflichkeit in der Kommunikation: Small Talk dient dem Kennenlernen und als Gesprächsabschluss und beansprucht eine gewisse Zeit, denn auch in Polen gilt eine gute persönliche Beziehung als beste Grundlage für einen erfolgreichen Geschäftskontakt.

Nehmen Sie Rücksicht auf eventuelle Empfindlichkeiten: Zum einen ist Polen ein ausgeprägt katholisches Land, zum anderen reagiert man sehr sensibel auf allzu heftig demonstriertes deutsches Selbstbewusstsein. Religiöse Diskussionen und alles, was mit der deutsch-polnischen Geschichte im Allgemeinen und dem Zweiten Weltkrieg im Besonderen zu tun hat, sind im Small Talk tabu.

Die Körpersprache: Schon bei der Begrüßung gibt es im Vergleich zu Deutschland viel Körperkontakt: Während Männer sich die Hände schütteln oder sich umarmen, bekommen Frauen von Männern oft einen Handkuss. Als Frau sollten Sie sich darauf einstellen, damit Sie nicht überrascht werden.

Russland

Falls Sie beim Stichwort Russland Bilder im Kopf haben, die einen rauen, aber herzlichen, ausgesprochen emotionalen Umgang miteinander zeigen – vergessen Sie es. Das gilt für private Feiern, nicht fürs Geschäft: Hier herrscht ein ruhiger und zurückhaltender Kommunikationsstil vor. Emotionen, egal ob positiver oder negativer Art, werden kaum ausgedrückt. Macht ist etwas, das auch in der Kommunikation bewusst gezeigt und ausgeübt wird.

> *Achten Sie daher in Gesprächen auf die bestehenden Hierarchien, die sehr ernst genommen werden.*

Meiden Sie beim Small Talk politische Themen und Kritik am Land oder der politischen Führung.

Die Körpersprache zeigt viele Ähnlichkeiten mit den deutschen Gepflogenheiten. Lediglich das Begrüßungsritual fällt etwas anders aus: Männer schütteln sich kräftig die Hände; kennt man sich gut, gibt es Umarmungen und Wangenküsse. Das Händeschütteln mit Frauen fällt weniger kraftbetont aus, auch ein Handkuss ist üblich.

Durch Winken, Nicken und körperliche Nähe während des Gesprächs wird Zustimmung und Zufriedenheit signalisiert, ebenso durch ein intensives Händeschütteln nach einem Gespräch. Lächeln als Zeichen von Sympathie im Gespräch ist dagegen eher selten.

Poland

In Poland, a **balance between cordiality and politeness** in communication is appreciated: small talk serves in getting acquainted and as the conclusion to a discussion, taking a certain amount of time, because in Poland as well, a personal relationship is seen as the best basis for a successful business contact.

Take possible sensitivities into consideration: Poland is a very Catholic country, so religious discussions are best avoided.

Body language: in comparison to the West, there is a good deal of physical contact, even during introductions: while men shake hands or embrace one another, women are often greeted by men with a kiss on the hand. So as a woman, be prepared in order to avoid being unpleasantly surprised.

Russia

In case the catchword "Russia" brings a particular image to your mind, depicting rough but hearty and distinctively emotional dealings with one another – forget it. That may be true for private parties, but not in business: **a calm, reserved communication style** is what you can expect. Emotions, either positive or negative, are scarcely expressed. Power is something that is also consciously demonstrated and exercised in communication.

> *So pay attention in discussions to the existing hierarchies, which are indeed taken very seriously here.*

Avoid political topics and criticism of the country or its political leaders in small talk.

Body language is largely similar to that of the Germans. Only the greeting ritual is somewhat different: men shake hands vigorously, and if they know one another well, there are embraces and kisses on the cheek. Shaking hands with women is less vigorous and a hand kiss is customary.

Motioning, nodding and physical closeness during the conversation signify agreement and satisfaction, as does an intensive handshake following the discussion. In contrast, smiling as a sign of sympathy during the discussion is rarer.

Schweiz

Der Kommunikationsstil der Schweizer ist dem der Deutschen in vielen Punkten sehr ähnlich: Halten Sie den Small Talk ruhig etwas knapper, führen Sie Geschäftsgespräche zielgerichtet und direkt, drücken Sie sich klar und deutlich aus. Vermeiden Sie potenziell kritische politische Themen wie etwa den EU-Beitritt oder Vor- und Nachteile der Neutralität.

Skandinavische Länder

In den skandinavischen Ländern wird der Small Talk eher kurz gehalten – er dient lediglich als höflicher Einstieg in das eigentliche Geschäftsgespräch. Der Kommunikationsstil ist offen, klar, unkompliziert, zielorientiert und sachlich. Zurückhaltung kommt besser an als überschwängliche Emotionalität. Ironische Bemerkungen und Witze sollten Sie nur gegenüber guten Bekannten machen. In Norwegen oder Dänemark sollte man die Themen Alkohol und europäische Integration meiden. Generell gilt: Was Sie erzählen, muss immer Hand und Fuß haben und verlässlich sein.

Das Gesagte gilt – nicht nur Schriftliches hat hier eine hohe Verbindlichkeit.

Die Ansprache mit dem Vornamen und Duzen ist in Schweden und Dänemark üblich, in Finnland und Norwegen siezt man sich eher und benutzt den Nachnamen.

Die Körpersprache ist freundlich, aber distanziert: Direkter Blickkontakt ja, allzu heftige Mimik und Gestik nein. Berührungen, selbst die Begrüßung mit Händeschütteln, sind selten, die Distanzzonen mindestens so groß wie in Deutschland.

Süd- und Mittelamerika

Bevor die geschäftlichen Themen angesprochen werden, macht man erst einmal ausgiebig Small Talk. Bei Geschäftsessen in Brasilien sollten Sie sogar erst nach dem Kaffee das Gespräch auf Geschäftliches lenken.

Unterhalten Sie sich über unverfängliche Themen wie die Anreise, das Land und seine Sehenswürdigkeiten, über Sport, Essen und Trinken, Interessen oder Hobbys Ihres Gesprächspartners. Erzählen Sie auch etwas von sich; rechnen Sie mit persönlichen Fragen, die Sie aber nicht detailliert beantworten müssen. Status ist wichtig; stapeln Sie nicht zu tief – nennen Sie Ihre Titel (falls vorhanden) und sprechen Sie Ihre Gesprächspartner mit Titel an.

Switzerland

The communication style of the Swiss is very similar to that of the Germans in many respects: keep the small talk rather brief, conduct your business discussions in a targeted and direct fashion and express yourself clearly. Avoid potentially controversial political topics such as entry into the EU or the advantages and disadvantages of neutrality.

Scandinavian Countries

In the Scandinavian countries, small talk tends to be kept brief – it only serves as a polite opener for the actual business discussion. The style of communication is open, clear, uncomplicated, target-oriented and businesslike. Being reserved makes a better impression than overt emotionality. Ironic comments and jokes should only be made with good acquaintances. In Norway or Denmark, one should avoid the subjects of alcohol and European integration. Generally speaking, whatever you say should make sense and be reliable.

> *What is said counts – a high degree of commitment is associated here with words, and not just those that are in writing.*

Addressing someone by their first name is customary in Sweden and Denmark, while in Finland and Norway, dealings are more formal and one uses the last name.

Body language is friendly but distanced: direct eye contact, yes, but overly dramatic facial expressions and gestures, no. Physical contact, even greeting with a handshake, is rare, and the distance zones are at least as large as they are in other northwestern European countries.

South and Central America

Before one gets "down to business", an extensive small talk session is first up on the menu. At business meals in Brazil, you should even wait until after the coffee to steer the conversation toward business.

Talk about uncontroversial topics such as the trip, the country and its many sights, sports, eating and drinking and your discussion partner's interests or hobbies. Also tell them something about yourself and be prepared for personal questions, which you are nonetheless not obliged to answer in too much detail. Status is important,

Wichtig im Kommunikationsverhalten sind Respekt, Höflichkeit, Freundlichkeit und Geduld. Üben Sie keine direkte Kritik (schon gar nicht vor Dritten) und sprechen Sie keine kontroversen politischen oder historischen Themen an. Dazu gehören z.B. das frühere Pinochet-Regime in Chile, die Kämpfe Argentiniens und Großbritanniens um die Falkland-Inseln und die Drogenmafia in Kolumbien.

Die Körpersprache: Die Distanzzonen zwischen den Gesprächspartnern sind deutlich geringer als in Deutschland; Körperkontakt, z.B. Berührungen an Arm oder Schulter, ist keine Seltenheit. Dieser körperlichen Nähe auszuweichen, sich zurückzuziehen, würde unhöflich wirken.

Eine lebhafte Gestik und Mimik gehört zur Kommunikation, ebenso der Blickkontakt, der allerdings häufig etwas kürzer ist als in Deutschland. Die Hände bitte nicht in die Hosentaschen stecken oder energisch in die Hüften stützen – diese Haltung könnte als aggressiv, als Herausforderung interpretiert werden.

Tschechische Republik

Hier kommen Sie mit zurückhaltender, höflicher und sachorientierter Kommunikation am weitesten. Kritik wird nicht direkt geäußert; generell lehnt man allzu intensives Selbstmarketing als Besserwisserei, Überheblichkeit und Prahlerei ab. Lange Monologe und Unterbrechungen des Gesprächspartners sind ebenfalls verpönt. Meiden Sie im Small Talk politische und geschichtliche Themen der jüngeren Vergangenheit. Außerdem sollten Sie unbedingt auf die als sehr verletzend empfundene Bezeichnung „Tschechei" verzichten. Geeignete Small-Talk-Themen sind z.B. Kultur, die Anreise, Sport, aber auch die Familie.

Die Körpersprache: Kommunizieren Sie auch nonverbal zurückhaltend und halten Sie Distanz. Langer und direkter Blickkontakt gilt als unhöfliches Starren; Mimik und Gestik sollten eher zurückhaltend sein. Die Begrüßung erfolgt per Händedruck, Männer machen häufig zusätzlich eine leichte Verbeugung.

Ungarn

In Ungarn herrscht ein formeller, höflicher Kommunikationsstil vor, der von Understatement (sowohl was Erfolge, als auch was Missgeschicke angeht) geprägt, aber auch durchaus expressiv und beziehungsorientiert ist. Small Talk ist wichtig und dient dem Aufbau der persönlichen Beziehung, geeignete Themen sind z.B. Essen, Wein, Pferde und landestypische Kultur.

so don't be overly casual – state your title (if applicable) and address your discussion partner by their title.

The important things in your communication conduct here are respect, politeness, friendliness and patience. Don't express direct criticism (above all, in front of third parties) and don't inquire about controversial political or historical topics. These include, for example, the former Pinochet regime in Chile, the hostilities between Argentina and Great Britain for the Falkland Islands and the drug cartels in Columbia.

Body language: the distance zones between discussion partners are significantly smaller than in most of the West; physical contact, e.g., touching the arm or shoulder, occurs often. To avoid or withdraw from this physical proximity would be perceived as impolite.

Lively gestures and facial expressions are a part of communication, as is eye contact, which nevertheless is frequently somewhat briefer than you may be accustomed to. Please don't conceal your hands in your trouser pockets or energetically prop your hands on your hips – this posture can be interpreted as aggressive or even as a challenge.

Czech Republic
Here is where reserved, polite, factually-oriented communication will get you the furthest. Criticism is not expressed directly, and generally speaking, overly intensive "self-marketing" is looked down upon as "knowing-it-all", arrogance and boasting. Long monologues and interruptions of the discussion partner are equally frowned upon. Avoid political and historically-related topics of the recent past. Culture, sports, the journey, but also the family are all suitable topics.

Body language: also communicate non-verbally in a reserved manner and keep your distance. Longer, direct eye contact is considered as impolite staring; facial expressions and gestures should be more reserved. A greeting is conducted by handshake, with men often additionally bowing slightly.

Hungary
In Hungary, the customary communication style is formal and courteous, distinguished by understatement (in regard to both success as well as failure), but which is nonetheless thoroughly expressive and relationship-oriented. Small talk is important and serves in building up personal relationships. Suitable topics consist, for ex-

Ablehnung wird nur indirekt formuliert, das klare Nein ist selten. Blickkontakt ebenso wie Berührungen werden im geschäftlichen Bereich dosiert eingesetzt.

USA

Vor allem zum Kennenlernen und bei offiziellen Anlässen ist Small Talk wichtig, wird allerdings vor Geschäftsgesprächen eher kurz gehalten: „Time is money." Wie in Deutschland gilt: Nicht tiefschürfende, sondern unkomplizierte Themen eignen sich für Small Talk, z.B. Sport, die Herkunft der Familie, falls sie europäische Wurzeln hat, Essen (inklusive Diäten), Beruf, Filme oder Musik.

> *Der Kommunikationsstil ist generell eher humorvoll und auf jeden Fall positiv, eine optimistische Sichtweise ist von Vorteil.*

Offene und direkte Fragen sind üblich. Machen Sie Komplimente, verteilen Sie großzügig Lob und Anerkennung: über das Land, über das Aussehen Ihres Gegenübers usw.

Zu den Tabu-Themen gehört der Patriotismus der US-Amerikaner und die Innen- oder Außenpolitik der USA, aber auch Religion, Rassendiskriminierung oder Waffenbesitz sind keine geeigneten Themen. Fragen nach dem Einkommen bzw. den Vermögensverhältnissen sollten Sie nicht überraschen – anders als in Deutschland ist es in den USA nicht unhöflich, über Geld zu reden. Die typische Begrüßungsfloskel *„How are you?"* sollte kurz und positiv beantwortet werden: *„Fine, thanks."*

Bei aller Lockerheit sind US-Amerikaner aber auch konservativ – es gibt eine Business-Etikette, die es einzuhalten gilt: Pünktlichkeit gehört zum Beispiel dazu, ebenso wie die Beachtung hierarchischer Strukturen.

Die Körpersprache: Zur Begrüßung ist ein kurzer, fester Händedruck üblich. Er gilt dann ebenso wie Lächeln, direkter Blickkontakt und eine offene Körperhaltung als Zeichen von Aufgeschlossenheit und Selbstbewusstsein. Anders als in anderen Ländern ist es kein Problem, wenn Sie eine Hand in der Hosentasche haben – beide Hände sollten es aber nicht sein.

Vorsicht beim Unterschreiten von Distanzzonen: Zwar ist ein Schulterklopfen, gerade unter Männern, akzeptabel; mit einem Abstand von 60 bis 80 cm sind Sie aber in jedem Fall auf der sicheren Seite.

ample, of dining, wine, horses and cultural matters typical of the nation.

Rejection is formulated only indirectly and a clear "no" is rare. Eye contact and physical contact in the field of business occur in measured amounts.

USA

Small talk is important here primarily for getting acquainted and at official functions, but is generally kept brief prior to business discussions: "Time is money". Here the small talk rule is: no deep, complicated topics, but instead light subjects such as sports, the origin of the family in the event that it has European roots, eating (including diets), the job, films or music.

> *The communication style generally tends to be humorous and in any case positive and an optimistic attitude is a plus.*

Open, direct questions are the norm. Be generous with compliments, praise and acknowledgement: about the country, your conversation partner's appearance and so on.

Topics to avoid include the patriotism of the Americans and the domestic and foreign policy of the US government, religion, racial discrimination or gun ownership. Don't be surprised by questions about your income or your financial standing – in contrast to Europe, it's not considered impolite to talk about money in the USA. The typical greeting phrase, *"How are you?"* should be answered briefly and positively with *"I'm fine, thanks"*.

For all their easy-going nature, Americans also have a conservative side – there is a business etiquette that is to be complied with: punctuality is one of its provisions, for example, as is the observance of hierarchical structures.

Body language: a brief, firm handshake is customary upon introduction. This, along with a smile, direct eye contact and an open physical posture are viewed as signs of openness and self-confidence. In contrast to other countries, having one hand in your trouser pocket is no problem, but you should avoid having both hands concealed.

Be careful of overstepping distance zones: while a pat on the back is acceptable, particularly among men, you're still on the safe side with a distance of 60 to 80 cm, or roughly 2 to 3 feet.

Vielleicht fragen Sie sich, warum Sie sich die Mühe machen sollten, all diese kulturellen Unterschiede kennen zu lernen und Ihr Verhalten dementsprechend auszurichten. Nun ...

- Wenn Sie mit Geschäftspartnern aus dem Ausland kommunizieren, tun Sie dies, weil Sie Ziele erreichen wollen – und das können Sie effektiver und effizienter, wenn Sie in der Lage sind, Fettnäpfchen und die daraus resultierenden Konflikte und Probleme zu umgehen.
- Wenn Sie die Regeln kennen und anwenden, werden Sie von Ihren Gesprächspartnern schneller akzeptiert. Und Akzeptanz ist eine wichtige Grundlage für den Aufbau von (Geschäfts-)Beziehungen.
- Wenn Sie wissen, worauf es ankommt und worauf Sie achten müssen, können Sie das Verhalten Ihrer Gesprächspartner besser abschätzen und interpretieren – und das verhilft Ihnen z.B. in Verhandlungen zu Vorteilen.
- Sie fühlen sich sicherer und Ihr Auftreten ist souveräner. Und wer souverän und selbstbewusst auftritt, ist meist erfolgreicher.
- Und nicht zuletzt ist interkulturelle Kompetenz ein wichtiger Karrierefaktor:

   Wer mit Menschen unterschiedlichster Kulturen erfolgreich kommunizieren kann, genießt im Unternehmen hohes Ansehen.

10 Wie kann ich Small Talk – höflich! – beenden?

„Ein guter Abgang ziert die Übung." Friedrich Schiller (1759–1805)

Sie haben es geschafft, einen Kontakt zu knüpfen und sind schon eine Weile im Gespräch, aber ...

- jetzt ruft der „Big Talk", d.h., der Small Talk, der das eigentliche Gespräch eingeleitet hat, hat seinen Zweck erfüllt: Die Gesprächsatmosphäre ist entspannt und Ihr Gegenüber auch – jetzt können Sie Berufliches besprechen.
- der Small Talk entwickelt sich nicht wie erhofft.
- Sie wollen (und sollen) ja nicht Stunden mit diesem Menschen verbringen, selbst wenn er noch so sympathisch ist.

Wie also beendet man den Small Talk – und das so höflich wie möglich?

Perhaps you're asking yourself why you should go to all the trouble of learning all these cultural differences and to adjust your behaviour accordingly. Well ...
- When you communicate with business partners from abroad, you're doing so because you want to achieve particular aims – and you can do this more effectively and efficiently if you're able to avoid embarrassing situations and the resulting conflicts and problems.
- If you know and apply the rules, you will be accepted by your discussion partners more quickly, and acceptance is an important basis for building up (business) relationships.
- When you know what's important and what you have to be aware of, you can weigh up and interpret the behaviour of your discussion partner better – and that gives you advantages, for example, in negotiations.
- You feel more confident and you make a more competent impression. And people who are competent and self-confident are usually more successful.

> And last but not least, intercultural competence is an important career factor: people who can communicate successfully with other people from a variety of cultures enjoy a high level of esteem within a company.

10 How can I end small talk – politely?!

"A good conclusion adorns the exercise."
    Friedrich Schiller (1759–1805)

You have succeeded in establishing contact and have been chatting for a while, but ...
- now the "Big Talk" is calling, i.e. the small talk that opened the actual conversation has now fulfilled its purpose: both the discussion atmosphere and your conversation partner are relaxed – now you can talk about business.
- the small talk isn't going as you had hoped.
- you don't want to and certainly shouldn't spend hours chatting with this person, even if they are genuinely nice.

So, how do we end the small talk phase – and end it as politely as possible?

Wie kann ich Small Talk – höflich! – beenden?

Wenn der „Big Talk" folgen soll ...

..., beenden Sie den Small Talk nicht abrupt. Sagen Sie also nicht: *„So, dann lassen Sie uns mal übers Geschäft reden.", „Um zur Sache zu kommen ...".* Vielleicht finden Sie anhand dessen, was Ihr Gesprächspartner gerade erzählt hat, eine elegante Überleitung:

> *„Apropos Kundenorientierung ..."*
> *„Wie Sie gerade schon sagten, ist Pünktlichkeit natürlich etwas ganz Entscheidendes. Unser Unternehmen ..."*

Oder Sie beenden den Small Talk, indem Sie betonen, wie nett und interessant es war – und dass man sich jetzt ja leider wieder dem Geschäftlichen zuwenden muss:

> *„Das ist ein wirklich spannendes Thema, ich würde mich gern noch länger darüber unterhalten. Aber Ihre Zeit ist sicher begrenzt – sollen wir uns jetzt mal dem Geschäftlichen widmen?"*
> *„Jetzt haben wir uns so interessant unterhalten, da fällt es schon fast schwer, über das zu sprechen, weswegen wir uns eigentlich getroffen haben."*

Wenn Sie sich höflich verabschieden wollen ...

..., sollte Ihr Gegenüber niemals merken, dass Sie z.B. genervt oder gelangweilt sind. Blicke zur Uhr und unruhiges Umherschauen sind tabu. Unterbrechen Sie Ihren Gesprächspartner nicht mitten im Satz, warten Sie, bis sich eine natürliche Gesprächspause ergibt, und leiten Sie dann den Abschied mit einem freundlichen Satz ein:

> *„Ich habe mich gefreut, Sie kennen zu lernen."*
> *„Das war wirklich ein sehr anregendes Gespräch."*
> *„Es war nett, mit Ihnen zu plaudern".*

Was aber, wenn Sie es mit einem Dauerredner zu tun haben und es keinerlei natürliche Gesprächspausen gibt? Nun, dann sollten Sie etwas tun, das man sonst aus Gründen der Höflichkeit vermeidet: Unterbrechen Sie Ihr Gegenüber.

> *„Tut mir leid, dass ich Sie unterbrechen muss, aber ...*
> *– ... ich muss jetzt los."*
> *– ... ich muss noch einen dringenden Anruf erledigen."*
> *– ... ich sehe da gerade jemanden, mit dem ich noch etwas besprechen muss."*

How can I end small talk – politely?!

When it's time for "Big Talk" …

…, don't end the small talk abruptly. In other words, don't say: *"So, let's get down to business.", "And now getting down to brass tacks …"* Maybe what your discussion partner has just said provides you with an elegant bridge:

> *"Speaking of customer orientation …"*
> *"Like you just said, punctuality is of course a very decisive factor. Our company …"*

Or you end the small talk by noting how pleasant and interesting it was – and that unfortunately the discussion should now focus on the business matters at hand:

> *"That sounds really interesting and I'd love to talk about it longer. But I'm sure your time is probably limited – should we move on to the business side now?"*
> *"We've been enjoying talking with each other so much, it's almost hard to move on to discussing what we're actually meeting for today."*

When you want to politely say "goodbye" …

…, your conversation partner should never notice that you're annoyed or bored, for example. Glances at your watch and nervous looks around the room are out of the question. Don't interrupt your discussion partner in the middle of what they're saying; wait until a natural pause comes, and then introduce your farewell with a friendly statement:

> *"I've really enjoyed meeting you."*
> *"That was really a very productive discussion."*
> *"It's been great talking to you."*

But what do you do if your discussion partner is a motormouth who goes on without a break? Well, then you should do something that you otherwise wouldn't do out of courtesy: you interrupt your conversation partner.

> *"I'm really sorry to interrupt you, but …*
> *— … I've got to go."*
> *— … I've really got to make an urgent call."*
> *— … I see someone over there that I've got to discuss something with."*

> *Wie kann ich Small Talk – höflich! – beenden?*

Es empfiehlt sich, eine Begründung anzugeben, warum Sie das Gespräch nun beenden müssen:

> 👁 *„Sie wollen ja sicher noch ein paar andere Leute begrüßen."*
> *„Ich würde mich jetzt gern verabschieden, denn ich sehe da gerade jemanden, den ich noch begrüßen möchte."*
> *„Ich muss mich jetzt leider verabschieden, ich muss nämlich morgen sehr früh raus."*

Und dann äußern Sie, idealerweise begleitet von einem Lächeln, eine vorläufige Abschiedsfloskel:

> 👁 *„Vielleicht können wir unsere Unterhaltung ja später fortsetzen."*
> *„Wir sehen uns ja sicher später noch."*
> *„Bis später!"*

Wenn es eine endgültige Verabschiedung werden soll, gibt es auch noch einen Händedruck:

> 👁 *„Auf Wiedersehen!"*
> *„Dann wünsche ich Ihnen noch viel Spaß, auf Wiedersehen."*
> *„Falls wir uns nicht mehr sehen sollten, noch einen schönen Abend."*

Eine weitere, sehr diplomatische Möglichkeit, sich höflich zu verabschieden: Sie binden eine weitere Person in das Gespräch ein und verabschieden sich dann. So steht Ihr Gesprächspartner nicht ganz allein da.

> 👁 *„Darf ich Sie meiner Kollegin Beate König vorstellen? Beate, das ist Frau Heineke – sie ist ebenfalls begeisterte Hobbygärtnerin."*

Der Abschluss eines Gespräches bleibt im Gedächtnis. Wenn Sie als sympathischer Mensch in Erinnerung bleiben wollen, sind folgende Abschiedsvarianten daher nicht zu empfehlen:
- Sie stehlen sich davon, als Ihr Gegenüber gerade abgelenkt ist: *„Jetzt habe ich aber Hunger – ich glaube, ich gehe mal zum Buffet."* Kann gut sein, dass Ihr Gesprächspartner sagt: *„Ach, ich auch, dann lassen Sie uns doch gemeinsam gehen."*
- Sie geben vor, jetzt endgültig gehen zu müssen – und dann trifft Sie Ihr Gesprächspartner eine halbe Stunde später woanders wieder: *„Ach, Frau Rietmeyer, Sie sind ja immer noch da!"*

How can I end small talk – politely?!

It is recommended that you provide a reason why you have to end the discussion now:

> *"I'm sure you want to say hello to a few other people."*
> *"I'm going to have to say goodbye now. I see someone over there that I need to say hello to."*
> *"I'm afraid I'm going to have to go now. I've got a very early start tomorrow morning."*

And then, ideally with a smile, say a preliminary farewell:

> *"Maybe we can continue our chat some other time."*
> *"We're sure to see each other later on."*
> *"See you later!"*

When it's time for a final farewell, accompany it with a handshake:

> *"Goodbye!"*
> *"Have fun. Goodbye!"*
> *"In case we don't see each other later on, have a nice evening."*

Another very diplomatic way of saying goodbye to someone is to include someone else in the conversation and then say your farewells. This avoids leaving your discussion partner standing alone.

> *"May I introduce you to my colleague, Betty King? Betty, this is Ms Henkel – she's also an enthusiastic gardener."*

The conclusion of a conversation stays in one's memory. If you want to be remembered as a congenial person, then the following farewell methods are not recommended:
- Disappearing while your conversation partner is distracted for a moment. *"Boy, I'm hungry now – I think I'm going to check out the buffet."* This could result in your discussion partner saying, *"Yeah, I'm hungry, too. Let's go together."*
- You pretend that you really have to go now – and then you run into your discussion partner half an hour later somewhere else: *"Ah, Ms Riddle, you're still here!"*

Und jetzt?
Jetzt geht es los – jetzt üben und perfektionieren Sie Ihre Small-Talk-Fähigkeiten. Das Schöne ist ja, dass es dazu reichlich Gelegenheiten gibt – immer und überall. Nur anfangen müssen Sie – denn:

„Das ist alles, was wir tun können: immer wieder von Neuem anfangen, immer und immer wieder."
   Thornton Wilder (1887–1975), amerik. Dramatiker und Romanautor

Viel Spaß und viel Erfolg dabei!

> How can I end small talk – politely?!

And now?

Now it's time to start – now you can practise and perfect your small talk skills. The best thing is that you've got plenty of opportunities to do just that – everywhere, all the time. You just have to get started – because:

"That's all we can do: keep starting over, again and again."
   Thornton Wilder (1887–1975), American dramatist and novelist

Here's wishing you lots of fun and success in the process!

Stichwortverzeichnis

Afrika 162
Aggressiv-entwertender Stil 32, 34
Alternativ-Fragen 58
Anpassungsbereitschaft 154
Anrede 110
Anteilnahme 50
Arabische Länder 162, 164, 166
Aufmerksamkeitslaute 50
Aufnehmendes Zuhören 48, 52
Ausländische Kunden 154 ff.
Ausstrahlung 100
Australien 166

Bedürftig-abhängiger Stil 24, 26
Beneluxländer 166
Bestimmend-kontrollierender Stil 38, 40
Beziehungsebene 12, 18, 40
Blickkontakt 50, 94, 96, 102

Cultural Awareness 154

Dialogzone 90
Distanzzonen 86 ff.

Eindruck 8, 14, 18, 50, 80
Einfühlungsvermögen 50
Eisbrecher 108

Frageketten 58, 60, 66
Fragetechnik 56 ff.
Frankreich 166, 168
Fremdwahrnehmung 18, 20

Geschäftsessen 150
Geschlossene Fragen 58
Gesichtsausdruck 80
Gesprächsablauf 14
Gesprächsatmosphäre 12, 54, 186
Gesprächseinstieg 104
Gesprächstechniken 48 ff.

Gestik 8, 80, 84, 92
Glaubwürdigkeit 82
Großbritannien 168, 170

Händedruck 80
Harmonie 160
Helfender Stil 26, 28

Integrativer Anpassungsstil 156
Intimzone 90
Israel 170

Johari-Fenster 18, 20

Kanada 172
Karriere 6, 140 ff.
Killerphrasen 74 ff.
Kollegen 144, 146
Kommunikationsregeln 160
Kommunikationssperren 64 ff.
Kommunikationsstile 20 ff.
Kommunikationsverhalten 16, 18, 22
Kommunikative Grundkompetenzen 22, 48 ff.
Konzentration 50
Körperhaltung 8, 80, 84, 86
Körpersprache 80 ff., 102
Kulturelle Kompetenz 154
Kunden 146 ff.

Lob 74, 120

Manipulationsstrategie 74
Manipulative Fragen 58
Mimik 8, 80, 84, 92, 94
Mitteilungsfreudig-dramatisierender Stil 42, 44
Mittelmeerraum 172, 174

Networking 6, 12, 140

Offene Fragen 56
Offenheit 154
Ostasiatische Länder 174, 176
Österreich 176

Paraphrasieren 52
Polen 178
Positive Rhetorik 60, 62

Reizformulierungen 78
Respektzone 90
Rhetorische Fragen 58
Russland 178

Sachebene 12, 18, 40
Schweiz 180
Selbstloser Stil 28, 30
Selbstwahrnehmung 18, 20
Sich distanzierender Stil 40, 42
Sich selbst beweisender Stil 34, 36
Skandinavische Länder 180
Small-Talk-Partner 10
Small-Talk-Themen 112 ff.
Stimme 96, 98
Süd- und Mittelamerika 180, 182
Suggestive Fragen 58

Tabu-Themen 132 ff.
Taktgefühl 34
Timing 12
Toleranz 154
Tonfall 80, 96, 98
Trigger 78
Tschechische Republik 182

Ungarn 182, 184
Unvoreingenommenheit 50
USA 184

Verbalisieren 52, 54
Vorgesetzte 142, 144
Vorstellungsgespräch 152

Zuhören 8, 22, 42, 48 ff.

Index

Absorbent listening 49, 53
Africa 163
Aggressive-demeaning style 33, 35
Alternative questions 59
Arab countries 163, 165, 167
Attentive comments 51
Australia 167
Austria 177

Benelux countries 167
Body language 81 et sqq., 103
Business meals 151

Canada 173
Career 7, 141
Charisma 101
Closed questions 59
Colleagues 145, 147
Communication conduct 17, 19, 23
Communication roadblocks 65 et sqq.
Communication styles 21 et sqq.
Communicative competence 23, 49 et sqq.
Concentration 51
Conversation starter 105
Course of a conversation 15
Cultural awareness 155
Customers 147 et sqq.
Czech Republic 183

Determining-controlling style 39, 41
Dialogue zone 91
Discussion atmosphere 13, 55, 187
Discussion techniques 49 et sqq.
Distance zones 87 et sqq.

East Asian countries 175, 177
Empathy 51

Eye contact 51, 95, 97, 103

Facial expression 9, 81, 85, 93, 95
Factual level 13, 19, 41
Foreign customers 155 et sqq.
France 167, 169

Gestures 9, 81, 85, 93
Great Britain 169, 171
Greeting 111

Handshake 81
Harmony 161
Helpful style 27, 29
Hungary 183, 185

Ice breakers 109
Impartiality 51
Impression 9, 15, 19, 51, 81
Inflection 81, 97, 99
Integrative adaptation style 157
Intercultural competence 155
Interest 51
Intimate zone 91
Israel 171

Job interviews 153
Johari Window 19, 21

Killer phrases 75 et sqq.

Listening 9, 23, 43, 49 et sqq.

Manipulation strategy 75
Manipulative questions 59
Mediterranean region 173, 175

Needy-dependent style 25, 27
Networking 7, 13, 141
"News Flash"-dramatising style 43, 45

Open questions 57
Openness 155

Paraphrasing 53
Perception of others 19, 21
Physical posture 9, 81, 85, 87
Poland 179
Positive rhetoric 61
Praise 75, 121
Provocative formulations 79

Question chains 59, 61, 67
Questioning technique 57 et sqq.

Relationship level 13, 19, 41
Respect zone 91
Rhetorical questions 59
Rules of communication 161
Russia 179

Scandinavian countries 181
Self-distancing style 41, 43
Selfless style 29, 31
Self-perception 19, 21
Self-praising style 35, 37
Sense of tact 35
Small talk partner 11
South and Central America 181, 183
Suggestive questions 59
Superiors 143, 145
Switzerland 181

Taboo topics 133 et sqq.
Timing 13
Tolerance 155
Topics for small talk 113 et sqq.
Triggers 79
Trustworthiness 83

USA 185

Verbalising 53
Voice 97, 99

Willingness to adapt 155

Wortschatz Deutsch-Englisch / German-English Vocabulary

Afrika	Africa
Aggressiv-entwertender Stil	aggressive-demeaning style
Alternativ-Fragen	alternative questions
Anpassungsbereitschaft	willingness to adapt
Anteilnahme	interest
Arabische Länder	Arab countries
Aufmerksamkeitslaute	attentive comments
Aufnehmendes Zuhören	absorbent listening
Ausländische Kunden	foreign customers
Ausstrahlung	charisma
Australien	Australia
Bedürftig-abhängiger Stil	needy-dependent style
Beneluxländer	Benelux countries
Bestimmend-kontrollierender Stil	determining-controlling style
Beziehungsebene	relationship level
Blickkontakt	eye contact
Dialogzone	dialogue zone
Distanzzonen	distance zones
Eindruck	impression
Einfühlungsvermögen	empathy
Eisbrecher	ice breakers
Frageketten	question chains
Fragetechnik	questioning technique
Frankreich	France
Fremdwahrnehmung	perception of others
Geschäftsessen	business meal
Geschlossene Fragen	closed questions
Gesichtsausdruck	facial expression
Gesprächsablauf	course of a conversation
Gesprächsatmosphäre	discussion atmosphere
Gesprächseinstieg	conversation starter
Gesprächstechniken	discussion techniques
Gestik	gestures
Glaubwürdigkeit	trustworthiness
Großbritannien	Great Britain
Händedruck	handshake
Harmonie	harmony
Helfender Stil	helpful style
Integrativer Anpassungsstil	integrative adaption style
Intimzone	intimate zone
Israel	Israel
Johari-Fenster	Johari Window
Kanada	Canada
Karriere	career
Killerphrasen	killer phrases
Kollegen	colleagues
Kommunikationsregeln	rules of communication
Kommunikationssperren	communication roadblocks
Kommunikationsstile	communication styles

German-English Vocabulary

Kommunikationsverhalten	communication conduct
Kommunikative Grundkompetenzen	communicative competence
Konzentration	concentration
Körperhaltung	physical posture
Körpersprache	body language
Kulturelle Kompetenz	intercultural competence
Kunden	customers
Lob	praise
Manipulationsstrategie	manipulation strategy
Manipulative Fragen	manipulative questions
Mimik	facial expression
Mitteilungsfreudig-dramatisierender Stil	"News Flash" dramatising style
Mittelmeerraum	Mediterranean region
Offene Fragen	open questions
Offenheit	openness
Ostasiatische Länder	East Asian countries
Österreich	Austria
Paraphrasieren	paraphrasing
Polen	Poland
Positive Rhetorik	positive rhetoric
Reizformulierungen	provocative formulations
Respektzone	respect zone
Rhetorische Fragen	rhetorical questions
Russland	Russia
Sachebene	factual level
Schweiz	Switzerland
Selbstloser Stil	selfless style
Selbstwahrnehmung	self-perception
Sich distanzierender Stil	self-distancing style
Sich selbst beweisender Stil	self-praising style
Skandinavische Länder	Scandinavian countries
Small-Talk-Themen	topics for small talk
Stimme	voice
Süd- und Mittelamerika	South and Central America
Suggestive Fragen	suggestive questions
Tabu-Themen	taboo topics
Taktgefühl	sense of tact
Toleranz	tolerance
Tonfall	inflection
Tschechische Republik	Czech Republic
Ungarn	Hungary
Unvoreingenommenheit	impartiality
Verbalisieren	verbalising
Vorgesetzte	superiors
Vorstellungsgespräch	job interview
Zuhören	listening

Literaturverzeichnis/Bibliography

- Bonneau, Elisabeth: Stilvoll zum Erfolg. Der moderne Business-Knigge. Hamburg 2004.

- Fichtinger, Heinz / Sterzenbach, Gregor: Knigge fürs Ausland. 2. Auflage. Planegg bei München 2006.

- Fine, Debra: The Fine Art of Small Talk: How to Start a Conversation, Keep it Going, Build Networking Skills, and Leave a Positive Impression. New York 2005.

- Gordon, Thomas: Leader Effectiveness Training (LET). The Proven People Skills for Today's Leaders. New York 2001.

- Klein, Hans-Michael: Cross Culture – Benimm im Ausland. 2. Auflage. Berlin 2004.

- Kollermann, Nicole: Spinn ich oder spinnen die? Über den konstruktiven Umgang mit interkulturellen Irritationen. In: Kumbier, Dagmar / Schulz von Thun, Friedemann (Hrsg.): Interkulturelle Kommunikation: Methoden, Modelle, Beispiele. Reinbek bei Hamburg 2006.

- Mole, John: Mind Your Manners: Managing Business Culture in a Global Europe. London 2003.

- Morrison, Terri / Conway, Wayne A.: Kiss, Bow, or Shake Hands: The Bestselling Guide to Doing Business in More Than 60 Countries. Avon, Massachusetts 2006.

- Schulz von Thun, Friedemann: Miteinander reden. Stile, Werte und Persönlichkeitsentwicklung. Reinbek bei Hamburg 1981 (Originalausgabe).

Die Autorin

Dr. Susanne Watzke-Otte ist Trainerin, Moderatorin und Beraterin mit den Arbeitsschwerpunkten interne und externe Kommunikation, Selbstmanagement, Projektmanagement und Führung. Seit einigen Jahren bildet sie zudem Trainer/-innen für Unternehmen der Technologiebranche aus.

The Author

Dr. Susanne Watzke-Otte is an experienced trainer, presenter and consultant in the fields of internal and external communication, self-management, project management and leadership. For a number of years she has been coaching trainers for companies in the technology sector.

Überblick.
Sprachkompetenz als Klimafaktor

Wo Englisch Geschäfts- oder Verhandlungssprache ist, besteht die erste Herausforderung darin, Besprechungen sprachlich und vom Klima her optimal zu bewältigen. Mit diesem zweisprachigen Band lässt sich die entsprechende Kompetenz mit überschaubarem Aufwand erwerben.

Jochem Kießling-Sonntag

Meetings und Moderation
200 Seiten, kartoniert
ISBN 978-**3-589-23904-7**

Weitere Informationen zum Programm erhalten Sie im Buchhandel oder unter
www.cornelsen.de/berufskompetenz

Cornelsen V
14328 B
www.cornelse